EMBATTLED BANNER

A Reasonable Defense of the Confederate Battle Flag

DON HINKLE
TURNER PUBLISHING COMPANY

TURNER PUBLISHING COMPANY
412 Broadway, P.O. Box 3101
Paducah, KY 42002-3101
Phone: (502) 443-0121

Turner Publishing Company Staff:
Publishing Consultant: Douglas W. Sikes
Designer: Herbert C. Banks II

Library of Congress Catalog Card Number: 96-62025
ISBN: 1-56311-354-6

Additional copies may be purchased directly from
Turner Publishing Company.

Printed in the U.S.A.

CONTENTS

DEDICATION

To Dad, who is in Heaven.
To Mom and Joe for their love and support.
To Jeff, Kelley, Heather, Hillary, Leann, and Bryant
for being my loving family.
To Jesus Christ, my Heavenly Father, Lord, and Savior.

*Take away a nation's heritage
and they are more easily persuaded.*
--KARL MARX

6

ACKNOWLEDGMENTS

It is with pleasure that I acknowledge the assistance that made this book possible.

I would like to thank Turner Publishing for taking a chance on an unReconstructed Confederate. It's been a long and winding process, but the support provided by everyone at Turner — and particularly Doug Sikes — is greatly appreciated.

I was fortunate to have two talented ladies editing my manuscript. I would like to thank Connie Hudson of Columbia, Tennessee, who took time from her teaching and writing to remind me how to properly use a comma. She caught a number of boo-boos and offered many valuable suggestions. But more than anything, she was a major source of encouragement. She is a valued friend who can do a pretty mean stir-fry. Maureen Poole, also of Columbia, deserves kudos for her work on the manuscript as well. She tightened sentences and helped me keep my focus. This book would have been impossible without her support. I especially appreciated the T-bone and Bennie's homemade ice cream. Both came along on days when I was about to pull my hair out. I would also like to thank my pastor, Reverend Mike Dawson, at First Baptist Church, Columbia, for his review of the manuscript. He's a valued friend and a great proclaimer of the Gospel.

I am grateful to the 23,000 members of the Sons of Confederate Veterans. This is their story, too.

Many members of the SCV contributed information, pictures, and suggestions. I would like to thank former Commander-in-Chief Norman Dasinger, former Adjutant-in-Chief Ralph Palmer, ex-Judge Advocate-in-Chief Jeff Massey, SCV Executive Director Ronald Clemmons, Tennessee Division Commanders Gene Andrews and James Turner, former Georgia Division Commander Jim Reynolds, South Carolina Division Commander Chris Sullivan, North Carolina Division Commander Frank Powell, Ohio Division Commander Robert Croye, compatriot Jim Zeirke of the SCV's Wisconsin division, former Georgia spokesman Charles Lunsford, author and compatriot Devereaux Cannon Jr., of Gallatin, Tennessee, compatriots Wes Shofner of Nashville, Mike Corley and Bill Jennings of Woodbury, Tennessee, Lotz House Museum Director Ronnie Mangrum of Franklin, Tennessee, and J.E.B. Stuart IV of Richmond, Virginia.

Members of Sam Watkins Camp No. 29 of the SCV in

Columbia, Tennessee, provided great support as well. Compatriots Bob Duncan, Chuck Byrne and Neal Pulley read the manuscript for historical accuracy and provided valuable suggestions. Russ Cothran supplied much needed newspaper clippings and great moral support. Dear friends Dr. Bobby Bain and wife, Kathy, lifted my spirits on many occasions. When I needed seclusion they provided it with their cabin at 1861 Nathan Bedford Forrest Memorial Parkway in the heart of Glenfiddich.

I must also thank the entire staff at the international headquarters of the Sons of Confederate Veterans located at the historic Elm Springs mansion in Columbia. They provided valuable support and unlimited access to the General William D. McCain Memorial Library. I would especially like to acknowledge the assistance provided by staffers Connie Morris, Lynn Bradley, Sandy Hardison, Bill Young, Patricia Copley, and Collette Crowley.

My sincere appreciation goes to Dr. John Shelton Reed at the University of North Carolina-Chapel Hill for the valuable information he provided on the battle flag. I would also like to thank John Coski of the Museum of the Confederacy in Richmond, Virginia. Marion Lambert, chairman of the Tampa Bay Chapter of Preserving Our Heritage, Inc., supplied valuable information as well.

I am grateful to Betty Krimminger of Chapel Hill, North Carolina, for her research assistance on the William Porcher Miles Papers at the University of North Carolina. I must also thank the staffs at the Tennessee State Archives and Library in Nashville, the John W. Finney Memorial Library at Columbia State Community College in Columbia, Tennessee, and the Maury County Public Library in Columbia.

Finally, I would like to express my deepest gratitude to David and JoAnn Westerman of Trenton, Kentucky. They welcomed me into their home, fed me, and turned over virtually every public and private newspaper clipping, picture, video and tape that addressed the tragic death of their son, Michael Westerman.

Don Hinkle
1 February 1997

INTRODUCTION

"Mr. Hinkle, I sure enjoy your Sunday columns defending the South," I heard a soft voice say from behind as I walked out of my office where I once worked as the editor of a small daily newspaper in Tennessee. I turned to find a familiar, little silver-haired lady. She was well known in our county of 60,000 citizens. She had a reputation for being deeply concerned about the preservation of Southern heritage in our area.

I knew my writings defending the South's heritage had provoked quite a bit of discussion around town. Among my columns drawing the most comments were the ones written in the weeks following the death of Michael Westerman, a 19-year-old white man from Todd County, Kentucky, who was shot and killed for flying a Confederate battle flag in the back of his pickup. As one might expect, the crime was major news throughout the South and it was clearly on this little lady's mind the day she came to see me.

"I just wanted to let you know that I've turned my flag over to the Sons of Confederate Veterans for safe keeping," she said in almost a whisper.

"Why don't you fly it?"

"Oh, no, no," she replied. "I couldn't do that. I'm afraid they will shoot me."

The sincerity of her words stunned me. I felt sick, then angry, then sad. This is America, I thought. You know, free speech, First Amendment and all that stuff.

I was unable to get her words off my mind as the days went by. Questions besieged me at every turn — What has happened to our country? Are my fellow Southerners and I so out of touch with the world that we've lost our heritage? Can anything be done or is it too late? What has caused this? Is it "open season" on Southerners and anything Confederate?

Were our Southern forefathers racists? Did they fight under a "rebel" banner as the news media loves to write tirelessly? Are the people of the South evil just because they want to cling to their heritage?

Did my great-great grandaddy die in a Yankee prison because some folks down the road had a few slaves? Did my great-great uncle die for no reason on a bloody battlefield called Chickamauga?

Where did the battle flag come from? What does it stand for?

Has its meaning changed? Who is uncomfortable with it — and why?

These questions sent me on a quest for answers concerning the Confederate battle flag — a flag my great-great grandfather and at least two great-great uncles, fought under (by the way, they owned no slaves).

What is it about this flag that has caused it to endure for 130 years? Why can it trigger cheers as well as jeers?

Some say it's a divisive symbol, reflective of racism. Others say it is a symbol of the South's regional pride. Politicians love to focus on it as a source of political expendiency, while others shun its very shadow. Interest groups spend thousands of dollars in court costs to have it removed from public display, while others struggle for its preservation. Many college professors fail in their attempts to explain it fairly, the most liberal wanting it banished to advance their politically correct agenda — and in so doing— revise our history; yet others, fearful of losing their jobs, tenatively defend it.

The debate over the Confederate battle flag is nothing new. Its opponents have attacked it from its earliest days, so it should not come as a surprise that it is still an emotionally charged issue.

It seems to me, that if someone wants to understand what a symbol means, then they should go to the people who own the symbol. To do that with the battle flag, one must go back to the Confederate soldiers. After all, they are the ones who fought and died for it.

Flag opponents often attack with this reasoning: "The Confederate soldiers are dead and the Confederacy is dead, too. So why don't you just let it go?"

On the surface, such questions sound reasonable, but after some thought they should be recognized for what they are: utter nonsense. It's interesting that the people who attack the flag are often heard accusing Southerners of wanting to "cling to the past." Yet these same people seem to be obsessed with recalling the past themselves. Rarely a day goes by that the anti-flag people don't throw the "Jim Crow" South and slavery in the faces of Southerners. The anti-flag groups are the ones who won't let the past go because it would not be in their political interests to do so. But they are being hypocritical. On one hand they claim to support the cultural diversity of America, unless of course, it is a culture they don't like. It is the South they bully today, but who will they bully tomorrow?

But literally, their question concerning the death of the Confederate soldier misses the target. The Confederate soldier is not dead.

"Well, yes, he is," they retort. "He died at Appomattox."

That's not true. The army surrendered its arms, but when the war was over the soldiers who survived formed an organization called United Confederate Veterans and they continued to meet until they died (the last Confederate veteran passed away in 1959).

But the men of the UCV had sons, and another organization was born out of their brotherhood: the Sons of Confederate Veterans, the rightful heirs to — and protectors of — the battle flag.

So the memory of the Confederate soldier lives — not to fight with bullets, but with the true words of history.

As the first UCV Commander-in-Chief Confederate Lt. Gen. Stephen Dill Lee, said in 1906,

"To you, Sons of Confederate Veterans, we submit the vindication of the Cause for which we fought; to your strength will be given the defense of the Confederate soldier's good name, the guardianship of his history, the emulation of his virtues, the perpetuation of those principles he loved and which made him glorious and which you also cherish. Remember it is your duty to see that the true history of the South is presented to future generations."

But that explanation still doesn't satisfy flag opponents, so they attack the battle flag from another angle.

"What about the Confederate government? It's dead, so why not let it go?" they say. The answer can be found in history.

The battle flag was never the official national flag of the Confederacy. It was reserved only for use by the army, though it was eventually incorporated into the national flag in 1863. But their question still deserves an answer because it lingers on the periphery of the battle flag issue. While it is true the Confederate government no longer functions (the Confederate army surrendered, but President Jefferson Davis never formally surrendered the Confederate government), it is only natural that Southerners would want to fly a flag connected to their once proud and independent nation, not as a symbol of defiance, but as a symbol of regional pride. Many other subjugated regions in the world fly their once proud colors. So why should the South be any different? Like it or not, the South was an independent nation from 1861-1865.

The South is the only region of the United States to have its own flag — and that likely bothers some people. It is clear there is an element that wants the flag erased from history unless it suits their political purpose at any given moment. Whether it is because of jealousy, fear, ignorance, political expediency, or downright bigotry remains a mystery to the world, but as this book suggests, it's likely a combination of them all.

Some current day "intellectuals" say the fight over the Confederate battle flag is the South's attempt to find its identity because it is undergoing such massive change. I disagree. Southerners — of all ethnic backgrounds — have always known who they are. They knew that a Southerner, General George Washington of Virginia, led a group of rag, tag scarecrows to victory over an oppressive government that was infringing on their personal rights and taxing them to death. In the hour of secession, Southerners saw themselves as the guardians of the Constitution and defenders of what the Founding Fathers had actually intended. The fiery Georgia secessionist, Thomas R.R. Cobb, led the charge to name the new nation "The Republic of Washington because its founding represented a return to the principles of George Washington." Even though Cobb and his allies failed in the efforts, Washington was placed on the new nation's official seal. All of this is but a small portion of the evidence which shows how closely Southerners identified themselves with the Founding Fathers.

Some Southerners even argued to keep the "Stars and Stripes," and felt that it was the other side who should adopt a new flag. "Logically the Union belongs to those who have kept, not those who have broken, its covenants," said Virginian Henry A. Wise in 1861. The North was the one who should have seceded, he argued, and if there was to be a fight over the issue he was willing to join the fray with "the star-spangled banner still in one hand and my musket in the other."

Wise ended up on the losing end of the debate. The Confederate Congress adopted the so-called "Stars and Bars" (a term wrongly used by the news media to refer to the battle flag), or first national flag of the Confederacy, on March 4, 1861. That day was purposely selected so the new banner could "fly in the face" of Abraham Lincoln's inauguration, which was the same day.

The first "Stars and Bars" had only seven stars in its canton (top left corner). But as Southern states continued to secede, the number of stars grew to 13 (11 were for the seceded states, while the two additional stars represented the exiled Confederate governments of Kentucky and Missouri). Some historians, like James M. McPherson of Princeton University, contend the 13 stars in the "Stars and Bars" evoked memories of the first 13 colonies and the first American war for independence.

Identifying closely with the principles of the Founding Fathers may partially explain why Southerners remain among the most patriotic of all Americans. Since losing their bid for independence, Southerners have gone the extra mile to prove themselves loyal to the United States, often in the face of oppressive Reconstruction and non-stop ridicule. The first war America fought after the Civil War was with Spain. It was an ex-Confederate general, Joe Wheeler of Alabama, who led U.S. forces to victory. Interestingly, most people think of Teddy Roosevelt and his band of troopers when they hear the nickname "Roughriders." But it was a Confederate unit in the Western frontier who were the original "Roughriders."

Yes, Southerners know exactly who they are.

Our homeland is often referred to as "The Bible Belt" because it refuses to compromise the tenets of the Christian faith. The majority of Southerners have always believed in a two-parent family (headed by a man and woman), strong penalties for felony crimes, the right to bear arms, love of the land, and a unique obsession with storytelling and music.

Much of the dislike for Southerners stems from jealously because the South's culture is a dominant culture.

For example, the South has produced some of our nation's greatest leaders: George Washington, Thomas Jefferson, Patrick Henry, James Madison, Andrew Jackson, Sam Houston, Winfield Scott, Zachary Taylor, Martin Luther King Jr., Billy Graham, Booker T. Washington, Supreme Court Chief Justice John Marshall, W.C. Handy, and Admirals David Farragutt and Chester Nimitz. Southerners occupied the White House for 45 — and the office of secretary of state for 40 — of this nation's first 57 years.

In the arts, Helen Keller, Robert Penn Warren, Flannery O'Conner, Sequoyah, William Faulkner and Grantland Rice set standards with their writings; while Southern musicians created bluegrass, western and country music, rock and roll, jazz, blues and an assortment of gospel music.

Indeed, the Southern culture is so dominant that it may be the only one in the United States that can absorb large numbers of new people and promptly turn them into "Southerners." This may explain why the anti-flag troopers, disguised in their politically correct fatigues, run into stiff resistance at the Mason-Dixon Line.

Southerners are sickened when one of their own lowers themself to profit at the expense of their heritage. Hollywood is notorious for encouraging anti-Southern views. The entertainment industry learned the lesson of Reconstruction well: stomping the South is profitable. But even with a 135 years of bashing, the Southern culture still flourishes. Which brings us back to the battle flag.

The attacks on the battle flag are perceived by a large majority of Southerners as an attack on our culture and homeland. What the anti-flag agitators refuse to understand is that the South cannot be strong if it is robbed of its past. A weak South weakens the United States. Or is that what they want?

Many Southerners are beginning to respond to the attacks on their heritage in a variety of ways. Forming heritage preservation groups, writing state legislators, and being more visible in their communities is impacting public opinion.

But there remains a good portion of Southerners who dearly love their homeland, the battle flag, and their ancestors who fought it; yet they don't know how to respond when confronted with emotional, but shallow, appeals by anti-flag, anti-Southern culture groups. They feel helpless as they watch the character assassination of their ancestors unfold. This book is for them.

I am among those who want some answers, but I refuse to go to the demagogues with my questions. The place to go is history. This book will show how history comes down squarely on the side of the South, its culture, and people — all of which is wrapped up in the one most defining and enduring symbol of the South: the Confederate battle flag. Supporters of the battle flag also know that the attacks on the flag are just the beginning. This book will show that the flag is not the only Southern symbol under siege.

The issue has reached a critical stage. If the anti-Southern establishment can be stopped at the battle flag, the rest of Southern culture can be saved as well. But it is time for the sons and daughters of the South to make their stand. As a Southern writer recently put it, "When the barbarians are at the gate, you don't lower your voice and invite them in for a hot meal. You grab your swords and pistols and pitchforks — and shout 'bloody murder!'"

I am not a historian. This book is partisan, but true. It has been written from a Southern perspective and — like so many others — is a statement of fact. Having gone through public schools and college, I can attest to the Northern side of the story. That's the version that has been widely taught in American educational institutions since Reconstruction. Remember, the victor always writes the history, and it is often one-sided.

I've written this book to find some answers for myself about the battle flag and to help others — especially Southerners — understand its meaning. But I want even more than that. I want blacks to feel at ease with the battle flag and with being Southerners, too. I don't want them to feel threatened. I want the path to be clear and straight for all Southerners as we work together to make the Southland the best it can be. I want us to take equal pride in our accomplishments.

I want our relationship to be much like the one I had as a little boy with a black man while growing up in rural Middle Tennessee during the early 1960s. I would often play with Civil War toy soldiers in the house or with a toy dump truck in the back yard until around 4 p.m. For me, that's when everything stopped. Nothing could keep me from my daily visit with my friend, Ewing.

Ewing was a middle-aged black man who worked on a nearby farm. He drove a tractor and always wore a dilapidated fedora, overalls, and a smile as big as the fields he tilled.

Mom knew how important it was for me to meet him, so if I got sidetracked with my Civil War soldiers, she would always holler if she heard Ewing's tractor coming down the road. At the sound of her voice, I would bolt out the front door, often gasping for air while I stood on the front porch gazing down the road. We lived far enough out in the country that I had no playmates, making Ewing's visit take on greater significance.

Ewing would turn into the dirt road next to our house, smiling and waving like crazy. He was as happy to see me as I was him. He would never think of proceeding to the fields without stopping to see me first. Neither one of us ever discussed our commitment to meeting each day, for it was simply understood that I would be out there and he would stop. Color meant nothing to us. I respected him because of the way he could handle his huge tractor. I guess he liked me because I was so faithful in waiting for him to come by. I begged him to let me ride along, but he would kindly brush aside the question by saying, "Now, Don, your mother says you're too little, but you'll be driving your own tractor soon enough."

I'll never forget the joy I felt as we finished our five-minute conversations and he fired-up his tractor. It was noisier than anything I'd ever heard, and I'd jump and clap with approval as its exhaust pipe belched plumes of smoke. Then with a grin and a wave Ewing would head down the road. I'd stand there until he disappeared behind the dust clouds. My memories of Ewing are among the fondest of a happy childhood growing up in the South.

We eventually moved to the city, and I lost touch with him. Ewing was the first black friend I ever had. I've had many since then, and I hope to have many more.

I detest seeing a small group of malcontents and bigots making them feel uncomfortable when they see a Confederate battle flag. Slavery was wrong, but it must be examined within the proper historical context. We are all thankful that God has rid us of such behavior in America. But even a mistake like slavery is no reason to exterminate a culture because of lies and revisionist history.

I want to help expose the untruths because I cannot — and will not — banish or dishonor the memory of my Confederate ancestors. To do such a thing would be to accept a lie, place a blot on my family's name, and deny who I am — a Southerner.

CHAPTER ONE

ORIGIN OF A BATTLE FLAG

They are waving OUR flag above us,
With the despot's tyrant will;
With our blood they have stained its colors,
And they call it holy still.
With tearful eyes, but steady hand,
We'll tear its stripes apart,
And fling them, like broken fetters,
That may not bind the heart.
But we'll save our stars of glory,
In the might of the sacred sign
Of Him who has fixed forever
One "Southern Cross" to shine.
                        —The Southern Cross
                        E.K. Blunt

On September 11, 1863, President Abraham Lincoln ordered the publishers and editor of a Baltimore newspaper arrested for printing the poem "The Southern Cross," which was another often-used name for the Confederate battle flag. Those arrested were not allowed to communicate with anyone and were sent across the battle lines with the understanding that they should not return during the war.[1] The arrests — and subsequent exile — of the newspapermen were made possible by Lincoln's 1861 suspension of the writ of *habeus corpus* — an action Federal Circuit Court

Judge Roger B. Taney ruled unconstitutional on May 28, 1862.[2] Some Southerners, like United Daughters of the confederacy Historian Mildred Rutherford, maintain that the suspension of the writ was one of 10 constitutional violations committed by Lincoln prior to — and during — the war.[3]

Lincoln wasn't about to preside over the break-up of the United States, though it is widely accepted that secession was within the constitutional rights of each state. In the weeks following the secession of the 11 Southern states, Lincoln proclaimed martial law. He was fearful of Confederate clandestine operations in border states like Maryland, widespread uprisings by Northerners who opposed the military draft, and others who wanted to let the South go in peace. Many Northerners were afraid of losing their jobs to emancipated blacks from the South.

"A large majority can see no reason why they should be shot for the benefit of niggers and abolitionists," wrote an Ohio newspaper editor in 1862. If "the despot Lincoln" attempts to force abolition and a draft upon white men in Ohio, "he would meet with the fate he deserves: hung, shot, or burned."[4] Many scholars agree that the 1862 elections — won mostly by Democrats against the abolitionist-supported Republicans — is evidence that most Northerners opposed the Emancipation Proclamation.[5]

Things continued to go badly for Lincoln in 1863. A riot by Irish immigrants opposing the draft in New York forced Lincoln to deploy 20,000 federal troops — just 10 days after Gettysburg — to quell the uprising. Order was restored after two days of street fighting that left 105 people dead. Historians still call it the worst riot in American history.[6]

So it was amid this upheaval that "The Southern Cross" was published and the battle over the Confederate banner reached a new level of intensity. The defiant Baltimore newspapermen knew they would be arrested. Lincoln had been on a rampage in their city well before the poem was ever published. Among those arrested were a grandson of Francis Scott Key (who wrote the "Star Spangled Banner"), Baltimore's chief of police, and four commissioners.[7] Much of the Key family were known Confederates, though at least three served in the Union army. One was Major John J. Key whom Lincoln personally dismissed from the Army. Lincoln suspected Key of making a treasonous statement implying that Union General George McClellan was intentionally dragging the war out until a peace accord could be reached. Lincoln was already suspicious of McClellan who had failed to attack the retreating Confederate army after the battle of Antietam on September 17, 1862.

Major Key maintained he was loyal to the Union, noting his son had just been killed while fighting for the Union at the Battle of Perryville. Lincoln, also paranoid that the popular McClellan might launch a *coup d'etat*, rejected Key's defense (Key's statement appears to have been innocent gossip). Lincoln used Key to "send a message to all of McClellan's staff." He threw the distraught Key out of the army despite appeals in Key's behalf by Lincoln cabinet members.[8]

Lincoln was anything but the mild-mannered emancipator, a reputation northern historians moved quickly to establish immediately following the war and his assassination. The arrests made in connection with the "The Southern Cross" were in keeping with his ruthless actions at the time. There was no way Lincoln could tolerate such writings that openly glorified the relatively new battle standard of the Confederacy. So attacks — and ill feelings — toward the Confederate battle flag are nothing new.

Though people are rarely arrested anymore for flying the Confederate battle flag, attacks against flag supporters have intensified in recent years. Southern children are now being expelled from school for wearing T-shirts featuring the flag. Some people have lost their jobs for displaying or defending the flag. The flag has been removed from public properties, and a vocal minority — supported by the news media — routinely slanders the flag, calling it a racist symbol. The most heinous attack occurred when two black men shot and killed a white man from Kentucky in 1995 for flying a Confederate battle flag in the back of his pickup.

There have been some near arrests like the 1994 incident involving Charles Lunsford, the former Georgia spokesman for the Sons of Confederate Veterans and three friends who were carrying a battle flag at Alexander Stephens State Park in Georgia. Several other people, including six Georgia state troopers, showed up when park officials threatened to arrest the group if they did not remove the battle flag. The state troopers reminded the park officers that carrying the battle flag was within the constitutional rights of those wishing to do so. The park officers retreated, and the flag was permitted in the park.

"We wanted them to arrest us," Lunsford said, noting that such a move would have brought more attention to the issue. "They were wrong."

Not only were people's constitutional rights nearly violated, but the whole episode raised another important issue: Why were officials banning the Confederate battle flag from a park that honors the vice president of the Confederacy? The likely answer: A resolution passed in 1991 by the National Association for the Advancement of Colored People (NAACP) calling for the abolishment of everything Confederate. (More on this later.)

The defiant reaction by the pro-flag group should not have surprised park officials. The battle flag has always stirred the hearts of Southerners, particularly those whose ancestors fought for the Confederacy. Eye contact with the flag can make Southerners' chests swell with regional pride, while its desecration can cause them to quickly draw battle lines. An attack upon the Confederate battle flag is an attack upon the South.

The flag is the embodiment of the South: patriotism, family, religion, farms, local autonomy, hospitality, "Bear" Bryant, chivalry, grits and Goo-Goos, banjos, fiddles, honor, bravery, Moonpies, and "Dixie." To call for the removal of the battle flag is to herald the banishment of everything that is quintessentially Southern. Equally as sinister is the blatant attempt by anti-flag supporters to rewrite America's history to fit their modern-day political goals. The battle flag is a key target in their quest.

Some ask, "Well what about all the immigrants and Northerners flocking to the region?" As I wrote in the introduction, the South's culture is a dominant culture. Southerners tend to make new arrivals more like themselves. For example, 22 percent of non-Southerners under age 25 now say they use the term "y'all" very often. That is up from the four percent of their grandparents' generation.[9] I recently complained to a friend, who had moved to Tennessee from the North, about how it seems that Southern women are trying to rid themselves of their native accent. "You obviously haven't heard my little granddaughter," my friend said with a grin as she rolled her eyes.

The South's dominance is apparent in entertainment and religion. Country music, a truly Southern form, has exploded in popularity. And the South's evangelical Protestantism has shaken the foundations of politics, while scaring the wits out of the secular news media. Woe unto the news organizations that attacks those filling the pews in Southern churches on Sunday.

Newcomers to the South often learn quickly that the region is unique and that Southerners' passion for their heritage is paramount. A few newcomers have tried to change the South, but they become bitterly frustrated when they fail. They forget that an occupation army sent by Lincoln supporters during Reconstruction couldn't turn the trick either. At the heart of Southern heritage is the Confederate battle flag. The South's history is woven through the sacred threads composing the beloved banner, threads forged in bravery and paid with the blood of its Fathers.

Most Southerners know their history, much to the chagrin of the politically correct revisionists who want it rewritten, and ultimately suppressed. The politically correct movement has gotten the attention of Southerners who have always been protective of how history is taught in their public schools. Many Southerners feel the attacks on the battle flag are just the first step toward branding white Southerners as mean and evil people. It was done to Southerners once before, circa 1860, so it's understandable that they think it could be done again. The politically correct demagogues want history from the Southern perspective to be taught in very restrictive terms. They want any discussion concerning the South's constitutionally protected right to secede in order to gain its independence to be distorted, focusing solely on the slavery issue. For example, new proposed standards for teaching history to American school children have been written in recent years by a national committee of teachers, historians, and administrators. It was funded by four philanthropic foundations and issued by the National Center for History in the Schools at the University of California at Los Angeles. The original draft was severely criticized because it virtually ignored white male heroes like George Washington while containing 17 references to the Klu Klux Klan and 19 to McCarthyism.[10]

While most Southerners know their history, such teaching has had an effect on young southerners. They are ashamed of who they are and their homeland. Ask your children if they know who J.E.B. Stuart or Sam Davis were? As a result, there are likely to be more confrontations like the one that occurred between a gentleman and historian Mildred Rutherford earlier this century: Mrs. Rutherford," the man said, "my father was a Confederate soldier, but had he lived, I am sure he would have regretted having fought for the wrong side." To which Rutherford replied: "Far more probably, he would have regretted having a son so disloyal to the principles for which he was willing to give his life."[11]

There also is evidence that the "politically correctniks" are threatening Civil War sites around the country. The leftist Organization of American Historians and the National Park Service have discussed adopting the new liberal teaching standards for the National Park Service. Just imagine having some government paid scholar, at a national battlefield, detailing how many Union "multiculturalists" charged the "racist" Confederate breastworks.

Don't laugh.

The United Daughters of the Confederacy dedicated a six-foot, four-ton, granite monument honoring free black Heyward Shepherd at Harper's Ferry, Virginia, on October 10, 1931. Shepherd was killed by two of John Brown's thugs during their raid on the United States Arsenal at Harper's Ferry on October 16, 1859. Northern and Southern historians have identified the gunmen as Oliver Brown and Stewart Taylor.[12] Among the guests at the dedication were descendants of Shepherd. The ceremony's speaker was Henry T. MacDonald, president of the all-black Storer College in Harper's Ferry. The Storer College singers provided music. The monument was originally located on property owned by the Baltimore and Ohio Railroad, but was later moved to West Virginia property. West Virginia then gave the property to the National Park Service. The monument remained undisturbed until the 1970s, sitting just outside the firehouse where John Brown's men held hostages.

By the way, the National Park Service removed five iron plaques the U.S. War Department had erected commemorating Stonewall Jackson's capture of Harper's Ferry (the largest mass surrender of the U.S. Army prior to World War II). They have never been returned.

As politically correctness reared its ugly head in the late 1970s, Shepherd's monument became the next target. The Park Service asked the UDC in 1976 if it would object to the monument being moved while construction was completed on a nearby building. No objection was made. Five years passed without the monument being returned to its original site. A UDC investigation found the monument lying in a nearby Park Service storage area. A July 1, 1981 letter to the UDC from a Park Service official said Shepherd's monument "has become a subject of discussion among representatives of the National Association for the Advancement of Colored People (NAACP)." The Park Service, the official said, "has decided to relocate the stone in approximately its original position with an adjacent interpretive plaque depicting it in the context of the time it was erected." The new plaque failed to identify Shepherd's killers and was an obvious attempt to rewrite history. When the UDC and other heritage organizations strongly objected to the new plaque, the Park Service returned the monument to its site, but covered it with a wooden box — out of public view — for more than a decade as the controversy went unresolved. It's interesting to note that Storer College placed a stone slab nearby honoring Brown and his men as "freedom fighters" in 1918. But of course, there is no "interpretive" plaque with Brown's stone.[13]

But all is not lost! Some Southerners, like many in the SCV, have hit the public speaking circuit by visiting civic clubs and classrooms. In some cases, near Atlanta, Georgia, they have received permission by the local school board to write history courses based on proven fact. Southern colleges, such as the University of Georgia and the University of North Carolina have established programs focusing exclusively on the South's past and present. This is in stark contrast to the anti-flag minority which tries to create an emotional atmosphere (with the issue of slavery) while suppressing historical truths that do not support their self-serving political agendas. As this book attempts to show, there is a wide gulf between a people's true history and petty politics based on distortion and bigotry.

In vexillological terms most experts rate the Confederate battle flag among the most beautiful banners ever designed. Next to the Stars and Stripes, it remains the second best-selling flag on the American market. Shaped like a square, the original battle flag featured a red field with a blue St. Andrew's cross edged in white, extending the full length and width of the flag. Thirteen white, five-pointed stars, each one representing the 11 states of the Confederacy and the exiled Confederate governments of Kentucky and Missouri, were located inside the cross.

It gained immediate popularity with the Confederate soldiers. As the death toll mounted, the flag took on a more profound meaning with each passing battle.

But to get a better understanding of any symbol, and particularly with the Confederate battle flag, one must consider its origin. By examining its parts and going to the people to whom the flag belongs, one gains confirmation as to its meaning and purpose. In the case of the Confederate battle flag this means going to the Confederate soldiers or their ancestors.

It does not, and will never, belong to hate groups such as the masquerading Nazis known as the Klu Klux Klan. The battle flag was never the Confederacy's national flag. It was only approved by the War Department as the "official banner" of the Confederate army and navy. And as you will see in a later chapter, the soldiers' explanations offer far more insight into the meaning of the battle flag than any of the shallow revisionist demagoguery being spewed today.

Most debate over the Confederate battle flag begins with its issuance following the battle of First Manassass on July 21, 1861. Confederate field commanders had trouble identifying their units on the battlefield because the Confederate national flag (the so-called "Stars and Bars"), which the army was using, looked too much like the Stars and Stripes. The chaos prompted Confederate General Joe Johnston to order the design of a new flag for his Army of Northern Virginia. The result was the battle flag. Today, Southerners fly the rectangular version (which was actually the navy jack of the Confederate fleet). The history of the Confederate battle flag will be covered more extensively later. It is only mentioned here because First Manassass is where exploration of the flag traditionally begins.

No examination of the battle flag should be undertaken without beginning with its most distinguishable feature: the Cross of St. Andrew. The Cross of St. Andrew is nothing new when it comes to flags. The Hapsburgs introduced it to Spain in the 16th century.[14] More recently it has been adopted by Poland, Lithuania, Ukraine, Hungary, and East Germany. Alabama has a red Cross of St. Andrew on a white field as its state flag. The states of Georgia and Mississippi have the Confederate battle flag incorporated in their state banners, while Florida and Hawaii feature variations of the St. Andrew's Cross. The Cross of St. Andrew easily precedes the Hapsburgs as well as the others just mentioned.

To fully understand the Cross of St. Andrew, one must go back to the time of Jesus Christ. The first disciple Christ called to assist with His ministry was a fisherman named Andrew, the brother of Simon Peter, who would become Jesus' second disciple. Andrew was born in Bethsaida, Galilee, the son of a fisherman. He was a hard worker as evidenced by his burned, dried, coarse hands, which he used to cast nets all day. Fishing and religion were Andrew's primary interests.

He was a faithful listener to John the Baptist and was present the day John saw Jesus and proclaimed, "Behold the Lamb of God

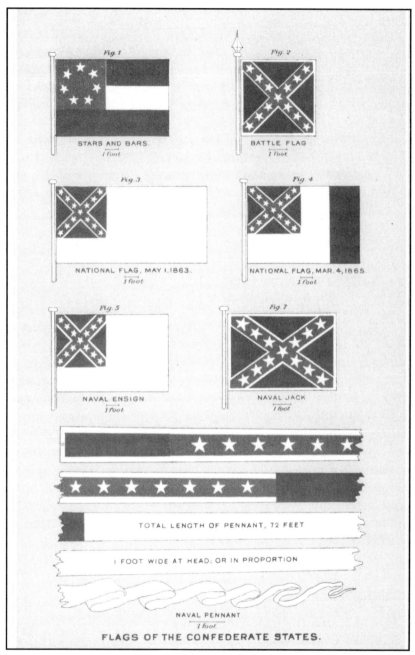

Taken from The Flags of the Confederate States of America published in 1907 by William E. Mickle and United Confedrate Veterans. This scarce pamphlet was written to "set the record straight" regarding the flags used by the Confederacy.

who takes away the sins of the world." Andrew was stunned, for here was a prophet proclaiming not the coming of the Messiah, but His arrival! Andrew ran to Jesus, upon which Jesus said to him, "What are you looking for?" Scholars say Andrew's likely reply was: "You."[15]

Andrew became a faithful follower of Christ and boldly preached the Gospel following Jesus' crucifixion, resurrection, and ascension into Heaven. He preached in many Asiatic nations and in what is now Russia. Andrew was crucified circa 69 A.D. in Patrae, Greece. Unlike Jesus, he was not crucified on a Latin cross. Andrew persuaded his prosecutor, who objected to Andrew's Christian preaching, to crucify him on a cross made of two intersecting pieces of wood of equal length, the ends of which were fixed in the ground. He convinced the prosecutor not to nail him to the cross as the Romans had Christ, but rather to tie him to the cross with cord, even though he knew it would mean a slower, more painful death. Andrew's reason: He felt unworthy of being crucified in the same manner as Christ.

For three days Andrew, who was at least 90 years old at the time, hung on the cross and continued to preach the love of Jesus. An ancient writer describes what happened:

"The people as they listened (to Andrew) began to believe his words, and asked the governor to let him be taken down from the cross. Not liking to refuse them, he at last ordered the ropes be cut, but when the last cord was severed, the body of the apostle fell to the ground quite dead."[16]

Andrew died a Christian martyr and became the patron saint of both Russia and Scotland. Russia is understandable, since historians place a portion of Andrew's ministry in that country. When Peter the Great became czar, he incorporated the Cross of St. Andrew into his nation's national banner in 1699.[17] Andrew's connection with Scotland is equally strong. Andrew had amassed a number of disciples and they continued to spread Christianity throughout Europe following his crucifixion. As the Christian faith grew, so did the number of missionaries throughout Europe. With the arrival of St. Patrick to Ireland and St. Columba to Scotland, Christianity reached among the last of the Celtic tribes around 500 A.D.[18] (Interestingly St. Patrick, the patron saint of Ireland, was actually the son of a Scottish deacon. Patrick was kidnapped as a boy and sold into slavery before escaping and rising to prominence in the church.).[19]

The converted Scots eventually built a church on their country's east coast in honor of Andrew. Today, the area around that church has become a bishopric and town of St. Andrews, which is also known as the international headquarters for the game of golf.

An examination of Scotland's ties to St. Andrew is important because such a large percentage of Southerners trace their ancestry to the Scots or other Celtic-influenced peoples like the Scots-Irish.

Little wonder Glasgow, Scotland, has its own "Grand Ole Opry," a barbeque restaurant that features country music entertainment and a stage adorned with Confederate battle flags.

> *Toward midnight the Committee prepared for the last official duty of the night: closing ceremonies," wrote guest and reviewer Steve DuRocher. "The Confederate battle flag was presented... with a member holding each of the four corners and one member standing close by. They were immediately surrounded by the rest of the Committee, who were encircled by as many patrons as could fit on the floor. They held hands and guarded the flag as the band started to play Elvis' 'Trilogy'... . Elvis was followed by a raucous rendition of "Dixie."*[20]

Some people have suggested that the War For Southern Independence was "the last great rising of the Scottish clans." With the strong ties (as we will see) between the two lands there is little wonder why.

How St. Andrew became so revered in Scotland is shrouded in legends. One of the more bizarre is where Christian monks recover the bones of Andrew in 370 A.D., in order to prevent them from falling into the hands of Emperor Constantine. During their escape with the relics, the monks were shipwrecked along the east coast of Scotland. They encountered natives and began preaching the Gospel. They eventually built a church to house the relics.[21] The ruins of the abbey are all that remain today.

The earliest reference (in the 1100s) to the Cross of St. Andrew imputes an origin going back to Hungus, king of the Picts, in the eighth century.[22] Another, also dating to the eighth century, claims that Achaius, King of the ancient Scots, saw the Cross of St. Andrew in the sky the night before a battle with Athelstan and his Saxon horde. Upon the defeat of the Saxons, Achaius vowed to make the Cross of St. Andrew Scotland's national device.[23] Whether

tradition, or historical fact, Andrew took on monumental importance to the Scots.

Tradition has always been important to the Scots, a fact that did
not go unnoticed by Confederate President Jefferson Davis. "St.
Andrew's, it is claimed, is the oldest military order in the world,
dating back to the time of Achaius, and Hungus, at least, so
tradition goes, and I have more faith in tradition than in history.
Tradition usually rests upon something which men did know;
history is often the manufacture of the mere liar," Davis said in an
1875 speech to the Scottish Society of Memphis.[24] Davis' words
would be appropriate even amid today's distorted view of the
Confederate battle flag. (Davis, by the way, was of Welsh descent,
which is also Celtic.)

Though 1385 appears to be the first reference to the St.
Andrew's Cross, it is widely held that theScots used it much
earlier. It was ordered in 1385 that every soldier of a combined
French and Scottish army, fighting Richard II of England, should
wear "a white St. Andrew's Cross, and if his jack is white or his
coat white he shall bear the said white cross in a piece of black cloth
round or square."[25] Blue slowly replaced black as the standard
background color for the cross. That would be logical since the
original inhabitants of Scotland were the Celtic tribe known as the
Picts, dating back to 297 A.D.[26] The color of the Pictish nation was
blue. This should come as no surprise because blue dye could be
easily made from Highland vegetation.

Today's Scottish Cross of St. Andrew is white on a blue field.
The cross is also incorporated into the Union Jack, the flag of Great
Britain. The Cross of St. Andrew continues to fly today throughout
Scotland. The Confederate battle flag's Cross of St. Andrew is
exactly like that of Scotland's.

Another key point concerning the original meaning of the St.
Andrew's Cross: The shape of the cross upon which Andrew died
was the same as the Greek letter "X," which in English is the letters
"CH" or the first two letters of "Christ."[27] As the decades went by,
the St. Andrew's cross, or "X," evolved into an international
symbol of "good faith," one that was binding on legal documents
and understood by the uneducated and well educated alike. This
particular point becomes very important in understanding the St.
Andrew's Cross on the Confederate battle flag and the flag's
meaning to the soldiers.

When the massive migrations of Scots to North America began

around 1700, many found their old nemisis, the English, already
settled in the New England states. Most of the Scottish immigrants
entered through the ports of Philadelphia; Norfolk, Virginia;
Charleston, South Carolina; and Savannah, Georgia. Those who
landed in Philadelphia traveled inland and then turned south.

Thousands migrated to the vast, untamed Southland through
the mid-1700s. The South provided them with plenty of land and
game, and a climate much milder than they had endured in the
Scottish Highlands. They were joined by lowland Scots who had
moved to the north of Ireland during the 17th century and immi-
grated to America by the thousands between 1717 and the early
1780s. These particular immigrants are known as the Scots-Irish.[28]
They were followed by a massive influx of Irish and Welsh settlers.

Unlike the New Englanders, who were primarily of English
stock and who were greatly influenced by the Germanic tribes of
the Saxons and Jutes, the "new Southerners" maintained their
Celtic culture and the influences of the ancient Scots, Britons,
Angles, Scadinavians, and Picts. The Celts, one of the most
dominant civilizations in the history of the world, controlled much
of Europe for centuries well before — and after — Christ. They
were herders who depended on the land for survival. They were
also fierce fighters who frequently fought with just about everyone
on the European continent, including themselves. They were
cocky, much like the haughtiness Southerners are often accused of
displaying.[29] To understand the Celts is to further understand
Southerners, the cause for which the South seceded, and even the
flag that symbolized that cause.

An interesting argument has advanced in recent years concerning how strongly the South's culture has maintained its Celtic
roots, while with the North, though possessing some Celtic blood-
lines, just the opposite is true. This argument was introduced by Dr.
Grady McWhiney, the Lyndon Baines Johnson professor of history at Texas Christian University in Fort Worth, Texas.

> *More than a decade of research and analysis…*
> *convinced me that fundemental and lasting divi-*
> *sions between Southerners and Northerners began*
> *in colonial America when migrants from the Celtic*
> *regions of the British Isles — Scotland, Ireland,*
> *Wales and Cornwall — and from the English up-*
> *lands managed to implant their traditional customs*
> *in the Old South. By 1860 they far outnumbered the*

combined total of all other white Southerners and
their culture dominated the region.[30]

The first U.S, census in 1790 shows that Southerners of Celtic descent outnumbered Anglo-Saxons by two to one.[31] By 1850 scholars contend that 75 percent of the white population in the South was of Celtic descent.[32] United States Census Bureau statistics in 1990 showed that one in five Caucasian Tennesseans can still trace their ancestry to the Scots, Scots-Irish, Irish or Welsh.[33]

"The antebellum North, on the other hand, was settled and influenced principally by people who had migrated from the English lowlands," McWhiney contends.[34] It (antebellum American history) was "shaped far more by the differences between Northerners and Southerners than by any likenesses," he writes. "Their conflict in the 1860s was not as much brother against brother as it was culture against culture."[35] Indeed, the North had embarked on industrialization, while the South remained agricultural. This caused a number of problems that caused the two regions to grow apart.

Other scholars have noted the differences in the two regions, too. Joyce E. Chaplin, associate professor of history at Vanderbilt University in Nashville, Tennessee, says 16th century English took great pains to explain that extremely hot and extremely cold climates promoted "lassitude and barbarity" and that a moderately cool climate made them "superior."[36] Perhaps such thinking gave rise to the vile stereotype that Southerners are lazy and dumb.

The differences between the two regions became more pronounced in the 1860s. Until the invention of steamboats, railroads, and telegraphs, there was little opportunity for the two regions to communicate with each other. After all, they were separated by a vast unsettled territory.

Even a typical Confederate "webfoot" like Private Sam Watkins saw the stark contrasts in the two regions. "The South is our country, the North is the country of those who live there. We are an agricultural people; they are manufacturing people. They are the descendants of the good old Puritan Plymouth Rock stock, and we of the South from the proud and aristocratic stock of Cavaliers."[37]

The South knew a great deal about the North because that's where most of the literature was being produced. But the North knew little about the South because there was little literature available. This increased the opportunity for misrepresentation of Southern positions.[38] Northerners were — by and large — better educated, more well-read, and were more reserved in their demeanor. Southerners, on the other hand, were tough frontier people. They had to be to endure the Indians and harsh conditions. They enjoyed playing music, telling stories (William Shakespeare was from Wales), and just loved to have a good time, maybe too good a time. Early Southerners had an affinity for alcohol — and while gracious — could exhibit a quick temper — often to the point of dueling. For example, President Andrew Jackson, a Tennessean of Scots-Irish descent, was in five duels.[39]

Confederate General Robert E. Lee would later acknowledge the more professional fighting skill of these descendants of Celtic tribesmen. When asked what race do you believe makes the best soldiers? Lee responded, "The Scots who came to this country by way of Ireland. Because they have all the dash of the Irish in taking up a position and all the stubbornness of the Scots in holding it."[40]

It is interesting to note that 31 of the 78 Medals of Honor presented to U.S. Army troops in the Korean War went to Southerners, half of them of Scottish descent.[41]

Lee should not have been surprised. The Celts' reputation as warriors was legendary. Referred to as "the people who came out of the darkness," by German author Gerhard Herm, the Celts terrified the Romans prior to the birth of Christ. Interestingly, Confederate Southerners were often looked upon with disdain by Yankee Northerners who were appalled at their haughty and cavalier attitude. Such behavior is strikingly similar to the way Greek historian Diodorus described the Celts prior to their clash with the Romans around 225 B.C.: "They look like wood-demons, their hair thick and shaggy like a horse's mane. Some are clean-shaven, but others... leave a moustache that covers the whole mouth... . At the same time they swing their weapons about to intimidate their foe... insulting and belittling their opponents... ."[42] The Celts prepared to attack by sounding "weird, discordant horns and then with a chorus of shouts, they broke ranks and charged forward."[43]

The Celts' "chorus of shouts" may have been the birth of the maniacal "rebel yell." "There is nothing like it on this side of the infernal region," a Union soldier said, recalling the yell after the war. "The peculiar corkscrew sensation that it sends down your backbone under these circumstances can never be told. You have to feel it."[44]. Some historians have suggested that the Celtic ranks' rapid movements toward their enemy was much like the heroic charges made by greatly outnumbered Confederates at Gettysburg and Franklin.

Behind Beauvoir, the Biloxi, Mississippi home of Jefferson Davis, is a Confederate cemetery. Near its center is a large Celtic cross. A Confederate battle flag flies just a few paces away, serving as a reminder that the two are forever linked. It only makes sense that the Celtic culture with all of its character, religion, and symbols would come to America through its Scot, Scots-Irish, Welsh, and Irish descendants. And with them came the Cross of St. Andrew. The cross appears to have first made its leap over the Atlantic Ocean onto a North American flag on January 2, 1776. That's when it was combined with a Cross of St. George (the patron saint of England) and 13 red and white stripes to form a flag flown in a Colonial Army camp at Cambridge, Massachusetts.[45]

Any examination of the tie between the Celtic desendants of Scotland and Ireland and the South must include religion. And the obviously religious aspect of the Cross of St. Andrew suggests some religious influence when it comes to the Confederate battle flag. Certainly religion was on the minds of some Southerners who wanted to help design a new flag for the Confederacy. One suggestion had a flag with a sun and shield with the words "The Lord God is a Sun and Shield." "It would seem to invite the blessings of God... to lift the standard of the Lord God — to acknowledge Him as Sun and Shield," Samuel Barrett of Washington, Georgia, wrote in a May 23, 1861, letter forwarded to South Carolina Congressman William Porcher Miles. Miles was head of the congressional committee tasked with adopting a flag for the Confederacy. Barrett said the flag should be "a token of humble acknowledgement of Him — and be a public testimony to the world that our trust is in the Lord our God."[46]

The acknowledgement of God went well beyond the individual Southerner. The Confederate government acknowledged God by including the words "guidance of Almighty God" in its Constitution. The U.S. Constitution does not specifically name God.

It is likely that as the war raged on, the religious meanings of the Cross of St. Andrew and the Confederate battle flag became much more pronounced in the Confederate ranks. Religion certainly became more important as a series of defeats made Confederates feel more dependent on the Almighty. The day in, day out facing of death on the battlefield took its toll as well.

The Scots and Scots-Irish were almost exclusively Presbyterian. Indeed the Presbyterian Church remains the national Church of Scotland and is the largest Protestant demonination in Northern Ireland.[47]

Though the South is deeply religious today, some historians suggest that the early South was anything but religious. That would be understandable given the sparsely settled territory and the inability for missionaries to travel over the rugged terrain. Things gradually changed as the Great Awakening hit the colonies between 1725 and 1770. Still by 1820 only one Southerner out of 10 was a member of a church.[48]

Then a second tidal wave of revival hit the South during the 1860s, cementing Christianity's hold on the region.[49] By the mid-1800s, Baptist and Methodist preachers had gained a foothold in the South.

"There was a great revival throughout the South in the 1830s," says Dr. Charles Estell Baker, former chaplain-in-chief of the SCV and the pastor of a Protestant church in Birmingham, Alabama. "And it continued during the war, particularly in the winters of 1862-63 and 1863-64. "Troops weren't moving as much during the winter, and there were a lot of religious tracts circulating through the camps."

So fervently religious were the Confederate soldiers that they would spontaneously erect crude log tabernacles that provided shelter for day long revival meetings. In one revival alone in 1863-64 in Dalton, Georgia, 20,000 Confederate soldiers accepted Christ as their Savior. An unknown Confederate soldier, who was stationed at Dalton during the time of the revival, reminisced about his experience in a January 1893 letter: "There has never been... a stronger religious feeling than there was in the army under Joseph E. Johnston. "Profanity, which is so common among soldiers, was almost entirely given up. There were no scoffers at the religion that had such a hold upon the army."[50] Some estimates place the number of conversions between 1861-1865 in the 600,000-man Confederate army at 100,000.[51]

Interestingly, the leaders of the Confederacy were affected by the revival as well. Jefferson Davis, Generals Dick Ewell, Braxton Bragg, John Bell Hood, and Johnston all entered the church during the revival.[52] During Christmas 1866, Pope Pius IX sent Davis a crown of thorns as a gift of sympathy as the Confederate president remained imprisoned at Fort Monroe, Virginia. The crown was woven by the Pope himself.

"We lost the physical battle, but we won the spiritual battle," Baker said. "That's why you see so many little country churches all over the South. Many of them, if you will check, were started right after the war."

While the Cross of St. Andrew is clearly a religious symbol on the Confederate battle flag, religion found its way on other Confederate battle standards as well. General Robert E. Lee, for example, arranged the stars on his headquarters flag to reflect the Ark of the Convenant. One of Lee's favorite songs, one he requested sung at his funeral, was the hymn "How Firm A Foundation." It is still a favorite in Southern churches.

"There was nothing that did more to promote the growth of Christian feeling and rectitude in the Confederate army than the spirit and bearing of its leaders," the late Rev. J.B. Hawthorne, pastor of First Baptist Church of Atlanta, told attendees at a United Confederate Veterans reunion in Nashville in the late 1890s. "Never did an army march into battle offered by men more loyal to Christ than Stonewell Jackson, Robert E. Lee, and many of their subordinates," he told the throng. "Who can calculate the power of Jackson's religious influence upon the men whom he led to battle? Gen. Ewell was so impressed by it that he was heard to say: 'If that be religion, I must have it.' After making a profession of faith in Christ, he confessed that his rebellious heart and will had been conquered by the power of Jackson's godly life."[53]

Jackson, who was of Scots-Irish descent, was a devout Presbyterian. He was reluctant to march his troops — or fight — on Sundays unless absolutely necessary.

Hawthorne gave another example of how religion had grabbed a powerful foothold on the Confederate army:

> I recall the case of Lewis Minor Coleman, a gallant young officer, who received his mortal wound at Fredricksburg," Hawthorne said. "For more than three months his sufferings seemed to be all that any mortal could possibly bear, yet it was endured with the utmost patience and resignation. When convinced that there was no hope of recovery, he was more than patient; he was happy; he was jubilant. He said to friends weeping at his

bedside: 'Tell General Lee and General Jackson they know how Christian soldiers can fight, but I wish they could be here that they might see how one of them can die.'[54]

The revival extended well beyond the Army of Northern Virginia where Lee and Jackson led. Revivals sprang up throughout the Armies of Tennessee and Trans-Mississippi. Thousands of brave men in these armies who had publicly professed Christ proved by their meekness and patience in suffering, and by their joy in death, that their professions were not spurious," he said.[55]

Some historians have argued that Confederates were able to endure the postwar indignities and hardships put upon them by the radical Republicans of the North largely because of their religious experiences during the war.

And then there was the Confederate Army's motto: "Help yourself and God will help you." Also, the latin words "Deo Vindice" appeared on the Great Seal of the Confederacy. It's English translation: "With God as Our Defender." The Confederates may not have considered the Cross of St. Andrew on their battle flag a religious symbol at the beginning of the war, but it's likely that changed amid the revivals and as it became consecrated in blood with each passing battle.

When the Southern states seceded (South Carolina being the first on December 19, 1860), the Provisional Confederate Congress established the Committee on Flag and Seal, tasking it with finding a suitable flag for the new nation. Word quickly spread throughout the South and hundreds of designs and models were sent to the committee. Some featured all kinds of animals, while others featured suns, plants, and shields.

Perhaps the most bizarre suggestion came from Samuel Morse, inventor of the telegraph. Morse felt the "Stars and Stripes" should be cut in half, with the North getting the top half and the South getter the lower half. "It prevents all disputes on a claim for the old flag by either confederacy," Morse wrote. "Each flag, being a moiety of the old flag, will retain something at least of the sacred memories of the past for the sober reflection of each confederacy, and if a war with some foreign nation or combination of nations, under our treaty of offense and defense, the two separate flags, by natural affinity, would clasp fittingly together... ."[56]

The flag committee said the designs were divided into two classifications: "Those which copy and preserve the principal features of the United States flag, with slight and unimportant modifications; and those which are very elaborate, complicated, or fantastical."[57] On March 4, 1861, four designs were presented to the entire Provisional Congress.[58] One was a design by William Porcher Miles of South Carolina, who chaired the flag committee. Miles' design was basically the Confederate battle flag as we know it today, though it only had stars for the seven states that had seceded at that time. Miles' design was rejected by the committee because some members thought it looked like a pair of suspenders, plus the odd number of stars would not balance on the cross.[59]

There also was great sentiment to adopt a flag similar to the United States flag. Congressman Walker Brooke of Mississippi offered a resolution to the committee calling for a flag designed "as similar as possible to that of the United States, making only such changes as should give them distinction. Let us preserve it as far as we can; let us continue to hallow it in our memory, and still say that: 'Long may it wave, O'er the land of the free and the home of the brave.'"[60] Brooke's eulogy was so full of favor for the old flag that it was considered treasonable and resulted in a severe rebuke from fellow lawmakers. Miles made it clear he had regarded the "Stars and Stripes" as an emblem of oppression and tyranny from his childhood days. His remarks were so warmly received with applause that a friend leaned over to Brooke and suggested he withdraw his resolution, which he did.[61]

But Brooke's reasoning was understandable, and it had some support. Brooke and his colleagues were not the ones violating the Constitution as it had been written by the Founding Fathers. They felt it was Lincoln and Northern agitators who were making a mockery of the Constitution. After all, it was abolitionist Senator Charles Sumner of Massachusetts who labeled the Constitution "a covenant with death and an agreement with hell."[62] Brooke, along with many other Southerners, felt it was the North who should be looking for a new flag.

One of the flag designs submitted — though it was not one of the four finalists — came from a Mrs. C. Ladd of Winnsboro, South Carolina. With her design was a letter stating she had offered her three boys in defense of the South and suggested the new nation be called the "Washington Republic," in honor of George Washington.[63] Washington was eventually put on the Confederacy's official seal.

Additionally, some members who agreed with Brooke reminded their colleagues that Southerners had paid with their blood defending the "Stars and Stripes" during the War of 1812 and in the war with Mexico. But Miles never hesitated with a rebuttal. "There is no propriety in retaining the ensign of a government which, in the opinion of the States composing the Confederacy, had become so oppressive and injurious to their interests as to require their separation from it," he said. "As to 'the glories of the old flag,' we must bear in mind that the battles of the Revolution, about which our fondest and proudest memories cluster, were not fought beneath its folds."[64] But then he eased off the pedal. "It must be admitted, however, that something was conceded by the committee to what seemed so strong and earnest a desire to retain at least a suggestion of the old 'Stars and Stripes.'"[65]

This was evident because two other designs presented by the flag committee resembled the "Stars and Stripes." One looked just like "Old Glory," except its seven stripes — rather 13 — were red and blue instead of red and white. In addition, the seven stars inside the canton formed a circle (just like the colonies had done during the Revolution). The other became known as the "Stars and Bars." It had a blue canton, with seven stars in a circle. It featured three stripes, the top and lower were red, the middle one in white. The fourth design was a red flag with a blue circle in the center. It was quickly rejected.[66]

In the end, the Provisional Congress approved the so-called "Stars and Bars" as the Confederacy's first national flag, though ironically no flag law was passed. The "Stars and Bars" was purposely first raised over the state capitol building in Montgomery, Alabama, shortly after the Provisional Congress approved it late in the day on March 4, 1861. It was no coincidence that Abraham Lincoln was inaugurated the same day.[67] The new flag was hoisted — among cheers, the playing of bands, and a seven-gun salute. Miss Letita Christian Tyler, granddaughter of President John Tyler, the only former living president in the Confederacy, did the honors.[68] In ensuing weeks, six more stars were added to the union of the "Stars and Bars," giving it 13 and further evoking memories of the first American war for independence.

Despite the adoption of the "Stars and Bars," Miles' battle flag design would not die. Five months later it would be resurrected. It would be an answer to the lamenting of Confederate General Pierre Gustave Toutant Beauregard following the battle of First Manassas on July 21, 1861. That day Beauregard's slightly outnumbered troops were holding their own against an equally "green" Union force, led by General Irvin McDowell, although as the day worn on the Yanks began to drive the Confederates back from Bull Run Creek. Only tremendous defensive stands by units like General Thomas "Stonewall" Jackson's brigade prevented a Union victory.

Finally reserves, supplied by Beauregard's commander, General Joseph E. Johnston, began arriving by midafternoon. All had deployed to the battlefield — or so they thought. Both armies had various colored uniforms, making it difficult to tell friend from foe. The problem was made considerably worse by the flags. The Confederate "Stars and Bars" — especially from a distance — was often confused with the "Stars and Stripes." Add the confusion wrought by these factors to the noise and smoke, and you can begin to understand the anxiety Beauregard must have felt as he struggled to see through the plumes of smoke bellowing from the artillery and small-arms fire as the battle reached a critical point around 4:00 p.m.

Spotting a body of troops moving toward the Union right flank, Beauregard, with great frustration, continued to peer through his glasses in an effort to determine the brigade-sized unit's identity. The lack of a breeze on that hot and hazy day caused the unidentified unit's battle standards to hang limp. Anxiety turned into anguish as the general begged staffers to look in hopes their eyes might be keener. No luck.

Finally a puff of wind spread the approaching colors. It was the "Stars and Bars"! Looking right and left to his staff, Beauregard screamed, "See that the day is ours!" as he ordered an immediate advance.[69]

In a letter after the war, Beauregard wrote: "At the Battle of Manassas,... I found it difficult to distinguish our *then* Confederate flag from the United States flag (the two being so much alike, especially when General Jubal A. Early made the flank movement which decided the fate of the day."[70]

Indeed Early's brigade, composed of the 24th Virginia, 7th Louisiana and 13th Mississippi regiments, slammed into McDowell's right flank. The surprised Union troops broke and ran, many of them not stopping until they got to Washington 25 miles away.[71]

"I... resolved to have ours (flag) changed... or to adopt for my command a battle flag which would be entirely different from any State or Federal flag," Beauregard wrote after the war. "After the battle it was found that many persons in both armies firmly believed that each side had used, as a strategem, the flags of his opponent."[72]

Soon after Manassas, Beauregard made a point of bringing up the flag problem. Johnston agreed that something had to be done and ordered that each regiment fly their appropriate state flag. But Johnston quickly discovered that only Virginia had furnished her regiments with state flags, so the idea was abandoned.

Meanwhile, Beauregard contacted Miles, who had served on his staff at First Manassas before being elected to the permanent Confederate House of Representatives. Beauregard requested a new national flag be adopted that did not look so much like the "Stars and Stripes." But Congress was unwilling to change the flag.

In a later meeting at Fairfax Courthouse, Virginia, Johnston, Beauregard, and General Gustavus W. Smith further discussed the flag dilemma. Their decision: Adopt a battle flag specifically for Confederate forces. Subsequently, Miles suggested the design he had presented to the Provisional Congress in March 1861.[73] Coincidentally, a design like Miles' was submitted by Edward C. Hancock of New Orleans and presented by Colonel J.B. Walton of the Louisiana Washington Artillery.[74]

By this time, word had gotten out that a new flag was needed for the army, prompting many other designs to come in. Beauregard had his draftsman make drawings of each design and presented them to Johnston and the rest of the headquarters staff.

"We gave the preference to one of those (designs) offered by Colonel J.B. Walton, commanding the Louisiana Washington Artillery, which corresponded closely to the one recommended to Congress by Colonel Miles," Beauregard wrote after the war. "Both were oblong; the field was red, the bars blue, and the stars white; but Colonel Walton's had the Latin Cross, and Colonel Miles' the St. Andrews (which was picked)... ."[75]

Johnston liked the selection of Miles' flag, but made one change. "I modified it only by making the shape square instead of oblong, and prescribed the different sizes for infantry, artillery, and cavalry," Johnston said.[76] It was immediately approved by the War Department in September 1861 and was first distributed to regiments of the Army of Northern Virginia a month later.[77]

What did the flag's design mean?

As stated earlier, the Cross of St. Andrew was derived from Andrew, a disciple of Jesus. It remains Scotland's national flag, and a large number of Southerners were of Scottish or Scots-Irish descent. The cross, in Greek, stands for "CH," the first two letters in "Christ." It also became a symbol of "good faith." The stars represented each of the Confederate states. Traditionally, the colors red, white, and blue are the true colors of a republic. In heraldry they are emblematic of the three great virtues — valor, purity, and truth.[78]

But most importantly, it was originally designed and adopted because it was easy to identify on the battlefield. Most of the battle flags were square, though today's rectangular version was flown late in the war by regiments in the Army of Tennessee. There were a few units (like those commanded by Generals William Hardee, Leonidas Polk and Patrick Cleburne) in the Western Theatre that never used the battle flag.

The battle flag was only adopted by the army — and that is important to note. After the war, Carlton McCarthy wrote an article about a speech Beauregard gave after the war for the *Southern Historical Society Papers*. In discussing the battle flag, McCarthy writes, "This article is penned... to place the battle flag in a place of security, as it were, separated from all the political significance which attaches to the Confederate flag, and depending for its future place solely upon the deeds of the armies which bore it amid hardships untold to many victories."[79]

It was never the national flag of the Confederacy. Disdain for the "Stars and Bars" grew to the point that a second national flag was adopted on May 1, 1863. The so-called "Stainless Banner," had the battle flag as a union, while the rest of the flag was white. But when the flag hung limp, it looked like a flag of surrender. Just one month before Appomattox, the Confederate Congress approved a third national flag which was just like the second, except that a red bar was added on the end of the flag. Some army units in the Western theatre did not get the battle flag until 1864. A few never adopted the battle flag.

The first three battle flags were made by Hettie, Jennie and Constance Carey of Richmond. They were made from silk dresses and presented to Beauregard, Johnston, and General Earl Van Dorn, who was commander of the First Division at that time.[80] Beauregard kept his for a short time at his winter headquarters in Centreville, Virginia. It remained there on display as a model for troops to see while they awaited the arrival of their new battle flags. Beauregard finally sent the flag to his home town of New Orleans for safekeeping. When the city fell in April 1862, the banner was taken to a French war steamer lying in port. It was transported to Havana, Cuba, where it remained under the care of a Spanish gentleman friendly to the Southern cause. It was returned to Beauregard shortly after the war. On May 28, 1883, Beauregard donated his battle flag — one of the first three ever made — to the Louisiana Washington Artillery. Beauregard was unable to attend the reunion that day, but Colonel Walton was there to accept the flag.[81]

> In the name of General Beauregard, under whose eyes you first went under fire at Manassas..., I have the honor to present to you this sacred emblem of Southern valor and patriotism," said Judge Alfred Roman. "Its colors are yet as fresh as when it received the parting look of its fair maker. Its value is enhanced by the fact that the upper portion of its staff is made of a piece of the flag-staff of Fort Sumter, shot down by the Confederate gunners, in April 1861 (gunners who were under the command of Beauregard). Unsullied though it be by the smoke of battle, it was, none the less, born in war, and the breeze first kissed it in the tented field. It is the genuine model of the glorious flag around which all of us fought, and so many of us bled, and so many of us fell.[82]

The Beauregard battle flag was eventually turned over to the Louisiana Historical Association, which owns Memorial Hall, a Confederate museum in the heart of New Orleans. It remained there until 1988. The flag is now in the hands of a private collector in the Midwest. Speculators say it could fetch as much as $2 million at auction.

CHAPTER TWO

A SACRED SYMBOL IS COMPROMISED

It speaks of men who fought so valiantly,
Now dead and forgotten, heroes unknown,
Who carried this flag, oh how bravely,
Until death claimed them his own.
It speaks of moments when all seemed lost
From our ranks an unforgotten shout arose,
With maddened rush, at any cost,
We wrenched our flag from the hand of foes.
                                    – Our Battle Flag
                                    H.L. Blanchard

Bill Jennings is known in the central Tennessee community of Woodbury as a gentleman dentist who stays active in community endeavors. Friends say he is gracious, but firm when it comes to defending his position in a debate. They say he's the kind John C. Calhoun would have liked.

Jennings is a descendant of Confederate soldiers and a member of the Sons of Confederate Veterans (SCV). He was among the majority who supported the local Cannon County Commission's July 1993 idea to adopt a new county flag. The banner was to be made of one-third county emblem and two-thirds Confederate battle flag. As soon as the measure passed, opposition surfaced, primarily from a nearby chapter of the NAACP and a gay rights group.

The issue ended up in court and details of what happened will be included in a later chapter (the battle flag design was upheld).

But on an autumn Saturday night — during the height of the court battle — a car carrying five Klu Klux Klan members showed up in the center of town. Jennings spotted them and — grabbing a pen and paper — walked behind their car and started scribbling. "They were antagonizing some kids, and one of them was walking down the street waving a battle flag and screaming, 'you're not going to take my flag away from me,'" Jennings recalled.[1]

Some of the other Kluxers, who were having no luck distributing their literature, walked up to Jennings and asked him what he was doing. "I'm writing down your license plate number because I want to know whose butt to kick if you make us lose our county flag," he replied as he was joined by compatriot Danny Nichols.[2] The shaken Kluxers left, but the Woodbury incident stands as a prime example of how defenders of the battle flag have had to contend with various groups trying to appropriate the flag for their own purposes.

Groups like the Klan, the Skinheads, and the Aryan Nation, have tried to redefine the flag — and in the process, have given other groups like the NAACP and the news media reason to howl. The whole mess has caused the news media to "revisit" 1861-1865 — and in typical fashion, they do so with predetermined bias and little knowledge of historical fact. They routinely address a complex issue like the War for Southern Independence in a few paragraphs or with a handful of disgustingly inflammatory pictures.

Every time the KKK parades with the Confederate battle flag, the small, but vocal anti-flag minority starts screaming that the battle flag is a racist symbol — and of course, cameras are always there to capture it for our living rooms. It has reached the point that Southerners cringe everytime the news media does a piece on Southern history.

"Everytime one of those bedsheeted buffoons opens his mouth and spews his ridiculous blather, I see our chances of saving our flag slip away," lamented James W. Zeirke, an SCV member from Sussex, Wisconsin.

"We need to openly challenge the Kluxers every step of the way if we are ever going to prove that our flag is not the racist banner that our enemies say it is."[3]

Is the Confederate battle flag a racist relic? Absolutely not!

What the anti-flag minority choses to ignore is that hate groups fly all sorts of flags. The KKK flies the Stars and Stripes, Nazi, and Christian flags. Is the NAACP and its supporters from the politically correct brigade calling for their banishment as well? Of course not — at least for now. The KKK and other hate groups dance around courthouse squares throughout the South with the Confederate battle flag because they want to gain favor with the Southern people. They know Southerners love the battle flag. What they don't realize is that Southerners view their organizations as repugnant and passe. That's not just the attitude of an overwhelming majority of Southerners today, but many in 1868 as well.

The KKK's first elected Grand Wizard, Confederate General Nathan Bedford Forrest, ordered the Klan disbanded when it veered from its original purpose of protecting war-ravaged and over-taxed Southerners at the start of Reconstruction from carpet-baggers, some out-of-control blacks, the Union occupation army, and the vindictively oppressive radicals of the Republican party.

Honor, valor, truth, and good faith are much of what the Confederate battle flag really stands for. One thing it never has done — or was ever intended to do — is make a political statement. And this is where Southerners, amid all their prosperity, have gotten apathetic.

A plethora of groups, not all of them of the hate variety, have tried to sieze control of the flag. The number of these groups have skyrocketed since the late 1940s. In fact, the number has grown so rapidly that traditional guardians of the battle flag (the United Daughters of the Confederacy and the SCV) have in some cases, been caught off guard, while in others, simply overwhelmed. Meanwhile, other Southerners have done little to protect the battle flag's true meaning.

Though flag supporters in South Carolina have been able to keep the battle flag flying over their state capitol, the issue remains in doubt as a waffling governor plays politics with history and the honor of the South's forefathers. Flag supporter and presidential candidate Pat Buchanan, himself a descendent of a Confederate soldier, was among the most vocal in challenging the South Carolinians to stand up for their heritage: "What kind of timidity and cowardice are today gripping South Carolina that so many of her sons will not defend the battle flag of kinsmen... ? What has happened to South Carolina that she would permit... noise-makers... frighten them into hauling down these colors of courage?"[4]

Find a Confederate battle flag in this photo. You won't because there's not one.
The Klu Klux Klan, as well as other hate groups, fly the Christian Flag and the
American Flag as well. Here they carry "Old Glory" during a 1926 march in

Washington, D.C. Since anti-flaggers claim the Confederate battle flag is racist because the Klan carries it, does that mean the "Stars and Stripes" is racist, too? (Culver Pictures)

Buchanan took dead aim at all South Carolinians, most notably, the politicians. Indeed, many Southern politicians like South Carolina Governor David Beasley, have contributed to the problem because they have failed to use their pulpit to defend their region's honor. A Southern lecturer recently chastised Southerners for not putting more pressure on its politicians over the battle flag issue. "The cruelest thing we can do to a politician is to trust him. Many of them want to do the right thing, but we don't give them a chance." We owe it to them to "threaten them every single day with political annihilation."[5] Such inactivity opens the door to revisionists, hatemongers, and political correctniks who are out to rewrite history in their image, suppress the truth, and control the classrooms of America. It is a frightening prospect as United Daughters of the Confederacy historian Mildred Rutherford warned in 1923: "False history accepted destroys civilization."[6]

Attacks upon the Confederate battle flag are nothing new. A Methodist bishop from Boston visited Baltimore in April 1897 and shocked a congregation with stinging criticism of the Confederate battle flag. He ranted that the brave Union soldiers fought against "the disgraceful, abominable, and infamous rag that floated over the Confederacy."[7]

Infamous rag?

Unlike today, where much of the Southern news media sides with the anti-flag minority; Southern newspapers wasted little time in drawing their sabres. *The Baltimore Herald* led the counter-attack.

> *We know nothing of the antecedents of the very learned, although somewhat pugnacious and atrabilious Bishop of Boston, except that he hails from one of the original slaveholding states and from the only American colony whose pious inhabitants indulged in the ignominious crime of burning witches; but it would require testimony to convince us that he was a soldier during the Civil War, and that he ever faced the 'infamous rag' under fire. Union soldiers, at least courageous ones, never refer to the Confederate (battle) flag in such ungracious and unchristianlike terms.*

The Baltimore World responded as well. "If he cannot find better things to preach about, he should abandon the pulpit and go into some other business, for he has evidently missed his calling."[8]

The Baltimore News was so shocked by the bishop's words that a reporter was sent to the cleric to obtain confirmation of his exact words. To their surprise, the bishop confirmed his remarks to the reporter and then autographed a transcript for further validation.[9] The whole episode caused a firestorm among Baltimore's business community which retaliated with its own withering responses through the newspapers.

"I have noticed for many years since the war that wherever or whenever any venom or vituperation is indulged in it nearly always comes from some Northern minister," Bartlett S. Johnson, a Baltimore businessman, wrote to *The Baltimore News*.[10] Baltimore attorney Skipwith Wilmer joined in the fray as well. "When the issues of the war are well-nigh forgotten it is a poor business for one that calls himself a messenger of the Prince of Peace to be tearing open the wounds of the past and referring in terms of contempt to what so many brave men died to serve and so many living regard as a sacred memory."[11]

But the mouthy Boston bishop was far from being the first to lambast the battle flag. More than 500 Confederate battle flags were captured by Union troops during the war. Generally they were handed over to regimental commanders, who passed them up their chain of command. At the end of the war, the battle flags were turned over to the Adjutant General's office in Washington. They were later moved to the War Department building and then to the Ordnance Museum before they were moved to the basement of the War, State, and Navy building in 1882.

In 1887, the Adjutant-General felt the time had come to turn them over to the former Confederate states as an act of goodwill. President Grover Cleveland agreed and issued an executive order to do so. But opposition mounted quickly, led by anti-Southern politicians and some Union veterans who harbored lingering bitterness over the war.[12]

"May God palsy the hand that wrote that order; may God palsy the brain that conceived it and may God palsy the tongue that dictated it," roared Union General Lucious Fairchild of Wisconsin.[13]

Cleveland abandoned the idea, and it wasn't until 1905 that President Teddy Roosevelt ordered the 514 battle flags in the possession of the government returned to the respective Southern states. Four northern states — Wisconsin, Iowa, Minnesota, and New York — plus the Chicago Historical Society, still have retained many of the 1,500 battle flags still in existence.[14] One of the flags, presently in the hands of the Wisconsin Veterans Museum in Madison, Wisconsin, is unique. It belonged to the First Tennessee Infantry and was the flag flown by regiments under General Leonidas Polk. It did not feature the Cross of St. Andrew, but rather the Cross of St. George (Polk was an Episcopalian bishop and the Episcopal Church was just one step from the Church of England, thus the Cross of St. George). The flag was captured at the Battle of Perryville, Kentucky, on October 8, 1862. The First Tennessee had 16 color bearers killed at Perryville. Private Sam Watkins, author of "Company Aytch," was a member of the First Tennessee and was at Perryville.

Following its capture, the flag was immediately shipped to Wisconsin as a war trophy, but it was never registered with the Union Army like most other captured Confederate battle flags. Therefore, it was not covered under the 1905 Joint Resolution of Congress authorizing the return of captured Confederate battle flags. While the flag has been transferred to the museum, it remains in control of the State Historical Society of Wisconsin. The society has refused all entreaties in recent years, including those by former Tennessee Governor Ned McWherter, the Tennessee State Museum and the Wisconsin Division of the Sons of Confederate Veterans, to return the flag to Tennessee. One person familiar with the discussions between officials of the two states, characterized them as being "heated" at times.

Wisconsin's reasons for not returning the flag include: Identification of the flag as the one captured at Perryville is "only tentative" since it is in poor condition and there is no unit identification on the flag. However, they concede all evidence points to the banner in their possession as the flag captured at Perryville and admit it is the First Tennessee Infantry's flag.

The Wisconsin Historical Society agrees the flag is important to those who fought and died for it, but that it is equally important to those who fought and died to capture it. They contend that returning captured artifacts is an issue best left alone as such transactions could "jeopardize the title to collections throughout the country." Apparently Wisconsin has had a problem with returning captured Confederate battle flags for quite sometime. Fairchild, who was so boisterous in his opposition to Grover Cleveland's attempt to return all flags to the Southern states in 1887, later served as the governor of Wisconsin.

Fortunately, the Wisconsin division of the SCV raised $1,800 to have the First Tennessee flag conserved. Meanwhile, the Wisconsin Veterans Museum has agreed to loan the flag to the Tennessee State Museum, but state officials still refuse to return the flag to Tennessee permanently. Wisconsin officials say they are not bound to the 1905 resolution. But their contention is based on technicality and is an unquestionable violation of the spirit of the resolution. The flags were returned to help heal the wounds of war. It was to demonstrate that the states were truly one nation again. So why has Wisconsin chosen to leave the wound open?

What would the Wisconsin Historical Society's response be to Union Corporal James Tanner, who lost both of his feet during the war? He had the following to say in a letter to the *Washington Post* in July 1898 about returning Confederate battle flags to their proper place: "It seems to me impossible that the people of the South should regard the flag under which their sons died with aught but veneration. The stars and stripes have gathered in their folds so much glory that brave men need not begrudge all the glory of endurance and achievement by valor that can justly be claimed for the late emblem of the late Confederacy.... . "With all of my heart I say, let us give them back their flags. They stood by them so bravely that we who captured them can well afford to see our late opponents treasure them as sacred relics... ."[15]

Other battle flags are in Southern museums or private collections. A rare 1st Alabama Volunteer Calvary battle flag fetched more than $65,000 at a Christie's auction in New York in May 1996. It was returned to its home state after it was purchased by a Tuscaloosa, Alabama, attorney. Could Wisconsin's reluctance to return the First Tennessee flag be motivated by money, or is it Wisconsin's childish way of sticking out its tongue at Tennessee — and the South?

It should be noted that Wisconsin's uncooperative spirit does not reflect the feelings of most Northerners, who support the South in its affection for its battle flags. A resolution calling for Wisconsin to return the flag to Tennessee was passed in 1992 at the national convention of The Military Order of the Loyal Legion of the United States, an organization composed of descendants of officers who fought for the Union.[16] About 78 percent of Americans say the Confederate battle flag is a symbol of Southern pride and that Southerners should be proud of Confederate ancestors who served in the war, according to a 1994 poll.[17] The SCV's Northern brother, the Sons of Union Veterans, have repeatedly passed resolutions supporting Southerners' right to fly the battle flag. So the battle flag controversy is not a North-South issue, and the attitude of the state of Wisconsin should be considered an aberration.

Up until 1905, one would have been hard pressed to have found a Confederate battle flag — and for several reasons:

First, everyone was tired of fighting. The war had taken its toll physically and emotionally. This was especially true in the South where 25 percent of all white males of military age — 260,000 all totaled — were killed.[18] An estimated 30,000 lost a limb as a result of the conflict.[19] "I had entered school in January (1861) for three years," said Marion Albertis Misenheimer of the Third Tennessee Infantry. Misenheimer lost a leg at Fort Donelson, Tennessee. "But the war coming on — knocked me out of an education such as I wanted as well as disabling me from manual labor. Therefore I have had kind of an uphill pull."[20]

Second, no one would dare fly the Confederate flag while under the yoke of Union occupation forces during Reconstruction. Union generals removed the governors of Georgia, Texas, Louisiana, Mississippi, and Virginia and replaced them with carpetbaggers and other Union officers. Soldiers patrolled the streets of Southern cities, the military ran the courts, laws were suspended, taxes were levied, newspapers suppressed, public meetings licensed and parades were forbidden.

Third, if anyone wanted to buy a flag, they probably didn't have the money to do so. Farms had been destroyed, land confiscated and heavy taxes imposed. At least 60 Southern cities and towns were completely destroyed. In Texas, the carpetbag government inherited a state that was debt free thanks to its Confederate governor and legislature. But when the carpetbag government left, Texas found itself shackled with $4 million in debt. Its property owners watched helplessly as their property taxes more than tripled between 1865 and 1876.

The South continued to suffer until the controversial 1876 presidential election involving ex-Union General Rutherford B. Hayes and New York Democrat Samuel J. Tilden. Tilden easily won the popular vote, but lost the disputed electoral vote after it was sent to Congress, who in turn appointed a special commission to decide the outcome based on disputed returns from South Carolina, Louisiana, and Florida. Hayes, a carpetbag Republican, won the electoral vote 185-184, but the manner in which it was handled so angered Democrats that there were threats of armed insurrection in South Carolina and Louisiana. Accommodations were sought by the Republicans, and it was ex-Confederate-General-turned-U.S.-Senator John B. Gordon of Georgia who led a contingent of Southern leaders to meet with some of Hayes' friends prior to Hayes' inauguration on March 5, 1877. In exchange for no more trouble, Hayes agreed to withdraw troops from the South, ending Reconstruction.[21]

Finally, in the 1880s, all the grizzled Confederate veterans, most of whom had been denied basic rights under carpetbag rule, began meeting for the first time since the war. A national organization was formed in 1890 called the United Confederate Veterans (UCV). They began having reunions and simultaneously battle flags started popping up again like wild daisies throughout the South. This pleased the proud Confederate veterans, and it did much to further reconcile the North and South.

Southerners wasted little time in joining veterans in expressing their affection for their Cross of St. Andrew. This was evident at a United Confederate Veterans reunion in May 1911 in Little Rock, Arkansas. More than 100,000 Confederate veterans attended the event marking the 50th anniversary of the firing on Fort Sumter. During the festivities, a silk battle flag was presented to the Lonoke, Arkansas Chapter of the United Daughters of the Confederacy. The chapter had raised $279 for needy Confederate veterans and their families.

"I am grateful for the honor and privilege to present you with a flag dear to every Southern heart," said the gentleman presenting the flag to the ladies. "Many a Confederate flag during the dark days of 1861 had been stained with the blood of the South and softened by the tears of weeping mothers and wives."

In accepting the flag, Lonoke's Mattie Trimble replied: "I assure you we will always regard this flag as the most precious of all our sacred possessions. I can't say more, for as you know when the heart speaks most the lips are dumb."[22]

But somewhere between the emotional flag ceremonies and the rapidly increasing number of flags, Southerners let the true meaning of their beloved banner slip from their control — some of it with good results, some bad. One of the more positive uses of the battle flag has been in the United States armed forces, where it has often lifted the spirits of Southern men fighting for the Stars and Stripes. It is only natural that the Southern soldier would continue to identify with the battle flag, while pledging allegiance to the United States. The battle flag frequently flew above World War I trenches. It was seen as a sticker on the outside of cockpits of World War II fighters. The battle flag flew over young Southerners fighting with Company H, 3rd Battalion, Seventh Marine Division, during the Korean War. It flew on the front lines for months, though shot down several times by Communist forces. When its owner was wounded, the flag accompanied him to a hospital where it was later destroyed in an accidental fire. A private in Company H, C.R. Sanders, wrote to the United Daughters of the Confederacy in Murfreesboro, Tennessee, explaining what had happened. The troops were soon flying a replacement.

Southern men, many from Army National Guard units stationed in the South called up for active duty during the Vietnam War, flew the battle flag throughout that conflict. "I was an engineer in the Marines in Vietnam in 1969, and I traveled all around," recalls Gene Andrews of Nashville, Tennessee. "It seemed like there was a Confederate battle flag flying over every fire support base I ever saw."[23] Unconfirmed reports say one of the first U.S. tanks to enter Kuwait City after the Persian Gulf War sported a battle flag on the vehicle's radio antennea.

Though Beauregard would have been displeased with today's abuses of the battle flag, its use by American troops would have made his chest swell with pride. "It (the flag) thus became in our armies the emblem of Southern valor and patriotism; and should we ever be compelled to have a foreign war, I trust that this standard will be adopted as our national battle flag, to which the Southern soldiers will always gladly rally to a just cause," he wrote in an 1872 letter.[24]

In other words, Beauregard felt the battle flag was worthy of being the official flag of the United States Armed Forces. Obviously, with the lingering bitterness at the time, that was not going to happen. But Beauregard also seems to have made another important point: Just as the Scottish Highlanders have always rallied to their Cross of St. Andrew in behalf of Great Britain, so should Southerners do likewise with their Southern Cross of St. Andrew in behalf of the United States.

The use of the battle flag shouldn't unsettle anyone. After all, protesters burned the American flag during the Vietnam War. In addition, Southerners are not the first to have their spirits lifted by displaying the colors of their once sovereign nation on a modern battlefield. Scottish troops, serving in the British armed forces, still wear the Cross of St. Andrew on their uniforms. It is only natural that Southerners on the battlefield would take pride in fighting under the colors of their brave forefathers. And that's exactly what they have done. The South has always answered the call to arms, often leading the nation in volunteer enlistments. From George Washington, Francis Marion, and Confederate General Joe Wheeler, who was entrusted with command of U.S. ground troops during the Spanish-American War, to Alvin York, George Patton, the Tuskegee Airmen, Audie Murphy and Chester Nimitz, Southerners have answered the call. Tennessee's nickname, the "Volunteer State," was conceived from the large number of volunteers who accompanied Andrew Jackson to New Orleans during the War of 1812 and distinguished themselves while defeating the British. America wouldn't be free today without the sacrificial blood of Southerner soldiers.

But something radically different began happening to the flag on the home front following World War II.

"The emergence of the Confederate battle flag (elevated in popular perception to become THE Confederate flag and erroneously dubbed the 'Stars and Bars') as a fixture in American popular

A U.S. Army tank, sporting a Confederate battle flag, roars across Germany during NATO exercises in June 1980. (Photo by Geoff Walden)

culture occurred in the 1940s," said John M. Coski with the Museum of the Confederacy in Richmond, Virginia. He has published a photo essay entitled *The Confederate Battle Flag in American History and Culture.*

"In the past half century, the flag has acquired a myriad of different meanings," Coski said. "It has served as a logo for the South and for those things southern, as well as a symbol of individual or collective defiance and rebellion, of resistance to civil rights and racism, of devotion to the principle of states rights and to a conservative political agenda, and of continuance of a Confederate heritage and the Civil War South."[25]

Some observers believe that middle-class intellectuals and working-class whites in the South feel like they've been on the losing end economically and politically in the last few decades. But they are most upset about their cultural losses, says John Shelton Reed, a sociologist at the University of North Carolina-Chapel Hill. "They feel that they don't get any respect, that their culture doesn't get any respect, and that their ancestors are being dissed," Reed said.

At the center of their concern over the loss of culture, is the battle flag. Reed says both black and white groups have found an endless source of debate in the flag. "It's a great issue for partisans on both sides to rally people around," he said. "There's no easy way to split the difference, and I don't know that anyone wants to. Either it's the school flag or not, the state flag or not. And, whether you win or lose, it keeps you in the public eye."[26]

It can also make you a buck. An unusual entrepreneurial endeavor surfaced at the 1996 Kentucky State Fair in Louisville. One vendor sold T-shirts defending the battle flag, while another next to him sold T-shirts opposing it.

In 1948, the battle flag began surfacing in the hands of people who opposed Civil Rights, or federal tyranny, depending on your perspective. It became the unofficial banner of the States Rights ("Dixiecrat") Party. Strom Thurman, now the senior senator from South Carolina, was the party's nominee and when asked what the flag meant to him he replied, opposition to "federal tyranny." Many Southerners agreed with Thurmond. In most cases only one generation had passed since Reconstruction. Many Southerners had been taught not to forget how their homeland was invaded, conquered, and subjugated. They equated the federalism of the late 1940s with the federalism that attacked their forefathers in 1861.

However, Southerners never stopped trying to rebuild their lives after World War II. "Coming out of World War II there were new opportunities in the South," said Norman Dasinger, who just completed a two-year term as commander-in-chief of the SCV. "The South became an anachronism in its quest for newness and expansion."

In short, it wasn't ready for what was to come.[27]

Flying the battle flag became popular among college students, particularly at the University of Mississippi whose athletic teams are nicknamed "Rebels." A 35-yard-long battle flag often covered the center of the football field at Ole Miss games in the mid-1950s. Huge battle flags were hung outdoors for Kappa Alpha fraternity Old South Balls at Auburn University as well.

By the early 1950s displaying a Confederate battle flag had become a national craze. "Everywhere along the Atlantic seaboard from New York to Miami and westward into the Mississippi watershed, pert little banners flap in the breeze — from car antennae, souvenir stands, bicycles or in the hands of youngsters, teenagers and grown-ups…," E. John Long wrote in October 1951. "Why fly it now nearly a century later? Why do cars of Northern states which defeated the Confederacy display it? And why is it being carried by Shriners in New York jamborees, at Atlantic City bathing beauty contests, or on planes in Detroit air races? Is there some deep underlying significance or political undertone or sectional significance to the movement?"[28]

In the late 1950s and early 1960s some Southerners grabbed the battle flag and waved it in the faces of federal troops sent to enforce federal desegregation orders for public schools in the South. Such scenes were flashed across newspaper front pages and television screens throughout the nation, first in 1956 in Little Rock, Arkansas, and then in 1963 during protests outside Birmingham, Alabama schools. They also surfaced on the steps of white college buildings whenever blacks rightly tried to enter.

Organizations like the United Daughters of the Confederacy tried to speak out against the battle flag being used in such a way. But they were largely ignored by those using the flag, and the news media which was fascinated by the emotion it generated between warring groups. There was certainly some racism involved, but remember, Thurmond had said it stood in defiance of "federal tyranny." In other words, some Southerners would have snatched up the battle flag no matter what the issue if it involved what they perceived as the federal government meddling in their personal lives. It is possible some of the older folks of that day were thinking, "Oh no, here comes the federal hammer down on our heads again."

Seymore Trammell, who was finance director for Alabama Governor George Wallace in 1963, said Wallace told him to have the battle flag raised over the Alabama State Capitol as a symbol of "defiance." It was purposely placed on top of the Capitol the day before U.S. Attorney General Robert Kennedy arrived for a visit with Wallace. In a dramatic meeting, Wallace not only ordered the battle flag flown, but directed state troopers to line the Capitol lawn upon the Massachusetts native's arrival.[29]

It has been suggested that Reconstruction ended in 1964 with passage of the Civil Rights Act, not 1876. This may be correct, but the politicizing of the battle flag by special interest groups and anti-Southern bigots have polluted the process. Southerners want to move forward, but it must be based on truth instead of distorted history.

Make no mistake, there was some serious damage done to the battle flag during the early 1960s. Those opposed to integration caused the flag to be "racialized," like certain phrases and words,

The Confederate battle flag flies over an U.S. Marine fire base in Vietnam. The battle flag has always been carried into battle by Southern soldiers, whether they were fighting for Dixie or the United States. (Photo courtesy of Gene Andrews)

said Larry Griffin, professor of sociology and political science at Vanderbilt University in Nashville. "Welfare, work ethic," and "law and order" are examples, he said. People who are not necessarily racists, often grab the flag as an expression of protest over the abuses linked to welfare and crime. "The flag," he added, "whatever else it is, is a racial symbol."[30]

It clearly was used that way by some in Selma, Alabama, in April 1960. "We are on the one-yard line," said one white radical at a Citizens Council meeting. "Our backs are to the wall. Do we let them go over for a touchdown, or do we raise the Confederate flag as did our forefathers and tell them... 'You shall not pass!'"[31]

Nothing could have been further from the truth when it came to the Confederate soldier or their beloved battle flag. Only about seven percent of Southerners owned slaves, and if they did, the overwhelming majority were well taken care of because they were so valuable to the wealthy planters.[32] "If it was so bad, then why did my granddaddy go back to his master and work for him for 12 years after the war?" asks Nelson Winbush, a black member of the SCV from Kissimee, Florida, whose grandfather fought in the Confederate Army. "He could have left any time he wanted, but he didn't."[33]

Predictably, in the 1960s, some black publications in the North began running cartoons depicting Confederate soldiers holding battle flags with the Klu Klux Klan. Clearly by that time, the true meaning of the flag had been distorted and disgraced.

Coski believes the meaning of the battle flag was further complicated when it surfaced in the early 1960s as part of the 100th anniversary celebration of the War for Southern Independence.[34] Little wonder Southern historian C. Vann Woodward wrote during those turbulent days: "It would be ironic, not to say a tragic, coincidence if the celebration of the anniversary (of the War for Southern Independence) took place in the midst of a crisis reminiscent of the one celebrated."[35] Percy Walker, at the same time, put it this way: "A peculiarity of civil war is the destruction not only of armies and nations but ideologies. The words and slogans may remain the same, but they no longer mean the same thing."[36]

By this time, it was clear that organizations charged with protecting the battle flag, (like the SCV and UDC) were being overpowered by forces and people beyond their control. They were joined by individuals who decried the growing abuse of the battle flag. "Today, the flag for which my grandfather fought is des-

The battle flag has been used for many things since 1865. It's seen here on a billboard advertising an upcoming Winston Cup racing event in Darlington, South Carolina. The battle flag is popular among NASCAR racing fans and is seen throughout the track infield at every race. (Photo courtesy of Gene Andrews)

ecrated," lamented Richmond Flowers, while serving as Alabama attorney general in 1966. "Our Confederate ancestors would spin in their graves if they saw their flags in the hands of those who trample upon everything they fought for. It deserves a better place in history than on car bumpers or on the bloody robes of the killers, floggers and night riders who call themselves the Klu Klux Klan."[37]

The Dixiecrat Party was not the last time Confederate battle flags would be seen flying in America's political arena. Supporters of Arizona Senator Barry Goldwater flew the flag during his 1964 presidential campaign. It also adorned campaign buttons for Wallace's unsuccessful presidential effort in 1968. It was flown at the Virginia State Republican Convention in 1994 by people supporting Oliver North in his bid for a U.S. Senate seat. "This (flag) is all about states' rights, and limiting the federal government," one of North's delegates said. "And I can tell you this: You're going to see a whole lot more of it."[38] Most recently it flew prominently at the traditional mock Republican Convention held by the student body at Washington and Lee University in Lexington, Virginia in March 1996.

Since the 1960s, the Confederate battle flag has been seen on business signs, bumper stickers and various products ranging from beer to grill covers and mud flaps.

Additionally, it has been spotted on stage with country music performers like Confederate Railroad. "We're not racists," said lead singer Danny Shirley. "I don't think we attract racists either — just people who like to drink beer and party and whoop it up. Being a redneck doesn't mean you're a racist."[39] Shirley speaks the truth (and I like their music), but being Southern does not necessarily mean one is a redneck either. The "redneck, bubba" stereotypes are still used frequently to degrade Southerners.

Anyone who uses the Confederate battle flag for any purpose other than to honor the Confederate dead is desecrating a sacred symbol. If anyone wants to use a relic of the Old South, use the Confederacy's first national flag (the so-called Stars and Bars) or the second national flag. Both were done away with by the Confederate Congress and replaced with the third national flag (or as some say the current national flag). States like Mississippi, Alabama, Florida, Louisiana and Georgia, which have laws making Confederate flag desecration a misdemeanor, should start enforcing them without exception.

How does a glorious battlefield banner carried by brave men end up in the hands of protesters, hate groups, and on T-shirts and other clothing? Obviously, they are protected by the First Amendment, but beyond that, how did it happen? "I have trouble answering that question," says J.E.B. Stuart IV, a direct descendant of the famous Confederate calvary commander. "It's sad to see the battle flag so terribly misinterpreted."[40]

Maybe the battle flag's true meaning just got swept away as our nation, over the last 100 years, endured the torment of six wars and redefining of "free but equal" at home. Yet while all the fighting was going on abroad — and the Civil Rights debate began at home — numerous things started happening that affected the battle flag. By the 1940s nearly all Confederate soldiers and their wives had died. The last Confederate veteran died in 1959. Even the SCV saw a decline in membership as Southerners went off to fight Nazis and Japanese. When they returned home, they were more interesting in rebuilding their lives and producing baby boomers. They had little time for — or interest in — heritage preservation.

Membership in the SCV has only rebounded in the past decade, largely because of the attacks against the battle flag. "As recently as 1978, membership in the SCV stood at only 6,000," says Ronald Clemmons, the SCV's national spokesperson. Membership now stands at 27,000.[41] "A lot of people stood by and didn't squawk when they should have," says UNC's Reed.[42] Dasinger added, "We let the soldier's flag be used as a political expression in the 1950s and 1960s. It suddenly began making social statements. Then it became a symbol of defiance of the Civil Rights movement and that was wrong. I don't blame them for waving the bloody shirt."[43]

Reed and Dasinger are both correct. With the end of the Cold War and relative peace covering the world, it should have come as no surprise that Americans would become less occupied with the rest of the world. We turned and looked inward, giving ourselves a thorough examination. It was an effort to check our bearings on a world map that had changed dramatically.

The Confederate battle flag, to the surprise of a lot of people, has become part of that on-going examination. "The real tragedy of the Confederate battle flag is that Southerners, white and black, have permitted it to be driven between them like a wedge, separating them from a common goal," wrote the late W. Earl Douglas, a black columnist from Charleston, South Carolina, who supported the flying of the flag. "The racism so evident in this controversy is not the flying of the flag but that we've permitted it to be designated as pro-white and anti-black."[44]

No one expected the NAACP to launch a pre-emptive strike on the battle flag. But that's exactly what happened when preoccupied Southerners stopped speaking up in its defense amid the rat race of the past 50 years. At the NAACP's southeast region convention in March 1987, the following resolution was passed:

> *Whereas, the delegates... consider the Confederate battle flag to be a symbol of divisiveness, racial animosity, and an insult to black people through the region; and... That the Association for the Advancement of Colored People, Southeast Region, requests the States of South Carolina and Alabama to take necessary action to remove the Confederate battle flag from the domes of their Capitol buildings; and... requests the state of Georgia to return to its standard state flag of pre-1956; and... the state of Mississippi to return to its standard state flag of pre-1894.*

South Carolina still flies the battle flag over its state capitol building, but the resolution convinced Alabama to remove it. Georgia and Mississippi, which have the battle flags as part of their state colors, have refused. (There will be more concerning the fights over the state flags in a later chapter.)

Interestingly, there was little — if any — news media coverage of the NAACP resolution, so the attacks on the battle flag and state flags got some pretty good results. It was helped along by another incident that got national attention and it just happened to occur in March 1987 as well. Forsyth County, Georgia, had no blacks living within its boundaries. But blacks suddenly showed up one day — and they had television cameras with them. That didn't discourage the idiots and racists who showed up with posters, mean dispositions, and — of course — Confederate battle flags. "It stands for the rights of white people," one protester shouted while waving the flag. "Call it a symbol of white supremacy if you like. It's a carryover from the Civil War."[45]

The whole mess was made for television, and it was these unsettling pictures and words of lies and hatred that were flashed into living rooms across America.

Some say Forsyth County has been known to have members of the KKK as residents and that the NAACP knew it. Others say the Klan's demonstrations were conducted by Kluxers from outside Forsyth County. At any rate, it was bad for the battle flag, the South, and America. Translation: Blacks marching into Forsyth County would be akin to the Klan marching into Harlem. No one could say for sure that the NAACP's resolution and the march in Forsyth were coordinated just because they happened in the same month, but if it wasn't part of the NAACP's strategy to use Forsyth as a launching pad for its all-out offensive against everything Confederate, it sure seemed as much.

Surprisingly there was still little reaction by Southern heritage preservation groups, some of which were just beginning to start building their numbers. At the time Georgia had only about a dozen SCV camps. Today it has more than 100. In 1986, North Carolina had only 500 members. Today it has more than 3,000.[46]

Perhaps more importantly, droves of Southerners were embarrassed and stunned at the antics in Forsyth. Of course the news media "loved" all the hate talk and — in the middle of it — the South's beloved battle flags. "When the controversy in Forsyth erupted, it brought the battle flag debate to a head," says Jeff

Massey, an Oklahoma attorney and the former judge advocate-in-chief of the SCV. "It laid the foundation of what was to come."[47] Dasinger put it this way, "We made ourselves (and the flag) a target."[48]

In 1991, the NAACP, which was being torn apart by internal strife, adopted the following resolution:

> *Whereas, the tyrannical evil symbolized in the Confederate battle flag is an abhorrence to all Americans and decent people of this country, and indeed, the world and is an odious blight upon the universe; and whereas, African-Americans, had no voice, no consultation, no concurrence, no commonality, not in fact nor in philosophy, in the vile conception of the Confederate battle flag or state flags containing the ugly symbol of idiotic white supremacy racism and denigration; and, whereas, we adamantly reject the notion that African-Americans should accept this flag for any stretch of imagination or approve its presence on the state flags; now therefore be it resolved that the National Office of the NAACP and all units commit their legal resources to the removal of the Confederate flag from all public properties.*

Finally, some Southerners started screaming bloody murder! "If we don't spread some education and truth, we're going to lose it (our heritage) all," Dasinger warned. "They want to culturally unhinge us."[49]

Once again, there was little if any news media coverage of the NAACP's hatred resolution. Meanwhile the news media continued to perpetuate the perception that it is biased when it comes to coverage of the battle flag.

For example, *The Tennessean* newspaper in Nashville recounted the murder of Kentucky teenager Michael Westerman in a story printed in April 1996. The story charged that the Sons of Confederate Veterans "attract white supremacists and separatists."[50] SCV members went ballistic. They felt the reputation of their organization had been damaged. Angry members called the newspaper, while others sent letters to the editor. An attorney representing the SCV wrote a letter requesting a retraction. The newspaper responded by offering to let an SCV member write an article explaining the organization's nature and purpose. Despite the newspaper's conciliatory tone, some members still felt the statement planted a permanent seed in the minds of "neutral" readers that the SCV — and the flag — are evil. In other words, it seemed like the same old badgering from the media: "Shut-up defending the flag and Southern history," they say. "It's time for Southerners to forget where they came from because a few people say it makes them feel uncomfortable. Southerners should stop talking about its region's great achievements and historic figures."

What will Southerners do? Will they succumb to bigots in the media? Are they going to surrender to the whines of the faddish politically correct movement? Will they bow to the demands of a small group of malcontents whose contrived argument against their blood-stained banner ignores historical fact?

It is hard to imagine the descendants of Celtic tribesmen not defending their honorable heritage as long as there is air to breath. The Celtic Cross has endured for more than 1,000 years. Do the anti-flaggers really think the Southern Cross of St. Andrew will have a shorter life span? This uncontrollable, inflammatory nonsense surrounding the battle flag — and Southern culture in general — has provided Southerners with a small taste of what their forefathers had to endure prior to 1860. While Southerners are known for their gentility, one should remember that they will "draw their sabres" in a second if they feel their honor has been questioned. Revisionists have mocked Southerners over this particular trait, but they would be wise to visit the Federal troops buried at Gettysburg, Arlington, or Shilch.

So why did the NAACP wait 135 years to launch an attack on the Confederate battle flag? Doesn't its membership know 68 percent of black Americans do not view the battle flag as a symbol of racism? Don't they know that 54 percent of blacks in South Carolina either support or don't care if the battle flag flies over the state Capitol?

Declining membership and internal controversy plagued the NAACP in the late 1980s and early 1990s under the leadership of Benjamin Chavis, who was eventually booted out the door by the membership. At the height of the battle flag debate in South Carolina, Chavis threatened South Carolinians by saying, "We will determine where we have to apply the heat. And I assure you, heat will be applied."[51] Pat Buchanan, one of the few flag defenders in the media, responded, "Now, to be fair, Mr. Chavis has a track record of 'applying the heat.' In 1971 he and nine chums were convicted of firebombing a white-owned grocery store in Wilmington, N.C., for which Mr. Chavis did 4 1/2 years in the state penitentiary. Who is this arsonist and ex-con to be preaching to anyone? The battle flag issue is synthetic and phony from the get go. A (1994) Harris Poll found that more than two thirds of black Americans have no problem with... the battle flag."[52]

It appears that the attack upon the flag by the NAACP was a calculated undertaking designed to whip blacks into an emotional tizzy and bolster the organization's pocketbook. Naturally the large liberal wing of the news media and the politically correct crowd hopped on board. Never mind at what cost. So what if they exterminate a culture? So what if they suppress — and ultimately — rewrite American history?

This orchestrated attack against Southern culture has moved the NAACP closer to becoming just another hate group. It should be less interested in rewriting Southern history and more concerned about fatherless children killing each other for a pair of Air Jordans. It should stop applying 1860 standards to today's South, while hypocritically looking the other way as black Muslims sell black Christians into slavery in Sudan.[53] What the NAACP and its allies didn't realize is that the historic truth would surface, exposing their misguided cause for what it is — a fraud. They also didn't anticipate Southerners rallying to their treasured banner. "Facile arguments that the Stars and Bars (sic) represented racism may be boneheaded, but they are also opinions that can be debated loud and long," a flag supporter wrote in a 1988 letter to the editor in *The Washington Post*. "But any attempt to tear down the flags takes aim at my heritage. That's when a debate becomes a good old-fashioned fight."[54]

The Scottish tie to the Confederacy becomes even more apparent with this replica of the flag used by the 9th Georgia Battalion, 30 Arkansas Regiment, 1st Mississippi Light Arillery and the East Tennessee and Central Kentucky Department of the Confederate Army. The Scottish national flag is just like this with the exception of being rectanagle. (Courtesy of John Bersot)

CHAPTER THREE

HATRED KNOWS NO BOUNDS

Furl it! for the hands that grasped it,
And the hearts that fondly clasped it,
Cold and dead are lying low;
And the banner, it is trailing,
While around it sounds the wailing
Of its people in their woe.
For, though conquered, they adore it.
Love the cold, dead hands that bore it,
Weep for those who fell before it.
Pardon those who trailed and tore it.
And, O, wildly they deplore it,
Now to furl and fold it so.
                    – Conquered Banner
                    Father Joseph Ryan

As we have seen, attacks against the Confederate battle flag began shortly after the war and continued for several years until dying off in the early 1900s. From 1905 — when President Teddy Roosevelt ordered Northern states to return the captured battle flags to the Southern states — until about 1970, the flag and other Southern symbols remained relatively free of condemnation. Even during the turbulent 1950s and 60s, when the flag was inappropriately waved in the face of school integration and the civil rights movement, it was never the target of scorn by leaders like Dr.

Martin Luther King Jr. and Dr. Ralph Abernathy Sr. However, the same can't be said about the news media and Hollywood. In the early part of this century, H.L. Mencken, who much of the print media considers a god, never missed an opportunity to indict everything Southern. His successors, while rightly calling for the end to segregation in the 1950s, did the same. And so it has been since the sanctimonious New England Transcendentalists began the trend in the 19th century.

Attacks on the Confederate battle flag — and other symbols representative of Southern culture — increased throughout the 1970s and early 1980s. It was during this period that "Dixie" stopped being played, most notably at the University of Georgia and then at a few high schools throughout the South. The attacks intensified over the past decade due in large measure to the orchestrated assaults of the NAACP. The American Civil Liberties Union, gay rights organizations and the politically correct movement — with the news media's encouragement — have joined the cause as well. Other attacks are being initiated by people who just hate the South or out of historical ignorance. The battle flag debate has been contaminated with opinions by people who have little or no knowledge of the history of the South. This ignorance can surface from almost anywhere. For example, I once commented to a Yankee friend that Abraham Lincoln may be getting a personal tour of the infernal region. (Some people, like Mildred Rutherford, contend Lincoln did not believe that Jesus was the son of God.) My friend responded by calling me a "Confederate jerk." Obviously she did not know Lincoln violated the U.S. Constitution perhaps as many as 10 times, was largely responsible for the deaths of more than 620,000 people, and may not have been a Christian (Lincoln's and the First Lady's passion for seances is well documented) — and that's just for starters.[1]

Attempts to assassinate the character of Southerners are nothing new. "The charge has been constantly made since the war that the Confederates were rebels and traitors, and the effort is continually being made to educate the rising generation into the belief that their fathers and their mothers were rebels and traitors, and therefore lawless criminals," lamented Judge John H. Reagan during a speech to the United Confederate Veterans reunion in Nashville, Tennessee, in June 1897.[2] Reagan's words still ring true today.

Initially the battle flag was the only target of these groups, but in recent years the attacks have expanded to include everything associated with the Confederacy. The anti-flag groups have bullied schools into banning the playing of "Dixie," called for the desecration of the graves of General Nathan Bedford Forrest and his wife in Memphis, expelled children from school for wearing Confederate clothing and lapel pins, demanded monuments be dug up, forced the firing of people from their jobs because of their love of Confederate heritage, smeared untold reputations, and demanded streets throughout the South be renamed. The whole thing smacks of cultural genocide. Isn't it ironic that a so-called civil rights group like the NAACP would lead the effort to exterminate another culture?

The battle flag "is a flag of slavery, symbol of racism and treason against our country," said Bobby Lovett, a black professor of history at the taxpayer-supported Tennessee State University in Nashville. "The soldiers were traitors against our nation and that should never be forgotten," he said, adding that the Confederacy should not be glorified or romanticized. "As Fredrick Douglass said, 'Death does not make an evil man moral.' And the Confederacy was evil then and it is still evil now."[3]

Lovett's decision to quote Douglass in this matter is interesting to say the least. Douglass, while opposing slavery, admired Southerners for what he called their life of leisurely contemplation, a lifestyle he said he wanted to replicate should he ever become a man of means. Douglass also admired Robert E. Lee and was given a chandelier from Lee's mansion at Arlington as a gift.[4]

Calling for the removal of the battle flags flying atop the state Capitols in South Carolina and Alabama have been among the more publicized attacks. The anti-flaggers also have tried to force the flag's removal from the state flags of Georgia and Mississippi. The attacks have been brutally divisive, costly financially, enormously painful, and widespread. All 11 of the states of the old Confederacy have been hit hard. States like Kentucky, Missouri, Oklahoma, Arizona, New Jersey and California have felt the sting as well. Many innocent people have been damaged — both physically and emotionally — by the vindictive assaults launched against Southern culture, symbols, and persons who defend them.

One can only wonder if the hysteria whipped up by the anti-flag and politically correct movements contributed to the murder of Kentucky teenager Michael Westerman in 1995. (More on Westerman later.) While the Westerman murder was by far the most heinous attack, there have been others of varying nature. Let's examine some of the more notable incidents:

The NAACP started howling about the Georgia state flag in the late 1980s, when internal problems with its leadership and apathy among its members mounted. After the Forsyth County episode, the NAACP set its sights on Atlanta because it was scheduled to host the 1994 Super Bowl and the 1996 Summer Olympics. They knew both events would give them a much needed stage.

"We see this Super Bowl as a prelude to the 1996 Olympics, and it would be a shame and a disgrace to stand under this flag when the world comes to Atlanta," wailed the Rev. Tim McDonald of Atlanta about a month before the 1994 Super Bowl. The Super Bowl was played at the state-owned Georgia Dome, where the state flag also flies. McDonald, who throws hateful words around as if they were Molotov cocktails, tried to get the players to join the cause with a pre-game protest march. He threw in a few more inflammatory remarks to get their attention. "The players must understand that whether they want to be or not, they are being used to support a racist past," McDonald said.[5] The Buffalo Bills' Bruce Smith, who is black, said he and his teammates didn't like playing under the Confederate flag, adding that "racism exists, period. It's unfortunate. It's ignorance. It offends me."[6] Even the activist organization Common Cause began badgering Georgians, declaring it was time for Georgia to "move on, move up and move out."

"It's becoming an atmosphere of hypersensitivity, and the sad thing is that it is cutting off bits and pieces of American heritage out of ignorance," said Bob Hawkins, who was commander-in-chief of the Sons of Confederate Veterans (SCV) at the time. "It's a sad thing to try to bury that heritage just to score a few present-day political points."[7]

As has come to be expected, it wasn't long before the adoring modern-day Transcedentalists ("USA Today" in January 1994 cried that the Confederate battle flag was "a symbol of ugly racial division") showed their support. About 60 reporters (out of 2,000 in attendance) covering the Super Bowl walked out in protest during the national anthem. Unfortunately for McDonald, his call for a "massive" protest prior to the Super Bowl turned out to be more bark than bite. Less than 100 people showed up.[8]

Meanwhile, the anti-flaggers turned their attention toward a possible economic boycott of Georgia. That too, met with limited success. Holiday Inn Worldwide called for all Holiday Inns to remove the state flag from their properties. Only three or four company-owned hotels obeyed in Georgia. A recent trip through Mississippi indicated that the order had been ignored by Holiday Inns in the Magnolia State as well.

Though McDonald's Super Bowl protest barely created a burp, the anti-flag minority began plans for another assault — at the Summer Olympic Games. The news media wasted little time in joining the cause. Local talk radio stations started mocking callers with Southern accents. Out-of-town reporters like Eric Harrison of the *Los Angeles Times* began showing up to write stories about the "Bubba Olympics," as he called it. He noted that pro-flag protesters were sure to keep alive the image of "tobacco-chewing good ol' boys driving pickups with Rebel bumper stickers." He also referred to Stone Mountain as a "freakish outcropping of granite" that has a history of racism and was sure to be an embarrassment to the Olympic Games. It wasn't.

The Atlanta Journal-Constitution couldn't resist not getting a piece of the action and denounced the flag while hysterically accusing the SCV of promoting sedition because its members observed Confederate Heritage Month in April. The editorial said Georgians should feel shame because the games were conducted under the Georgia state flag. Former Atlanta Mayor Maynard Jackson, who is black, said on July 19, 1995, that the Georgia state flag is a "constant negative reminder of slavery and segregation... an American swastika and an embarrassment."[9]

Nothing could have been further from the truth.

"This flag is not just a Southern symbol," said the SCV's Hawkins. "It is an American symbol and an international symbol. The SCV over the last few years has received numerous requests from the former Eastern Bloc countries for receipt of Confederate flags, which they viewed as an appropriate symbol of their struggle for independence against totalitarian control."[10]

Hawkins wasn't just whistling "Dixie." The battle flag was flown when the Berlin Wall came down, on independence day in Ljubljana, Yugoslavia, throughout other Balkan states as they sought their independence, and at the height of Quebec's quest for independence from Canada. The battle flag is also the centerpiece of the official coat of arms for the city of Vila Americana, Brazil.

The anti-flaggers may have cost the Atlanta area a lot of money when they hoodwinked the czars of Atlanta's tourism industry into believing that remnants of the Old Confederacy would be an

embarrassment during the Olympics. So Atlanta's tourism industry shunned the South's history in promoting the city for the
Olympics.

"Do they think people are coming in to see the new skyscrap-
ers?" said plantation owner K.C. Bassham in nearby Concord,
Georgia. "They're looking for Scarlett and Rhett."[11]

Bassham was correct. The South has international appeal.
"Gone With the Wind" remains the most popular movie in Japan
and Confederate battle flags are frequently flown throughout
Europe. In fact, it was Daimler-Benz, the German automaker, who
donated $4 million to restore the downtown Atlanta apartment
house where Margaret Mitchell wrote "Gone With the Wind."

"This was the great irony: The primary things they come
looking for is the one thing Atlanta chose not to give to them," said
Mary Rose Taylor, chairwoman of a non-profit organization that
has worked to restore the historic landmark. The Mitchell apart-
ment house, which was set to reopen prior to the Olympics, was
seriously damaged by an arsonist's blaze May 12, 1996. It marked
the second time the building has fallen prey to fire in recent years.

Coincidence?

"If it happens one time, you toss it off," Taylor said. "If it
happens a second time, are the two connected? The timing of this
particular one, suggests possible implications that are not attrac-
tive. We wanted to tell the story of Margaret Mitchell's life against
the backdrop of the city's history. I am stunned by the fear and
trepidation that the people in the tourist industry have of that
history. They tell me we can't talk about the Civil War. We go back
comfortably to the civil rights movement, but we can't talk about
the Civil War."[12]

The SCV responded to the anti-flaggers' cries about being
embarrassed by raising $20,000 to lease hot-air balloons the size
of billboards. They rose into the air everyday during the Olympics.
The balloons were strung from the tops of tall buildings at highly
visible locations around Atlanta. One side featured the SCV logo
with the battle flag, while the other solicited help in saving the South's
heritage while offering a 1-800-My-Dixie telephone number for
supporters to call. The organization also sponsored a large reenactment in Newnan, Georgia, which was included in most advertising
brochures distributed by area travel companies.

The Atlanta Committee for the Olympic Games (ACOG) was
thought to be neutral on the state flag issue until the fall of 1995.

That's when they directed the company — making lapel pins with the Olympic emblem and the flags of all 50 states — to omit Georgia and Mississippi because their state banners featured the battle flag. When people from Georgia and Mississippi protested — and the public showed no interest in buying the pins — the ACOG abandoned its plan. But an innovative Southerner marketed pins featuring the Olympic rings with pins of the Georgia state flag. When stacked, the two pins gave the appearance of one. "Call it Confederate ingenuity," quipped a happy Georgia pro-flagger. There were plenty of hurt feelings, though it came as no surprise, when "Dixie" was omitted from the portion of the Olympic Games' opening ceremonies which featured a collection of "traditional" Southern songs.

Meanwhile, a New Jersey company didn't boycott Georgia, but it issued a multimedia CD-ROM for elementary schools entitled "Story of the States." In the section about Georgia it said: "Recent research reveals that the St. Andrews Cross of the Confederate battle flag was added to the earlier, more neutral 1905 version to show contempt for the wave of desegregation rulings passing down from Federal Courts. Georgia has certainly come a long way, both economically and politically, but organizations such as the Sons of Confederate Veterans and the Klu Klux Klan still prove to be obstacles to its social progress."

An attorney representing the Georgia Division of the SCV wrote the company a letter requesting a retraction and apology. According to Jim Reynolds, who was commander of the Georgia Division of the SCV at the time, the company responded in April 1996, saying they were discontinuing production of the CD-ROM in question.

The anti-flag zealots were able to get Georgia Governor Zell Miller temporarily on board, but the SCV's Charles Lunsford made him look silly on a memorable Larry King "Live" telecast on CNN in 1992. King got in on the anti-flag act as well, opening his show by saying that "many will be embarrassed" if the flag flies during the Olympics.

Miller temporarily bought into the NAACP's argument that the current Georgia state flag, which was adopted in 1956, was a symbol of protest against integration in the South. In 1993, Miller called the flag a banner for "those who wanted to preserve a segregated South in the face of the civil rights movement."[13] The Associated Press seemed to confirm Miller's false contention, reporting on January 27, 1994, that the Georgia Legislature added the battle flag in 1956 "in a gesture of defiance over the U.S. Supreme Court's school desegregation ruling."[14]

But the facts show otherwise.

State Representative and Judge John Sammons Bell said it had always been his goal to convince lawmakers to accept the current flag — not as a symbol of defiance — but rather as a tribute to the thousands of Georgians who had fought for the Confederacy. Bell had known some Confederate veterans as a child in the 1920s.

Adoption of the current flag was also done in step with preparations for the 100th anniversary of the War for Southern Independence. The flag bill was linked to the Civil War Centennial Bill that paid for the placement of some 400 historical markers throughout the state. It should also be noted that the last Confederate veteran from Georgia died in 1952.

Polls began showing 70 percent of Georgians approving of the flag — with the rest opposing or voicing no opinion. That margin has held steady throughout the flag debate. National polls have shown approximately the same results.

Miller cooled his jets after he won re-election in 1994 by only 51-49 percent. He requested a meeting with SCV leaders in February 1995 in which he admitted to making a mistake in opposing the flag.

"He said he had come to realize that feelings ran deeper than he anticipated and that he would no longer support having the state flag changed," Reynolds said.[15] Miller validated his new stance by signing a proclamation declaring April 26 Confederate Memorial Day throughout Georgia. Pro-flaggers now affectionately refer to the governor as "Zig Zag Zell."

On January 11, 1996, the Georgia Division of the SCV held a reception for state lawmakers, with 90 of the 236 legislators showing up. The lobbying effort seems to have paid dividends. Just when it appeared the controversy might "take a breather" in late February 1996, a black legislator got an amendment — calling for the state flag to be changed — attached to a bill making English the official language of Georgia. Intense lobbying and a flood of phone calls to lawmakers were made as word quickly spread throughout the state. In the end, state Representative John White of Albany dropped his amendment amid pressure from House Speaker Tom Murphy. Murphy's concern: Changing the flag would create a disaster for Democrats in the 1996 election. The small anti-flag groups fumed, realizing nothing more could be done until 1997 — at least several months after the Olympics.

Meanwhile, the city of Atlanta continued its silly ways by flying the pre-1956 state flag on all municipal buildings. What's so funny is that the banner is essentially the Confederacy's first national flag (known as the "Stars and Bars") with the Georgia state seal included. The state flag continues to fly over state-owned buildings as required by state law.

One of the more bizarre "shots" taken at Georgia was by a Pennsylvania state legislator who introduced a resolution in January 1996, chastising the state for its flag. "What is offensive about the Georgia flag as it is now constituted is the Confederate symbol... one of the key things the Confederacy stood for was slavery and the idea that African-Americans are not equal," said Democrat Mark Cohn. "(Georgia is) dumb (and) afraid of change (for not removing the flag)."[16]

The matter did not go unnoticed along Peachtree Street. Georgia Legislator Sonny Watson responded, "I think Pennsylvania should tend to its own business. They have enough problems of their own. Maybe we should pass a resolution telling them to patch the crack in the Liberty Bell." Reynolds fired off a letter, charging Cohn with bringing into question the honor of his home and challenging the lawmaker to a "duel" (in reality a debate) "anytime, anywhere." Cohn never responded — even after Reynolds called him "a coward."[17]

With public opinion polls turning against them, and the political process and the call of an economic boycott failing to produce the needed results, the anti-flaggers decided to try the court system. A key ruling came after a lawsuit was filed by James A. Coleman, a black man who had moved to Georgia from Harrisburg, Pennsylvania. He claimed the state flag discriminated against him and that it should be removed from all public buildings. Coleman also asked for $12 billion in damages because he said he was afraid to enter any buildings flying the flag. But U.S. District Judge Orinda D. Evans dismissed the lawsuit. "There simply is no evidence in the record indicating that the flag itself results in discrimination against African-Americans," Evans said.[18] Aside from the inroads it made with the predominately black downtown Atlanta, the anti-flag groups seems to have accomplished little else other than to spend a lot of money and hurt a lot of feelings.

The news media loved the Georgia flag controversy because it made for great theatrics on television and inflammatory stories in newspapers. That translated into revenue — at the expense, of course, of the South's culture. Politicians used it only if it enhanced their standing with zealous constituents. Most of them viewed the issue like a cannibal gawking at animal innards. As for everyone else, it just made them mad. The whole mess prompted Pat Buchanan in March 1993 to write: "All over the world, men are attracted to The Lost Cause. Not because of the wrong of slavery, but because of the brilliance of her captains, the bravery of her soldiers, the character of her people, and the love they bore the country for which they gave all they had. If foreigners can understand, why can't we?"

The anti-flag groups tried to play the economic boycott card against South Carolina, too. Even though the battle flag is not part of the state flag, it flies on top of the South Carolina state Capitol as a memorial to South Carolinians who fought for Southern independence. NAACP board chairman William Gibson of Greenville, South Carolina, issued an ultimatum: "Take down the flag or face a boycott."[19] Companies like NationsBank and AT&T joined in condemnation of the flag. "We don't think that flag should fly there (at the state Capitol)," said Joel Smith, president of NationsBank of South Carolina.[20] Economically the effect was practically zero, but it made a lot of people mad, too.

Out of either fright from Gibson's threat or in concert with his views, a group of business and civic leaders filed a lawsuit in 1994, charging that the battle flag flying over the Capitol hurt the state's growth and served as a constant reminder of slavery. Once again, the statements of the anti-flag groups contradicted reality. Industrial investments stood at a handsome $5.4 billion in 1995 when nearly 24,000 new jobs were created. Nine percent of the firms in South Carolina are run by blacks — a ranking that is the third highest in the U.S. The battle flag didn't seem to bother British Motor Works, who announced it would build a new automobile manufacturing plant in the Palmetto State.

Then there was the Michael J. Carrier incident. Carrier, executive director of the Greater Columbia Convention & Visitors Bureau, was accused of having the battle flag on the state Capitol air-brushed off the city's tourism magazine cover photo in 1994. A storm of protests prompted a change in cover photos in later issues. The whole episode was strange considering the state's tourism trade was up eight percent in 1995, with blacks composing

30 percent of those visiting. A similar stunt was attempted in Mississippi. When the Mississippi Department of Tourism left the battle flag off an advertisement, irate Mississippians flooded the department with letters and jammed the department's toll free line. A revised ad — with the battle flag included — was distributed. Flag defenders in South Carolina were instrumental in convincing Harley-Davidson Motorcycles to reverse its decision removing the battle flag from its licensed products.

Predictably, during the South Carolina fiasco, the modern-day Trancendentalists resurfaced. Gannett News Service reporter DeWayne Hickman referred to the song "Dixie" as "sung by traitors who killed 140,400 soldiers who died defending the Union." He referred to the battle flag as "the noxious symbol of Southern rebellion that flies atop the South Carolina statehouse." Lead singer Darius Rucker of the South Carolina rock band Hootie and the Blowfish couldn't resist popping off about the flag either. He referred to South Carolina's Legislature as being "asinine" for keeping the Confederate flag. Rucker and the rest of the band were to receive the Order of Palmetto award from the state Legislature, but after Rucker's comments the award presentation was cancelled. Rucker said the band didn't want the Order of Palmetto anyway because it had become "political." He was right, and he had the NAACP and the politically correct movement to thank for making it so. They are the ones who made the battle flag a "political" issue. Speaking of "political," it should be noted that Rucker and the band recorded a song about the battle flag called "Drowning." It features a line that states, "I'm tired of all this s—t about Heritage not Hate."[21] A lot of Southerners are tired of Hootie and the Blowfish.

There was a time in 1994 when the battle flag's future was in jeopardy in South Carolina. Democrats stood opposed to the flag in an effort to recruit badly needed black votes for the upcoming election. The mayor of Columbia and the state attorney general both opposed the flag and were parties to the lawsuit looming before a receptive State Supreme Court.

But a sweeping Republican victory in the fall elections swung the issue in the other direction politically, though opinion polls still showed between 70 and 80 percent in favor of letting the flag stay at the Capitol. Pro-flag Republican David Beasley won the governor's race, defeating two other candidates by garnering 50 percent of the vote. The new Republican state Legislature passed a bill protecting the flag from future attacks, making the lawsuit before the State Supreme Court moot. It first passed in the House and then in the Senate without opposition in May 1995, giving the flag defenders a smashing victory. Nearly 2,000 spectators and 200 reenactors gathered on the State House steps to celebrate the victory and hold a memorial service for Confederate soldiers.

Some South Carolinians thought the issue was settled, but they were wrong. Rumors began circulating in 1996 that a few radical blacks were going to make another all-out effort, but in a new and sinister way; through the church. "They've lost in the courts, they've lost in public opinion polls, and you mark my words, they're going to try the churches next," predicted an SCV member in early 1996.

Then on Nov. 26, 1996, Beasley shocked South Carolinians - -if not the whole South--by going on statewide television and reversing his position on the flag. He had supported its flying during his successful campaign for governor in 1994. Even a non-binding referendum on the issue in 1994 showed that 75 percent of the voters wanted the flag to continue to fly. Yet Beasley announced that he would defy the majority of South Carolinians and seek to move the flag to a Confederate memorial on statehouse grounds. In typical fashion the news media, led by the New York Times, began writing stories about drive-by shootings by Klu Klux Klan members that seemed to imply a connection to the flag. Beasley cried that the state was getting a racist reputation. But not everyone agreed. "To me, personally, it's a symbol against political correctness," said South Carolinian Frank McGill. "What are they going to take next?"

No one can say for sure that appeals were made to Beasley through religious channels. But it is interesting that Beasley said he reached his decision after "much prayer." Then almost immediately, a divisive debate erupted within the state Baptist Convention in South Carolina. Beasley is a Southern Baptist. Pro and con editorials began running in South Carolina's State Baptist newspaper. Chris Sullivan, a South Carolinian, South Carolina SCV division commander, and lifelong Southern Baptist layman, had this to say in a December 12, 1996, guest editorial in *The Baptist Courier*, South Carolina's state-wide Southern Baptist newspaper:

> *Our state is plagued by abortion, legalized gambling, and the moral decay of communities. Our leaders, religious and secular, should be determined to cure these ills, not to stir old emotions*

everyone else thought were resolved. Unlike other denominations, our convention dare not be distracted by chasing political rabbits at the expense of winning souls.

Another theory is that Beasley is trying to position himself to run for president. Curiously, Ralph Reed, head of the Christian Coalition, told *Newsweek* magazine in late 1996 that he thought Beasley would make a good presidential candidate in the year 2000. Reed is no supporter of the flag and has made some questionable remarks himself concerning slavery and the South's legacy. All this makes it appear that the South's true history is being laid on sacrificial alter of political ambitions. Ironically, this whole sham has put Reed and Beasley, both historically conservative, in the same bed with the liberal Columbia, South Carolina newspaper, *The State*, which has been relentless in its attack against Beasley and the flag.

Beasley is a good man. But he may have jumped off a political cliff--and for nothing. He now stands accused of driving a wedge through his own Republican Party while his religious denomination seems bent on embarrassing itself by engaging in public debate over secular politics.

Republican State Senator Glenn McConnell of Charleston blasted Beasley, comparing him to ex-British Prime Minister Neville Chamberlain, who struck a deal with Adolf Hitler that failed to prevent World War II. "Our governor has asked you to give all to those who will give you nothing," McConnell told South Carolinians. Others charged Beasley with trying to look "politically correct."

Attorney General Charles Condon criticized Beasley, and in an eloquent statement published in the third quarter edition of *Southern Partisan* magazine, framed the battle flag issue for his home state and the whole South:

The root issue of this controversy is not where the Confederate flag flies. The issue is what the flag stands for. If that flag is a symbol of honor, as the governor and I agree that it is, then there should be no controversy. Why are we even here talking about it? On the other hand, if it is a symbol of racism and hate, then it shouldn't be flying at all, at any place or at any time.

Over 40,000 South Carolinians were casual-

*ties of that war. The tremendous loss of human life
touched every home and it broke every heart. And
the meaning of the battle flag was defined, for all
time, by the blood and the tears of the men and the
women whose remains now rest in graveyards all
across the state.*

*In death their voices are silent. Only we can
speak for them now. Only we can defend the meaning of their lives.*

*So let us ask ourselves this question: what is the
message of our past? Are we to regard our state's
heritage as essentially good and decent? Or shall
we agree with the extremist groups who define the
flag as a symbol of hate?*

*In my judgment, moving the flag would be a
victory for the extremist groups. They would immediately start planning their next crisis, their next
outrage, their next demand. That's what they do.
Controversy is their business. It is not possible to
appease the merchants of hate. And it is a mistake
even to try.*

Clearly Beasley did not learn the lesson of Georgia's Zell
Miller. The battle flag debate will rage on long after Beasley is
gone. South Carolinians will remember his reversal on election
day 1998, and of course, blacks will betray him in the voting booth.
At the time this book was printed, the future of the flag in South
Carolina was unclear.

Politicians pandering to the small anti-flag groups paid a price
in Alabama as well. Even though a lawsuit forced the removal of
the battle flag from atop the Alabama state Capitol, it will likely go
down as only the first round of other court battles to come. Pro-flag
groups led by the Confederate Heritage Fund and the SCV have
kept the issue alive, and a new bill returning the flag to the Capitol
is likely to surface.

After a 1994 vote by the House Ways and Means Committee
in which a bill to restore the flag was defeated 10-6, pro-flag
supporters in Alabama began focusing on the fall election. They
targeted three committee members who voted against the flag bill.
In the elections, two were defeated by whopping 65-35 percent
margins, while the third won by less than one percent. The
shockwaves were felt by politicians throughout the state. In

addition, Republican pro-flagger Fob James was elected governor of Alabama. Though the governor does not have the power to return the flag to the Capitol, James wasted little time in ordering the Third (current) National Flag of the Confederacy flown at all Welcome Centers and state parks. Opposition howled, but James refused to back down. He defended the Third National flag, saying it would fly with all other flags that have flown over Alabama during the state's history.

John Robertson, a tourist from Cleethorpes, South Humberside, England, took note of all the hullabaloo being made over the flag while

Anti-flaggers were successful in having the battle flag removed from the state Capitol in Montgomery, Alabama in 1995. But new governor, Fob James, ordered all state parks and welcome centers in 1996 to fly the Confederacy's Third (Current) National Flag which features the battle flag as its union. Note the Alabama state flag (second from left), which also features the Cross of St. Andrew.

visiting Montgomery in 1992. "Whilst staying in Montgomery... I detected a great deal of hostility," he wrote. "At that time a debate was taking place on whether or not the Confederate flag should be removed from the Capitol Building after renovation work was completed. I could not understand why a Southerner should not be proud of his or her heritage, and in my opinion to remove this very noble symbol was incomprehensible.... I am appalled at the way your history and heritage are being destroyed and politicized...."[22]

The anti-flag groups continued to focus on the courts, winning one of their few victories in 1995 when U.S. District Judge Robert B. Propst ruled that an Alabama school board could bar clothes featuring the Confederate battle flag. In dismissing the complaint, the judge ruled the case was controlled by a prior court decision, but went a step further, stating that Confederate symbols cause "dissension and disruption. The court further concludes that school administrators do not have to wait for an outbreak of such disruptions to forbid such Confederate symbols."[23]

The ruling frightened many Southerners who were fearful that the next step would be banning Confederate heritage and history from classrooms. Their fear was well-founded. Even before Propst's ruling, such bans were popping up. For example, in 1994, the 17th Tennessee Regiment reenactors went to Iowa City, Iowa, to participate in a memorial ceremony with reenactors of the 2nd Iowa Light Artillery. The ceremony was to honor a Confederate veteran buried nearby. The Confederate reenactors went to a local school to give a living history presentation but were told to leave their battle flags outside.[24]

Such incidents could multiply because of Propst. Indeed in the weeks following his ruling, many schools began banning students wearing clothes with Confederate symbols. Propst must have been unaware — or chose to ignore — a 1994 ruling by federal Judge William Hand of Texas who said the battle flag is not inherently racist. Yet school officials across the South seemed to panic and issued one ban after another.

As can be seen, bans are extending far beyond the battle flag. Here are a few examples of schools banning Confederate history and symbols:

— High school principal Tim Setterlund of Collierville, Tennessee, issued an order in late 1995 banning the Confederate battle flag and Confederate T-shirts from school.[25]

— In nearby Bartlett, Tennessee, a quotation by Robert E. Lee caused a stir. Quotations were supposed to have appeared under each student's picture in the high school yearbook, but when senior Will W. Reid III wanted Lee's quotation under his photo, the annual's staff and school faculty rejected it on grounds of possible racial overtones. Lee's quote, "If I had foreseen the use these people desired to make of their victory, there would have been no surrender at Appomattox, no sir, not by me. Had I foreseen these results of subjugation, I would have preferred to die at Appomattox with my brave men, my sword in this right hand." As a result, all quotations were removed from the yearbook.[26]

— Troup County High School in LaGrange, Georgia, implemented a ban on the Confederate battle flag.

— An assistant principal in Carroll County, Texas, reportedly threatened high school students in the fall of 1995 with dismissal if they were caught possessing "rebel flags and other racially inflammatory items."[27]

— Knoxville (Tennessee) Central High School principal Pat Mashburn prohibited about a dozen students from wearing Confederate battle flag shirts to school. Though no complaints had been lodged, Mashburn banned the shirts because "some people find them offensive." The students wanted to wear the shirts in memory of a classmate who had been killed in a jeep accident.[28]

— A 14-year-old Anderson County, South Carolina, student was suspended from school twice within a 10-day period in January 1996, for wearing a Confederate flag jacket to class. Jamie Kinley was suspended for three days the first time, then five days for the second. Assistant Superintendent Bill Dillard said the jacket jeopardized school safety. Kinley's parents, who began home schooling their child, said he would continue to wear the jacket until a court said otherwise. The school district had no dress code or formalized policy on what attire is deemed suitable.[29]

— A Dunn, North Carolina, high school student was told to leave school for wearing a Confederate lapel pin. Harnett Central High Principal Don Wilson asked John Denning Wood to leave February 8, 1996. He allowed the student to return to school with the pin unless "someone complained that the pin was offensive." Said Wood, who had worn the pin for two years, "It's just part of my Southern heritage."[30]

— A student at Montgomery County High School in the eastern Kentucky town of Mt. Sterling was threatened in November 1996 with suspension by the principal if she continued to drive her car onto school property. The reason: Her vehicle sported a Confederate battle flag license plate on the bumper. The county school board had no written policy with broad applicability and were told they were violating the student's First Amendment rights to free speech.

— Someone filed a complaint in 1995 with the Office of Civil Rights of the U.S. Department of Education against Haralson County High School in northwest Georgia for using the nickname "Rebels" and painting a Confederate flag on its gymnasium floor. When an overflow crowd opposing a change showed up at the

Board of Education meeting, the matter was dropped. The SCV immediately demanded an explanation from the U.S. Department of Education as to why it was involved in a local school matter.[31]

– In the fall of 1996, 15 high schoolers were sent home by the principal in Wentworth, North Carolina after wearing battle flag T-shirts to school. The students wore the shirts to protest a Rockingham County High School newspaper editorial criticizing the battle flag as a symbol of hate. The students returned to the school later that night for the homecoming football game wearing their T-shirts. The principal promptly had them arrested for trespassing. One child, who could not afford the $2,500 bail, spent two days in jail. The trespass charges were ultimately dropped, but the principal tried to get the district to indict the children for inciting a riot. In the end the district attorney refused to indict the kids.

From Carrollton, Georgia, to Ashland City, Tennessee, bans on Confederate clothing multiplied. The speed and volume of these actions shocked many people. Most of all, it caused needless confusion and misunderstanding.

The endless and senseless controversy over Confederate history and symbols at schools was not limited to clothing or quotations in yearbooks. A self-described Civil Rights activist named Louis Coleman filed a complaint in federal court in Kentucky against 18 state high schools which have mascots he claims are offensive to blacks and American Indians. Coleman, who is with the Justice Resource Center in Shelbyville, Kentucky, targeted Todd County (Kentucky) High School after two black men were convicted of killing Michael Westerman for flying a Confederate battle flag in the back of his pickup truck. "We feel that the school environment must be conducive for all people to learn," Coleman said. "But Todd County and several other Kentucky schools use a symbol that is repulsive to African-Americans. The Confederates fought to maintain slavery. And that flag... (is) a negative reminder that we don't need in our schools."[32]

Damaging court rulings, like that of Propst, against Southern heritage have given rise to pro-flag organizations like The Heritage Preservation Association in Georgia, the Confederate Heritage Fund in Alabama, the Southern Heritage Association in South Carolina, and Preserving Our Heritage, Inc. (POH), in Florida. All have become effective lobbying organizations and possess funds to fight selective court battles. Their actions, along with other organizations, have paid off. For example, seven Blackville (South

Carolina) Middle School students were suspended from school in 1995 for wearing Confederate flag T-shirts. A Civil Rights lawsuit was filed on behalf of the students against the school and Barnwell County School officials. The suit was settled in January 1996. Reports said the students were awarded $5,000.[33]

One of the most brutal attacks on a student by a school system occurred in December 1995 at Pine Ridge High School in Volusia County, Florida, about 100 miles east of Tampa.

Sixteen-year-old Wayne Denno was among five students suspended for three to nine days and had a "disciplinary" suspension action entered into their personal records after they carried Confederate symbols to school. Four of the students accepted their suspensions, but Denno refused. That prompted the school to turn Denno, who is a Confederate reenactor, over to the Department of Juvenile Justice in Deland, Florida, for prosecution for in-school "behavioral" transgressions. He faced criminal charges of "attempting to start a riot," said Marion Lambert, chairman of the Tampa Bay Chapter of the POH.[34] Of course, the only thing Denno had done was wear a four-inch Confederate battle flag to class, which he defended to an intolerate assistant principal. At the same time, a placement committee at the school was considering Denno's expulsion.

Meanwhile, Denno was articulate in newspaper interviews where he defended the battle flag. One irony about Denno: he's originally from Pennsylvania.

Naturally the Klu Klux Klan showed up at the height of the controversy, demonstrating across from the school in an effort to offset the NAACP who arrived and called for the firing of the principal and the banning of Confederate symbols in Volusia County. Three months went by while school officials tried to decide whether to expel Denno or transfer him to another school. "There really was no choice for us other than to stand with this young man who stood alone against a school administrator, a school system, and the legal system," Lambert said.[35] The POH provided legal counsel and was successful in getting the criminal charges dropped. The school rescinded its unwritten policy banning Confederate symbols and decided not to expel Denno, letting him instead return to Pine Ridge High.

All of the legal wrangling has required lawyers throughout the South to take up positions along the battle line. One example is Mike Corley of Woodbury, Tennessee, who like many of the

attorneys defending Southern heritage, is a descendant of a Confederate soldier. While Jennings and Nichols were running the
Klan out of town, Corley was in court battling the NAACP and a
gay rights group that had joined forces to prevent the Cannon
County Commission from adopting a new county banner featuring
the battle flag.

"The last thing I want to do is alienate anyone, but I'm proud
of my heritage," said Corley, whose family moved to Tennessee in
1815. "We've got to draw a line before Southerners are assimilated
into the mishmash of popular culture. They (the anti-flaggers)
smell blood. They are sincere, even though they are mistaken.
There also is political prestige that fuels the process."[36]

The anti-flaggers used the same tiring argument that the new
flag was a symbol of slavery and racism. But as is the case with all
Confederate battle flags, history tells a different story. The motives
of the Cannon County Commission were pure and strictly based on
history.

On July 12, 1862, Confederate General Nathan Bedford Forrest
and 1,400 of his troops rode into Woodbury in an attempt to get in
the rear of Union troops advancing out of Murfreesboro toward
Chattanooga. Upon their arrival in the Cannon County town of
Woodbury, Forrest and his men were met by female residents who
were extremely glad to see the Confederates. About 40 of the
town's men (mostly elderly and clergy since most men were off
fighting) and boys had been arrested by Union troops. Military
Governor Andrew Johnson had them unjustifiably arrested on
charges of aiding the Confederacy. They were taken to Murfreesboro
and jailed. Some were sentenced to hang the next day. Forrest
assured the women their men would be returned the next day alive
and well. The Confederates arrived outside Murfreesboro about
4:30 a.m., on July 13, Forrest's birthday, and immediately attacked
the Union force.

"The enemy, mounted and some 1,200 strong, with terrific
yells, dashed upon us from three directions, armed with double-
barreled shotguns and Colt's navy revolvers," a Michigan officer
reported later.

It was not long before some of Forrest's men shot their way
onto the public square where the courthouse and jail were located.
One of those jailed was a Baptist minister who said he — and four
other Confederate sympathizers — were ordered held and scheduled for hanging later that morning. The minister said they had

been arrested because a Union soldier had been killed near their homes. The other men were neighbors of the minister.

Among the others in jail awaiting hanging were Confederate Captain William Richardson and spy James Paul. Richardson later recalled what happened as the Confederates shot their way into town: Richardson was awakened by Paul "about daylight. (Paul)... caught me by the arm and was shaking me, saying 'Listen, listen!' I started up, hearing a strange noise like the roar of an approaching storm."

The two men leaped onto a box to look out their cell window.

"The roar grew louder and came nearer, and in a very few seconds we were sure we could discern the clatter of horses' feet upon the hard turnpike." Then "on the morning air there came to our ear with heartfelt welcome the... rebel yell... almost before we could speak, the advance-guard of the charging troopers came into sight and rushed by us on the street, some halting in front of the jail."

When the Union guard realized they were being surrounded, they took shots at some of the prisoners before running out the door. One Union soldier set the jail on fire before scampering out. The Confederates entered the blazing jail, using an iron bar to raise the jail door just enough so that the prisoners could be dragged out by lying on the floor.

Then, Richardson wrote, that Forrest ran in and "inquired of the officer in charge if he had rescued the prisoners. He said that they were safe, but added that the jail had been set on fire in order to burn them up, and the guard had taken refuge in the courthouse. Forrest said, 'Never mind, we'll get him.'"

Richardson said he would "never forget the appearance of General Forrest on that occasion; his eyes were flashing as if on fire, his face was deeply flushed, and he seemed in a condition of great excitement."

When the smoke cleared, Forrest and his men had captured 1,200 Union troops, 300 mules, 60 wagons, 200 horses, four cannons, burned $20,000 worth of stores, and destroyed the railroad and depot.

After the fighting stopped and the prisoners were gathered, Forrest approached Richardson and said, "They tell me these men treated you inhumanly while in jail. Point them out to me."

Richardson told Forrest he only wished to point out one man — "who had set fire to the jail in order to burn us up. Forrest asked me to go along the line with him and point that man out. I did so. A few hours later, when the list of private soldiers was being called, the name of this man was heard and no one answered; Forrest said, 'Pass on, it's all right.'"[37]

The battle flag that Forrest used was the Cross of the St. Andrew, but featured only 12 stars with a 13th star missing from the center of the cross. It is the Forrest-design battle flag that the Cannon County Commission wanted to adopt — not as a symbol of racism, but to honor the bravery of Forrest and his men whose daring raid saved the lives of innocent people from Woodbury and Cannon County.

How could anyone blame them for wanting to do that?

Corley was able to win the case in circuit court, but the opposition filed an appeal that went to the State Supreme Court. Fortunately, the appeal was denied for procedural reasons. As a result, the new flag flies at a downtown Confederate monument every day. It also flies over the courthouse on Confederate Memorial Day and on the birthdays of Nathan Bedford Forrest and Confederate President Jefferson Davis.

There were some other aspects of the Woodbury case that deserve examination as well. At one point the monument became the target of the anti-flaggers as well. As has been the case throughout the flag controversy nationally, they weren't satisfied with attacking just the flag. But when it was proven the monument was actually located on private property, they were forced to retreat. The monument, like so many others across the South, was hit by vandals. On October 23, 1993, the flagpole was bent in half and the flag stolen.

A spokesman for a group fighting the flag immediately denied members' participation in the theft and vandalism. "Our people had nothing whatsoever to do with what took place at the monument," Walter Alexander said. "We don't condone that type of action."[38]

Tensions heightened when a white woman — found by authorities in a secluded part of the county — claimed she had been attacked by a black man. The issue was well covered by area newspapers — until the woman confessed to police that her story was a hoax. That part of the story was largely ignored.

Corley, who is also a Confederate reenactor, often hosts reenactment drills at his farm. He places signs bearing the battle flag along the road to let participants know how to get to the drill location. Corley's signs were frequently the targets of vandals, so he started erecting cardbord signs with "Yankees" on them. The vandalism stopped.

One of the more highly publicized confrontations over the battle flag also occurred in Tennessee. Chattanooga Mayor Gene Roberts and the SCV squared off during the organization's reunion in July 1995. The SCV received permission from the city-owned Chattanooga Trade & Convention Center to fly the battle flag on the flagpole in front of the facility during the reunion. When a handful of people called to protest the flag, Roberts agreed with convention center officials and removed the flag.

"He chose to bow to the demands of less than two dozen people," the SCV's Norman Dasinger said after meeting with the mayor. "You make millions of dollars in this city off your heritage. This is hypocrisy."[39]

Roberts remained adamant about the flag coming down. "Raising that flag on a public flagpole in front of a public building was an affront to a lot of people in the community," he said.[40] In the end, Roberts made two serious miscalculations: first, it wasn't "a lot of people," who complained. Second, he failed to realize how seriously his anti-flag stand could hurt his city's tourism industry. When Dasinger mentioned the SCV might leave Chattanooga early, a defiant Roberts replied, "I would regret that, but that would not change my decision to ask the (Trade Center) board to take the flag down."[41]

As word of the controversy spread, Roberts was bombarded with calls and letters from flag supporters. Some SCV members erected the battle flag in front of the convention center atop a crane. "Other than the mayor, we're going to leave Chattanooga with a good taste in our mouths," Dasinger said during the controversy. "As time moves on — this being a new social era in this country — it's going to be OK to fly the flag. Chattanooga could have been on the cutting edge of that. This mayor really missed a marvelous opportunity. Chattanooga could have been the first city in the country to say, 'It's OK; these people are good people. It's a new multicultural era, and we recognize everybody's rights and freedoms.'"[42]

James Mapp, local branch president of the NAACP, eventually surfaced. "I think the mayor said and did the right thing; the board and its management did the right thing," he said.[43]

The SCV purchased full-page ads in both city newspapers,

88   CHAPTER THREE

blasting the mayor for removing the flag. "We are angry that city politics were more important to your community's public officials than the right of free speech guaranteed by the U.S. Constitution," said the advertisement addressed to the citizens of Chattanooga. "Yet, it's the citizens of Chattanooga who should be angry. Your city officials ran away from the issue rather than doing what was right and allowing the flag to be flown at our convention. Today, they permitted the banning of the Confederate flag. What will they compromise tomorrow? Just how much of this city's heritage are they willing to abandon due to politics?"[44]

As the days went on, the controversy continued to simmer. Roberts had one of his staffers call my boss at the newspaper to complain about an editorial I wrote criticizing his action. The staffer told my boss that the mayor did not order the board to remove the flag. But that contradicted both local newspaper reports and when I produced that proof, my boss dropped the matter and the mayor's flak retreated.

Then things really took a bizarre turn. About a month after the convention, reports surfaced that a Chattanooga police officer had been cited for insubordination by the city's Safety Administration for failing to leave an SCV rally being held outside City Hall while Dasinger and others met with the mayor. It seems the officer was seen roaming through the crowd, taking photographs of SCV members. He said he went to City Hall to help with crowd control, but the Safety Administrator said that taking photographs of SCV members was also part of the reason for the insubordinaton charge. The officer was a member of the Chattanooga Law Enforcement Officers Association, a union of predomiantly black police officers.[45]

Meanwhile, letters and criticism continued to roll into Roberts' office. More than a year after the incident, Roberts was still debating the action with SCV members. In a September 1995 letter to Lawrence Fafarman of Los Angeles, California, Roberts wrote, "Your rights do not extend to determination of what flies on a flagpole on publicly owned property."[46] Fafarman responded, "I would agree with your position if the Convention Center had a non-discriminatory, uniformly-applied policy of prohibiting all visiting organizations from flying their organizational flags on the center's flagpoles. However, it is apparent that the Convention Center had no such policy because the battle flag was initially allowed to be flown. The battle flag was taken down only after your office received a few anonymous complaints."[47]

The city of Chattanooga subsequently launched a massive advertising campaign to try to spruce up the city's tourism image.

Even the innocent United Daughters of the Confederacy have felt the sting of anti-flag attacks. U.S. Senator Carol Moseley-Braun, a black Democrat from Illinois, was successful in 1993 in denying the UDC its 14-year renewal on its patent for its emblem, which included the First National Flag, also known as the "Stars and Bars." The UDC has had the patent for the previous 100 years.

"Those of us whose ancestors fought on a different side in the Civil War, or who were held, frankly, as human chattel under the Confederate flag, are duty bound to honor our ancestors as well by asking whether such recognition by the U.S. Senate is appropriate," Moseley-Braun said.[48]

Republican North Carolina Senator Jesse Helms argued that the UDC is an organization of "delightful, gentle souls, most of them elderly women," who perform charitable work at homeless shelters, give awards at the nation's military academies, and fund thousands of scholarships for college students. "If a senator is going to use (inflammatory) tactics of this sort," Helms said, "it would be better if she would pick on somebody her size. Leave the United Daughters of the Confederacy alone."[49]

Moseley-Braun's motion was passed 75-25 by a Senate that was gutted by the 1994 election.

One final point on Moseley-Braun. The senator subsequently came under fire when it was discovered her campaign fund had apparently been padded by a British company who benefitted from a patent extension she helped get approved in the Senate. She was accused of accepting a $10,000 campaign donation from the company, flying to the corporate headquarters in a company jet, and receiving an honorarium of $15,000 just after her election. Critics claim the patent extension could cost Americans an estimated $3.6 billion.[50]

Comedienne Brett Butler, a native of rural Alabama, seemed to enjoy picking on the UDC, too. While a guest on "The Tonight Show," Butler said she had been performing at a comedy club in Mobile, Alabama, where a gathering of the UDC was taking place next door. "What's next?" she asked. "Stepdaughters of the Third Reich? Children of Ethnic Cleansing?"[51] Wonder if Butler knows what the term "scalawag" means?

There have been other, less publicized, attacks on the flag and other Confederate symbols. No one can say how many there have

been, but it is safe to assume there have been hundreds — and more
are on the way. The following examples are intended to give
readers the nature and breadth of the attacks being launched
against Southern culture. The outcome — if known — is included
after each incident:

— On a syndicated radio talk show in March 1996, Vincent
Ellison, representing the African-American Unity Congress of
Columbia, South Carolina, declared that the Confederacy equated
to "Nazism." Ellison said Jefferson Davis and Robert E. Lee were
traitors to the United States and should have been executed.[52]

— A white woman walked into Tom Tucker's Custom Flag
store in Columbia, Tennessee, and gasped when she saw a Confederate battle flag on display.

"You shouldn't sell that," said the woman.

"She jumped all over me about that," Tucker recalled. "I've
had other people come in and want to buy one, but back away
because they're afraid to fly it outside. The battle flag is part of our
history, and this just bothers the fire out of me."[53]

— In Hollywood, Florida, in 1994, the city commission
removed the Confederate battle flag from the All Wars Memorial
in Young Circle. When Southerners protested, all flags at the
memorial, including the POW/MIA flag, were removed — a clear
victory for the politically correct movement.[54]

— On June 3, 1993, the board of directors of the Danville,
Virginia, Museum of Fine Arts and History voted to remove the
Third (Current) National Flag of the Confederacy. The action was
taken after Joyce Glaise, a member of the city council, claimed it
was offensive to blacks. Despite a local newspaper poll showing
6,803 people opposing the move — compared to 345 agreeing with
it, the flag was replaced with the U.S. flag and state flag. Danville
was the last Capitol of the Confederacy. But the Heritage Preservation Association was successful in convincing the city to accept
a new 22-foot monument as a gift where the flag now flies every
day.[55]

— The black owner of a Biloxi, Mississippi, radio station was
joined by five other people in filing a lawsuit in August 1995
against the Harrison County Board of Supervisors. The lawsuit
asked that the Confederate flag be removed from Mississipi
beaches and other public property within Harrison County. The
lawsuit was dismissed by a judge, and the flag continues to fly over
Mississippi beaches.

— Navy Rear Admiral R.M. Mitchell removed the Georgia and Mississippi flags from a state flag display during an August 1995, change-of-command ceremony at the Mechanicsburg, Pennsylvania Navy Depot. Mitchell took the action after a black employee at the depot complained about the battle flags in the Georgia and Mississippi state flag designs. U.S. Senators Trent Lott of Mississippi and Sam Nunn of Georgia filed protests with the Navy. Admiral Mitchell was ordered to issue an apology, which he did, though he never explained why the flags were not included in the first place.[56]

— A small group of blacks called for the images of Confederate Generals Robert E. Lee and Thomas "Stonewall" Jackson on the face of Stone Mountain, Georgia, near Atlanta to be covered during the 1996 Summer Olympics. Their request was rejected.

— NBC's Bryant Gumble and former Virginia Governor Douglas Wilder launched an attack upon the Museum of the Confederacy in Richmond during the "Today" morning show. Wilder, protesting an antebellum fundraising ball being held for the museum, said the facility should have a slave ship on its lawn and compared Confederate soldiers to "Nazis," while Gumble repeatedly interrupted rebuttals by museum director Robin Reed. Prior to the "Today" show only about 100 tickets had been sold. About 400 were quickly sold in the days immediately following NBC's intolerate presentation.

— When members of the SCV went to reinter the remains of Jesse James (who was a Confederate soldier) in late 1995, they received permission to have the funeral in the chapel of William Jewell College near James' home of Liberty, Missouri. After all the arrangements had been made, the college said no Confederate flags would be allowed and no mention of the Confederacy could be made. The SCV moved the ceremony elsewhere. By the way, the college was founded by James' father, Robert James, who was a Baptist minister.

— A Nashville newspaper columnist howled when the Nashville Symphony played "Dixie" at Carnton Plantation near Franklin, Tennessee. Carnton was a field hospital during the Battle of Franklin. Blood stains from the Confederate dead can still be seen on the floors. About 1,500 Confederate soldiers are buried there as well. By the way, the Nashville Symphony received a standing ovation for its performance.

— A defiant Harvard law school student, Brigit Kerrigan from

Great Falls, Virginia, refused to remove the battle flag that hung from her fourth-floor dorm window in the spring of 1991. Opponents tried to pressure her into removing the flag by holding a protest march. She was the target of newspaper editorials and two university forums. One black student even painted a Nazi swastika on a white sheet and hung it from her window in protest of Kerrigan's display of her heritage.

By the way, it's been 135 years and Confederates are still the only Harvard alumni not listed in the university's memorial among the Americans who have fought and died in wars. Among those listed: a German who fought for the Axis powers in World War II. Since the deed to the memorial building prohibits Confederates from being named there, Harvard is considering a memorial for its 68 alumni who died fighting for the Confederacy at nearby Memorial Church in Harvard Yard.

— A dorm director attempted to have Baylor University (in Waco, Texas) student Allison Jill Wilson remove the battle flag that hung over her bed in her dormroom in 1994. The director said

A Biloxi, Mississippi man sued in 1996 to have the battle flag (third flag from left) removed from Mississippi's public beaches. The suit was dismissed and the battle flag continues to fly. Notice the Mississippi state flag (second from left) also flying.

some girls in the dorm had found her flag "offensive." Wilson refused, saying it was a symbol of her proud heritage.[57]

— Attorney Robert E. Patrick, who was an unsuccessful 1995 candidate for lieutenant governor of Louisiana, asked local government officials to remove an 80-year-old monument honoring Confederate soldiers from the Lake Charles, Louisiana, courthouse lawn. He suggested it be moved to a cemetery with "dead people" and that blacks be compensated for slavery. Patrick's argument against the monument: it was offensive to some blacks. Government officials rejected Patrick's request and then approved funding to restore the monument, erect a new historic marker, and make landscaping improvements.[58]

— Memphis City Councilman James Ford introduced a resolution in March 1994 to have the statue of Confederate General Albert Pike removed from Judiciary Square in Washington, D.C. The resolution was rejected.

— The ABC Thursday Night at the Movies' special two-hour presentation of the "Commish" involved white racists desecrating Jewish synagogues. The Confederate battle flag was prominently displayed and clearly connected to the white racists during numerous scenes of the show, which aired January 11, 1996. One irate Southerner, William D. Ferris Jr., of Orangedale, Florida, let ABC know how he felt: "I refer to the abuse of the Confederate battle flag, under which two of my ancestors served, by the racist hate group portrayed in the show. For many years the television media has portrayed Arabs as villains, Italians as members of the Mafia, and North American Indians as alcoholics. You are respectively requested in the future to refrain from stereotyping the Confederate battle flag. The SCV has repeatedly condemned the extremist and hate groups that have stolen our Confederate symbols. I call upon you to stop giving credence to our enemies by associating them with our cultural and historical icons."[59]

— The CBS movie, "Ruby Ridge: An American Tragedy," frequently showed Confederate battle flags at racist meetings, including a sickening display of the colors at an Aryan Nation meeting. In all of the news photo accounts of the actual Ruby Ridge standoff, I never recall seeing a Confederate battle flag flying in front of white separatist Randy Weaver's house. However, The producers made sure there was one in the movie which aired in May 1996.

— Other Hollywood-made movies have trashed the battle flag

as well. In "Forrest Gump," Gump is chased by bullies in a pickup bearing a Confederate license plate. In "Kalifornia," Brad Pitt plays a serial killer who has a Confederate flag on his cap. In John Grisham's "The Client," the crooked mafia attorney who commits suicide also has a Confederate flag license plate on his car. In Grisham's "A Time To Kill," the nuthead has a battle flag hanging in the rear window of his pickup (Hollywood changed it to a prominent sticker in the movie). All of this prompted columnist Sam Francis to write: "The cultural elite is engaged in a little psy-war. It is systematically linking the Confederate flag with images of evil, violence, backwardness and bullying; and in so doing it advances its self-appointed mission of erasing the symbolism and imagery — and therefore the memory — of America's past, which includes the South's past."[60]

— Crestview, Florida, Councilman Bill Kilpatrick made a motion to remove the battle flag flying at Lundy Park in the center of town. The battle flag had been flying under the American flag by a monument honoring William Lundy, the last living Confederate soldier from Florida. The city-owned park was dedicated by the Lions Club in memory of Lundy who died in 1957 at age 109.

"To have the American flag and the symbolic Confederate flag on the same pole is offensive to a good many people," Kilpatrick said. His resolution was defeated, 3-2, with the council's lone black member voting to keep the flag flying.[61]

— Belmont University in Nashville, Tennessee, announced September 23, 1995, that it would change its nickname from "Rebels" to "Bruins." Head basketball coach Rick Byrd said the change was made because "we wouldn't want anyone to equate the old nickname with something from the Confederacy, because that could offend some people."[62]

— A man who had recently moved to Tampa, Florida, from Chicago, demanded in 1993 that the Hillsborough County Commission remove the battle flag from the county's seal. Only one quarter of the seal, which was on the side of all county vehicles, contained the battle flag. The county bowed to his wishes. A new seal, without the Confederate battle flag has been adopted.[63]

— Army Specialist Richard Williams, a truck driver assigned to Fort Campbell, Kentucky, was ordered to remove a decal of a Confederate battle flag from the rear window of his truck in February 1996. Williams said he was told to remove the decal by his company commander who said the base was issuing a policy to ban the battle flag. But a superior officer said that was untrue and that the Army has no such policy. Said Williams, "I'm in the Army to protect the freedom of the American people, and now I'm being asked to give mine up."[64]

— Blacks want the Second National Flag removed from a display of flags in the state Capitol in Tallahassee, Florida. The display, which has been there 18 years, features all of the national flags that have flown over the state of Florida. Surprisingly, the issue was raised by the Southern Christian Leadership Conference and it took little time for state officials to respond.

"The Second National Flag of the Confederacy does not represent oppression or racism," Florida Secretary of State Sandra B. Mortham wrote in an editorial. "In fact, it does just the opposite. It represents the patriotism of both black and white Confederates and honors those men who fought in the Civil War for freedom and prosperity south of the Mason-Dixon line. If we ask Southerners to suppress their heritage, we are recreating the very ultimate injustice that critics of the flag condemn — oppression. The ultimate hypocrisy would be to remove this symbol. Be assured that should this matter come before the current governor and state Cabinet, due to the historic significance of the flag, I will do all within my power to keep the Second National Flag of the Confederacy flying over the Capitol."[65]

— Circuit Judge Don Mullins denied a request by a Tazewell, Virginia SCV camp to fly the Confederate "Stars and Bars" on Confederate Memorial Day, April 26 over the courthouse. The request had been approved by the board of supervisors. Mullins had removed the flag from the flagpole in 1995. His reason: it could cause divisiveness. A suggestion was made to move it to the county administration building, but the ACLU frightened the board of supervisors, who did not allow the flag to be flown there as well.[66]

— In Greenville, South Carolina, a lawyer who was handling a death-row inmates' appeal entered as evidence a drawing of the courthouse where the inmate had been convicted. The drawing showed a Confederate monument, cannon, and flag in front of the historic building. The judge asked the attorney, Mark Olive, if he was suggesting that everything connected to the Confederacy is racist. Olive replied yes. The judge then told Olive that his full name was Alexander Stephens MaCauley and that he was named after Confederate Vice President Alexander Stephens. MaCauley asked the attorney if he wanted him to disqualify himself from the bench. After a 10-minute recess the lawyer replied that the judge should stay.[67]

— A member of the Virginia House of Delegates introduced a bill to change the state song, "Carry Me Back To Old Virginny." Bob Marshall's effort failed after it raised a firestorm throughout the state. Marshall, who represents one of the Washington, D.C., beltway districts, wanted to replace the song, which was approved in 1940, with "The Old Dominion." A similarly unsuccessful attempt was made on the Maryland state song, "Maryland, My Maryland," as well.

— Dixie Youth Baseball dropped the battle flag from its baseball fields in 1994. A new logo replaces the stars in the Cross of St. Andrew with baseballs. It marked the first time the organization, which serves about 300,000 youth in 11 Southern states, had been changed since its founding in 1955. The organization and logo were labeled racist because of their connection to the Confederacy.

— Ed Hooper, an award-winning television reporter in Knoxville, Tennessee, claimed he was fired by WKXT-TV in April 1996 after he had completed a series of stories on the Confederacy. The television station would not say why he was fired just days after he had received a prestigious award from colleagues. Hooper claims some co-workers protested to management over his Confederate stories.[68]

— A Bladenboro, North Carolina, man claimed he was fired in 1994 for displaying a battle flag sticker on his toolbox after a few employees complained. Tony Johnson said he lost his job at Mayo Yarn because company officials said the flag was "racist." In an unusual move, the city council condemned the company for attacking Johnson's Southern heritage and demanded an explanation concerning its policy on such matters.[69]

— A whole fraternity was punished in 1994 at a college in New Jersey because one member brought a battle flag into the dining hall.[70]

— The North Carolina division of the SCV wrote a proclamation calling April "Confederate Heritage Month." It was sent to Governor Jim Hunt for his signature. He signed it, but not until he changed it to "Civil War Heritage Month." "We are disappointed that you chose not to proclaim April as 'Confederate Heritage Month' as we asked," said Frank Powell, SCV North Carolina division commander, in a letter back to Hunt. "The term 'Civil War' is offensive to most of our members and an inaccurate term for the War for Southern Independence. Since North Carolinians answered the governor's call and our state lost more troops than any other Confederate state, we feel 'Confederate Heritage Month' is a much better term."[71] Six other Southern governors signed similar proclamations — without removing "Confederate." Governors from all 11 of the former Confederate states, plus Oklahoma and Kentucky, wrote letters in July 1996 congratulating the SCV on its 100th anniversary.

— Ralph Meetze, a Columbia, South Carolina, businessman, came up with the idea of having checks printed featuring a lightly colored Confederate battle flag in the background. To his surprise, no one in the South would print it. Meetze finally found a printer, in of all places — California. "It's very popular; and it's going to be profitable," Meetze said. Interestingly, more than half of the checks sold are to people outside the South. The company is known as Old South, Ltd.[72]

— The Lynchburg, Virginia *News & Advance* called the battle flag a "racist symbol... of intolerance... that does not deserve to be flown. The Confederacy is dead."[73]

— Cheerleaders at the University of Mississippi can no longer carry the battle flag during athletic events. The school's athletic teams' nickname is "Rebels." University officials at Ole Miss and the University of Alabama have discouraged the sale of battle flags at games as well.

Ole Miss professor William Ferris, who is a darling of the liberal news media, once proclaimed that "white Southerners are holding onto the (Confederate) flag as a mystic symbol because they can't stop change.... Whatever the flag meant in the 1860s, in the 1990s it's about race. What we see today in a somewhat less violent way than during the Civil War era is the same wrestling with the issue of whether or not black people will have full participation in American culture and in the South." His comments were reported in a major northeastern newspaper.[74]

— The song "Dixie" has been banned by many high schools and is no longer played at athletic events at the University of Georgia and Virginia Tech University.

- A black man filed a $44 million lawsuit against the city of Franklin, Tennessee in December 1996 because the city square features a Confederate monument. He also asked that prints of Confederate soldiers in City Hall be removed. The monument, which is located where the Battle of Franklin occurred, was erected in 1899. The man said promoting the Confederacy was an act of sedition and treason against the United States. Originally, police department uniforms featured patches of the battle flag, but they were quietly removed about five years ago. The local Franklin newspaper, *The Review Appeal*, conducted a telephone poll asking residents if the monument was offensive. Of the people who were polled, approximately 90 percent said it was not.

Radical blacks seemed to have targeted Franklin. A few weeks before the lawsuit was filed, a black attorney and a handful of supporters walked into the Uncle Bud's Catfish Restaurant during the peak lunch hour one Sunday. The restaurant features various flags as part of its decor. On this particular day the attorney refused to leave until the battle flag was removed. The rattled manager complied in order to get him and his mob to leave, but put the flag back up three days later. Hundreds of SCV members have since patronized Uncle Bud's and the Todd Carter Camp of the SCV now holds its monthly meetings at the popular restaurant.

— For more than three decades a battle flag had flown in Memorial Hall between the Louisiana State House and Senate Chamber, that is until one day in September 1996. That is when Louisiana House Clerk Alfred Speer and Senate Secretary Mike Baer removed it. They denied charges that they removed it because of political pressure, saying they did so to be historically correct since the battle flag never flew over Louisiana. Their action angered many people, yet the flag was not returned. *Southern Partisan* blasted away, calling both men "weasels, cowards and liars." While it is true the battle flag never flew over Louisiana, thousands of Louisianians fought and died under the sacred banner. The removed battle flag was not replaced with another official symbol of the Confederacy.

— A newspaper reporter in nearby DeFuniak Springs, Florida, wrote a scathing attack in 1995 against Walton County officials for flying the battle flag at the county courthouse. Preservationists rallied and supported county officials who ruled that the flag will remain.

— A black hot dog vendor associated with the Redwood City, California Fourth of July Parade complained about the Confederate flag to the local NAACP. The vendor wanted the flag banned from the parade. A representative with the Heritage Preservation Association met with parade officials and told them that if they banned the flag the National Civil War Association (a reenactment group that marches each year and begins the parade with their cannon) and all other veterans' organizations would pull out of the parade. In addition, the HPA representative said his organization would not hesitate in filing a lawsuit against the parade for violating the first amendment rights of the people wanting to carry the battle flag. Parade officials said the flag would not be banned.[75]

— The local SCV camp in Hickory, North Carolina, repaired the wrought-iron fence around what may be one of the most beautiful Confederate monuments anywhere. The gates were gold-plated — until they were stolen. The monument is an angel carrying a dead Confederate soldier in his arms.

- The Motor Vehicle Administration of the state of Maryland were bullied into recalling 78 special license plates featuring the Confederate battle flag in January 1997. The flags, which were approved by the state and made in 1995, were sold to members of the Sons of the Confederate Veterans. Maryland recalled the plates after a few politically motivated blacks, led by the state's Legislative Black Caucus, alerted their news media allies and then launched their usual disinformation campaign. "Symbols are significant and important," said state Delegate Clarence Mitchell, who seemed to imply a connection between the battle flag and the Nazi swastika. "Ask a Jewish person about the significance of the swastika," he said.

SCV members tried to explain the organization's role and the true history of the flag while again condemning racist organizations like the Klu Klux Klan. But they were rebuffed by Ronald Freeman, Maryland's motor vehicle administrator, who promptly announced that SCV members had 60 days to return the license plates. If they did not comply, state investigators would be ordered to confiscate them. Freeman agreed to meet with SCV members, but added: "Anything that resembles a Confederate battle flag is not going to be acceptable to us."

As word spread, something unusual happened. Organizations began contacting the SCV about representing its members in a lawsuit against the state of Maryland. Among those wanting to represent the SCV: the American Civil Liberties Union. SCV officials declined their offer, but accepted one from the Rutherford Institute of Washington, D.C. The Rutherford Institute specializes in defending individuals and groups who are denied their First Amendment rights. SCV officials were confident that the Rutherford attorneys would make the state of Maryland eat this one and they did. The federal judge ruled in favor of the SCV members, who were able to keep their license plates.

One can only imagine the accumulative effect these incidents have had on Southern culture. There is no doubt that the Confederate battle flag is the anti-flag groups' main target. But their ultimate goal appears to be the cultural genocide of Dixie.

The battle flag flies daily at the Elm Springs antebellum mansion, which is the international headquarters of the Sons of Confederate Veterans. It is located in Columbia, Tennessee.

CHAPTER FOUR
The Truth Will Always Surface

Do it dishonor? That battle flag? Look on it with disdain?
No: never while our pulses beat our honor will we stain.
Yet will we touch our elbows close to yours, if comes the need
That we for our united land be called upon to bleed.
And North and South as friends again shall be to each so true
That both can march to "Dixie's Land" and "Yankee Doodle," too;
But never ask that we shall be so false unto our dead
That we can turn our backs upon the flag for which they bled.
> – The Southern Battle Flags
> Franklin H. Mackey

When Nelson Winbush talks about his Confederate grandfather it's like hearing fingernails slide down a chalkboard to the NAACP and its politically correct allies.

Hands cover ears, eyes shut, and heads turn away.

Winbush, a retired school administrator from Kissimmee, Florida, is an effective speaker and staunch defender of the battle flag and the Sons of Confederate Veterans, a heritage organization of which he is a member. Winbush can cause a stir because he is black.

Winbush's grandfather, Louis Napoleon Nelson, was a member of Company M, Seventh Tennessee Cavalry. Nelson saw action at the battles of Shiloh, Brice's Crossroads, Vicksburg, and Lookout Mountain (where he secretly entered a Union camp, stole a "jenny" mule, butchered it, and hauled its hind quarter back up the perilous mountain to feed his starving Confederate compatriots).

After the war Nelson attended 39 Confederate veterans' reunions — no matter where they were held. He was so respected in his community that all he had to do to raise travel money was to walk around the courthouse with his hat open. "He'd have enough after one trip around," Winsbush says proudly.[1]

When Nelson died in Lauderdale County, Tennessee, in 1934, his funeral included full military honors. He was buried in a Confederate uniform and a Confederate battle flag draped his casket. Winbush still has the battle flag and proudly displays it whenever he lectures on the subject. He is a potent defender of the Confederacy who bristles at anyone who tries to connect slavery with the battle flag by applying the morals of the space-age 1990s to the horse-and-buggy world of the 19th century. "Blacks went to war just like whites did, for much the same reasons, such as their rights, homes, families, and freedom," he says. "Contrary to what some people want you to believe, the war wasn't about slavery; it was about states' rights, and we still have that problem today."[2]

Winbush, who earned a master of science degree from Tennessee State University in 1955, is among a growing number of blacks who refuse to ignore historical fact. R.J. Wilkins of Miami is another example.

> *I am a black man who is not offended by the flying of the Confederate flag beside the Capitol in Tallahassee (Florida). The Confederate flag is as much a part of my history as of any white person's. It may not represent the best of my race, or be held by some as a contribution to this country's greatness, but it does to me. My great-grandparents were a part of the plantations. They worked the cotton fields, cleaned the big houses, and in many ways supported the development of the American society. We should let the Confederate flag fly as a reminder of our American history — both black and white.[3]*

Other blacks speaking out in defense of the Confederacy and its battle flag, have been targets of ridicule and even threats. Ernest Griffin, of Chicago's South Side, flew a Confederate battle flag outside his funeral home on Martin Luther King Drive for years —

often in the face of threats. Griffin flew the flag out of respect for the 6,000 Confederates who died at the infamous Camp Douglas Prison. His funeral home sat on the old Camp Douglas site. How serious were the threats? The following was a letter sent to Griffin in February 1994:

> *This will be put as bluntly as possible. That Confederate flag must come down. We are totally disgusted that such a racist symbol could be displayed at a South Side institution.... . Any African-American who waves a Confederate flag is a Tom. This is your initial warning. You have until March 1 to get that flag taken down. If by that time the flag is not removed, we will remove it ourselves.*[4]

Naturally, the anonymous authors sent copies of the letter to their allied news media to make sure they knew about Griffin. Such tactics are common by anti-flaggers who rely on the sympathetic media to pile on such people with inflammatory articles and editorial condemnation.

Griffin didn't budge.

"Anyone who objects to this flag being here reveals that they are not knowledgeable about the history of the subject matter," he said defiantly. "That flag is not a symbol of hate. It is a symbol of respect for a dead human being. When 6,000 people died on the site where you live and eat and earn your daily bread and butter, if you have any humility within your being, you have regard for the people who died."[5]

A local black publisher, Ron Carter, went to see Griffin about the flag after he received a copy of the threatening letter. "I see the Confederate flag and I get stomachaches," Carter said, prior to his visit. But after a four-hour conversation with Griffin, Carter's outlook changed. "I had an overall awakening regarding the Confederate flag," Carter said. "Even though I believe there are people who fly the Confederate flag to be spiteful and to use it as a racial type of symbol, I see now there is a history to it as far as America is concerned."[6]

Another black gentleman who defends the battle flag is Edward Smith, a history professor and director of American studies at American University, and study tour leader for the Smithsonian Institute. At a ceremony dedicating a Confederate monument and flag in Danville, Virginia, Smith said complaints that the Confederate flag represents slavery are "pure, unadulterated nonsense."[7]

It took little time for the demogogues to surface after his remarks. Former Virginia Governor Linwood Holton immediately denounced the event as an endorsement of white supremacy.[8]

When another black history professor in Virginia reminded black students that black Africans sold other black Africans into slavery, black students complained, prompting a rebuke by a black university administrator for stating "the unmentionable."

Smith finds such actions alarming and is concerned over what's happening on college campuses. He is particularly worried about students' lack of knowledge about the war. "I am amazed at the number (of students) who believe that all blacks who lived in the South were slaves and that all slaves picked cotton. I mean I don't know how in God's name this kind of mythology can continue. I mean I have had students (black and white) who didn't know whether Robert E. Lee was a Confederate or not. You can't imagine (some) of the things. I have ceased being shocked."[9]

Smith says students are surprised to learn that between 5,000 and 6,000 blacks fought with George Washington during the Revolutionary War and that thousands fought for the Confederacy. "A lot of these things don't get into the history books," he says. "The problem is that the people who make history books want to sell history books and what they've done is sanitize history to such an extent that you really don't have history anymore, you have journalism. So the students wind up going to these books and reading all this stuff. It really concerns me... so I have to re-educate them."[10]

Another outspoken defender was the late W. Earl Douglas, a black journalist from Charleston, South Carolina. He had this to say on the subject;

> *If hate had been the prevailing emotion between the races, then it is a safe bet that the Confederacy never would have been born. Fortunately there was love, understanding, and compassion. And the two greatest lies ever perpetrated by history (are) that the South instigated the war and that it was fought by the North for the purpose of freeing the slaves. The Negro was merely used as the excuse for that war, while the real reason for it is reflected in every area of our lives, where the tentacles of government form the bars of a new slavery. No! Don't furl that Confederate battle*

flag. Let it wave all across the South to remind
Americans that there exists here a yearning for
liberty, freedom, and independence that will not be
denied. Let it fly as a testimonial to real men and
real women who would rather work and fight than
shed tears and beg for government charity.[11]

The late Dr. Leonard Haynes, professor of philosophy at
Southern University in Baton Rouge, Louisiana, was also at the
Danville ceremony with Smith. Haynes frequently defended the
Confederacy amid much criticism from black peers. "Johnny Reb
was not only white, he was also black," he often said.[12]

At least four books detailing the often heroic exploits of black
Confederates have been recently published — one of them by
Ervin L. Jordan, a black history professor at the University of
Virginia. For the anti-flaggers, Jordan's research has meant more
fingernails sliding down the blackboard. He says that records,
showing the contributions blacks made to the Confederate Army,
have been intentionally ignored for "politically correct" reasons.

Smith sympathizes with Jordan's contention. "My job (as a
historian) is simple: make the past available to the present. But
sometimes historians don't ask certain questions of the past because they don't want to discover certain answers. So we develop
a conspiracy of silence."[13]

Jordan has been villified by some blacks for being so outspoken on the subject and friends have accused him of being an
"apologist" for Southern "atrocities."

"I've been told that Civil War history is white folks' history by
people upset that I'm a black man dealing with an evil empire,"
Jordan says. (Evil empire? That ought to give people a further idea
of the kind of rhetoric being hissed by the anti-flaggers.)

Jordan feels his book may be the most important he'll ever
write, despite the criticism. "Those publicly loyal to the Confederacy were pragmatically acknowledging who and where they
were," he says. "Their determination to stand with the South was
akin to free men consciously performing a civic duty. Black
Confederate loyalty was more widespread than American history
has acknowledged."

So why does Jordan think blacks fought for a flag that some of
their descendants now call a racist symbol?

"Anticipating post-war gratitude, some black property and
slave owners deemed their way of life threatened and wanted

whites to see them as patriots," Jordan contends. "Some considered the South their country." [14]

Remember, prior to 1861 Southerners often referred to their state as their country because their first allegiance belonged to their state. Southerners believed the Constitution defined the words "United States" to be a plural noun, as Princeton's James McPherson noted, "the United States ARE a republic." When the South lost the war, the words "United States" became a singular noun.[15] General Robert E. Lee personified the way Southerners felt about their states when he rejected the offer to command the Union Army, saying he could never draw his sword against his beloved Virginia. Many blacks, perhaps including the hundreds of free blacks whom Lee had freed before the war and employed on his Arlington plantation, felt the same way.

Smith points out that blacks fought in the army of George Washington — even after they were offered their freedom in exchange for fighting with the British. "If blacks served in the army of George Washington, then why should you be surprised if they served in the army of Robert E. Lee?" Smith asks. "Black people have always believed that military service and patriotic duty under fire would bring about rewards."[16]

So there is no reason why blacks shouldn't view the Confederate battle flag with as much pride as anyone if they so choose.

It is not known exactly how many blacks fought under the battle flag because so many of their records have been lost, destroyed, or suppressed. Jordan believes at least 180,000 assisted the Confederate Army, other estimates range from 30,000 to 300,000.[17] Though the exact number may never be known, historians agree that thousands of blacks helped build Confederate fortifications, produced war materiel, served as cooks, and played in military bands. The first chaplain in the Confederate Army may have been black. Winbush insists his grandfather often led the white troops in prayer and scripture readings.

Though banned by law, some blacks took up arms and fought as regular soldiers early in the war. General "Stonewall" Jackson had 3,000 black troops under arms at the Battle of Antietam in September 1862, according to Smith.[18] But most continued to serve in logistical and support positions until near the war's end when states finally gave their approval — at the urgings of generals like Lee and Patrick Cleburne — to let them fight. Once they entered combat, some fought effectively despite having little or no training. Many black Confederates captured black Union troops, often ridiculing them as "Lincolnites" before making them servants.[19] Many Southern blacks volunteered, joining local militia units to help defend Georgia and even the Confederate capitol of Richmond, Virginia.

Though it has been disputed, black Confederate troops may have unknowingly and indirectly helped thwart an assassination attempt on Jefferson Davis.

"Some who fought in my neighborhood, in the area I live in, saved Richmond when Colonel Ulric Dahlgren's Union calvary raided Richmond in February-March 1864," says Pat McSweeney of Virginia.[20]

Dahlgren was killed during the foray. Confederate troops were shocked to discover papers inside Dahlgren's uniform detailing the purpose of his mission. Among them were orders to shoot Davis and members of his cabinet on sight. When angry Confederate leaders confronted Grant and Lincoln with the papers, both men denied the plot. Because the "l" was in front of the "h" in Dahlgren's signature on the order, Northern historians maintain the misspelling suggests the order, which is nearly illegible, is not genuine. Southerners could counter that the order (which is at the National Archives) is illegible, and besides, Dahlgren's signature could have been intentionally misspelled in the event the papers were discovered and the illegal plot compromised. One other point about Dahlgren: he ordered a young black civilian, named Martin — who was probably innocent, hung for treason when the young man proved unable to help the raiders ford the James River as their ill-fated raid on Richmond began.[21]

So it is clear that blacks played a role in the defense of the Confederacy, though anti-flaggers argue that blacks served against their will. Some did follow their masters to the army, but Jordan contends that many joined voluntarily.

It should be noted that white Confederate soldiers, at least two-thirds of whom did not own slaves, were drafted and had no choice but to serve as well. Interestingly, blacks in the Confederate Army fought side by side with their white compatriots, while drafted blacks in the Union fought in segregated units. It is also worth noting that many rich whites in the North avoided the draft by paying a "stand-in" to take their place. Grover Cleveland, who would become president of the United States, was among the draft dodgers. Obviously the North's primary motivation to fight was far from the oft written moral outrage it supposedly felt over slavery, a "fairy tale" excuse offered in way too many school textbooks these days.

In June 1861, Tennessee authorized the enrollment of free blacks to fight for the Confederacy. Few were formally enrolled because Confederates, in their haughty Celtic ways, thought they could win without their help.

The whole issue of blacks serving in the Confederate Army is important in the battle flag debate. How could the flag be a racist symbol when thousands of blacks fought for it? The answer, Southerners believe, is in the question.

If anything the battle flag was a multicultural banner. It has been estimated that 10,000 Orientals, 40,000-60,000 Hispanics, and 50,000-70,000 American Indians joined blacks in defense of the Confederacy. The South had the only American Indian general, Stand Watie, and its secretary of war, Judah P. Benjamin, was a Jew (he also served as secretary of state and attorney general). About 20 Confederate staff officers were Jews and the first Confederate States marshal, bodyguard to Jefferson Davis, was black.[22]

Another Jew, Moses Ezekiel, produced the massive New South sculpture that draws so much attention at Arlington National Cemetery in Washington, D.C. Ezekiel, who served in the Confederate Army, had to have known the racial content of the army, so it should come as no surprise that the sculpture includes four Confederate soldiers, one of which is black.[23]

When you stop and think about it, it only stands to reason that many black Southerners would want to fight for the Confederacy. Their ancestors had been sold into slavery by other Africans, brought to America by New England slave ships, and forced to work in Northern factories and on farms. When Northern manufacturers realized they were not as productive as the new "free labor" immigrants entering the country from Europe, they sold them to wealthy Southern planters, most of whom took good care of them. History records the mistreatment of some slaves, but historians generally agree that such acts, like those described in *Uncle Tom's Cabin*, were rare.

Slave owners were reluctant to mistreat something they had paid a lot of money for, said Wisconsin historian William Hesseltine. "The capital investment in Negroes restrained masters from inflicting punishments that would injure the slave as a worker."[24]

The value of slaves in the state of Virginia prior to the war was about $100 million.[25] It had been a big, international business until it was outlawed in 1808. The slave trade was so lucrative that it helped build the early financial infrastructure of cities like New York and Boston. The oldest known slave cemetery in the United States is located in the Manhattan portion of New York City.[26] One of the missions of the pre-war U.S. Navy was to station itself off the African coast and intercept illegal slave runners, many of them headed to Northern ports. One of the first bills Jefferson Davis vetoed as president was a bill that tried to circumvent the Confederate Constitution's ban on slave imports to the South!

It is a shame we have to scrutinize the issue of slavery just because the NAACP and its revisionist allies make the battle flag a political issue. They wrongfully apply today's morals to a world that was vastly different. For example, in 1860 people believed that infection was part of the healing process for a wound. The telegraph was the speediest mode of communication outside the immediate neighborhood and people had lots of children because they knew some would never survive childhood. It was a tough, rugged world where people worked hard just to survive. It was hardly like today's world of open heart surgeries, fax machines, space shuttles, and central air conditioning.

"If they (the slaves) were so mistreated in the South, why did my grandfather return to his master after the war and work for him for another 12 years?" asks Winbush. "He could have left anytime during the war or after."[27]

The son of a Louisiana slave owner recalled his family's relationship with their slaves in an 1893 letter:

> I was familiar with the 'institution' of slavery, for my father owned quite a number of negroes — men, women, and children. Being forced to pay two large security debts, he was reduced to the alternative of selling his land or his negroes. The latter begged so earnestly not to be sold that the land was sold and all the negroes were held until they were set free at the fall of the Confederacy. At our house the white children were made to 'behave' respectfully to the old negroes and were punished for any breach of respect reported by black 'Uncles' and 'Aunties,' as we were taught to call them. I have also known families — but very few, I am thankful

to say — in which the negro slave was treated in a
very cruel and barberous manner.[28]

The main source of violence against the people of the South came from Sherman's army as it raped, burned, and pillaged Georgia and South Carolina. The number one victim of rape by Sherman's men were black women.

The issue of slavery, which the anti-flaggers like to reduce to a few stories about branding irons or bull whips, gets even more complex when the 500,000 free blacks, who lived in the South prior to the war, are examined. "Anyone familiar with the history of slavery around the world knows that its origins go back thousands of years and that slaves and slave owners very often were of the same race," says syndicated columnist Thomas Sowell, who is black. "Thousands of free blacks owned slaves in the antebellum South."[29]

In 1790, there were 48 Negro slave holders owning 143 slaves in Maryland. One of the South's wealthiest plantation owners was a free black named Cyprian Picaud of Plaquemine, Louisiana, who owned at least 200 slaves. Nat Butler, a free black farmer in Aberdeen, Maryland, bought and sold blacks to Southern slave traders. There were three black slave masters living in the District of Columbia as late as 1863.[30]

Free blacks owned more than $25 million in property in 1860. There is no question that most free blacks were impoverished, uneducated, and had no place to go; but a good many others gained middle-class status in the South working as carpenters, artisans, cabinet makers, and schoolteachers — who taught white children.[31]

The South is willing to bear its share of blame for the misfortune of blacks 130 years ago, but to place all blame on the South is grossly unjust given slavery's history.

"Those... who think of slavery in the United States as if it were the only slavery, go ballistic when anyone tells them that this institution was not based on race," Sowell says. "Blacks were not enslaved because they were black, but because they were available at the time. Whites enslaved other whites in Europe for centuries before the first black slave was brought to the Western Hemisphere."[32]

Despite the evidence to the contrary, some people still talk about the North and slavery from a moral point of view. In 1861, nothing could have been further from the truth. There were violent anti-war riots in Baltimore, New York and Wisconsin. The pro-South sentiments of the "copperheads" and the anti-war faction of the Democratic Party located mostly in western states in the North are well documented.

"Many and many a man deserted in the winter of 1862-63 because of Lincoln's Emancipation Proclamation," a magazine reported in 1893. "The soldiers did not believe that Lincoln had the right to issue it."

For the majority of pre-war Americans, the slavery question was over economics, not morality. Slavery was legal and had been an accepted practice since America's earliest days. Supreme Court Justice Henry Baldwin, a Pennsylvanian, declared in 1833 that "the corner stone of the American Union was slavery." But the abolitionists — which like the pro-slavery lobby in the South — were a minority, had influence, and were determined to impose their views on everyone else. They eventually became the radical wing of the new Republican Party and by 1864 were in control. Caught up in the religious fervor of camp-revivalism and the buoyant teachings of New England treehuggers known as the Transcendentalists, abolitionists began decrying slavery as a sin.

There was growing opposition to slavery in the South because there was no benefit to it for most Southerners who were small dirt farmers. They worked out in the hot sun just like everyone else (they were the original "rednecks"). They thought it was hypocritical for Northerners to raise the issue of slavery on moral grounds after they had brought them here, sold them to a relatively small number of big plantation owners — making more than $1 billion doing it — and then abruptly mocked the Constitution by abolishing it. For example, Boston's Faneuil Hall, known as the "Cradle of American Liberty," was given to the city by Peter Faneuil, a wealthy slave trader. Conversely it was the Virginia Legislature which passed 23 public acts protesting slavery to the British Crown prior to the Revolutionary War. In 1778 it passed a law forbidding further importation of slaves, while at the same time it was being sanctioned by the Commonwealth of Massachusetts.

Northern states also passed laws detrimental to blacks. Connecticut passed a law forbidding blacks from attending public schools because "it would tend to the great increase of the colored people of the state." Illinois enacted a law in 1853 "to prevent the immigration of free negroes into this state." Massachusetts had a law that permitted the flogging of blacks who stayed in the state for more than two months.[33]

Southerners resented the malicious attacks on their honor when 90 percent of them did not own one single slave. But what were they to do? It was legal. A shorter growing season in the North had made slavery less profitable, but just the opposite was true of the longer growing season in Dixie. It had been a way of life in North America for 100 years. It established deep roots in the South in the 1700s and spread like wild kudzu among the large plantations.

"Many Southern people at that time looked upon slavery as an institution, of which they would like to be rid if they only knew how," author John T. Derry wrote.

While Northern "hypocrites" made them angry, passage of the infamous Morrill Tariff of 1861 threw Southerners into a rage. The South, with "King Cotton" leading the way, was rolling in money after enjoying a decade of low tariffs. Between 1850 and 1860, the South exported about 75 percent of its goods. During that period Virginia increased its wealth 84 percent, South Carolina 90 percent, and Georgia 92 percent, according to U.S. Census Bureau statistics.[34] U.S. exports from the South in 1858 totaled $193 million, compared to $45 million from the North.[35]

As the Northern economy slowed, some states in the region, led by Pennsylvania, began screaming for a protective tariff, perhaps out of jealousy as much as anything else. The South was making a lot of money and they couldn't stand it. Lincoln promised during the presidential campaign to impose a new tax if elected. In March 1861, "Honest Abe" delivered on that promise by supporting the Morrill Tariff. The tariff was the work of Vermont Representative Justin Morrill, who spent more than three decades in Congress. He'd make an excellent poster boy for modern day supporters of congressional term limits. His other major accomplishment: Helping create the "beloved" Internal Revenue Act.[36]

So pompous were Northerners about imposing the tariff that after calling for separation on March 21, 1861, *The New York Times* declared nine days later that the material interests of the North would not allow for an independent South.

The *New Orleans Daily Crescent* rebutted: "When the North tells us that we have no right to withdraw from the Union, we answer that we are perfectly willing to stay in the Union if they themselves will withdraw! We will not question their right to secede, but on the contrary, will concede it cheerfully."

The Morrill Tariff meant that Southern wealth would end up in the pockets of Yankee industrialists and Lincoln coffers. It made Southerners feel like an agricultural colony that was being bled dry. The free-trade South had only one way to get even: strike out on its own. Free trade would ensure that the Northwest would deliver its goods through Southern ports like New Orleans, Savannah, and Charleston rather than New York, Boston, or Baltimore.[37]

Author Charles Adams puts it this way;

> *Secession was unquestionably the cause of the Civil War. Taxation was the most significant factor on both sides. Southern slavery was to be tolerated by the North; Southern free ports were not. In Lincoln's supposedly conciliatory inaugural address, there was one remark that is bound to have caught Southern attention. Lincoln promised that there would be no 'bloodshed or violence,' and 'no use of force' against the seceding states.... But taxes were another matter. Lincoln would 'collect the imposts, but beyond what may be necessary for these objects, there will be no invasion, no using of force against or among the people anywhere.' In other words, the South could secede as long as it paid its taxes to the North![38]*

Southerners were livid.

"The protective tariff had almost driven the country to war in 1833; it is not surprising that it brought war in 1861," said Virginia historian Lyon Tyler.[39]

The Morrill Tariff sent taxes skyrocketing. It damaged the South's export business and sent the price of Northern-made manufactured goods — which the South imported — through the roof. Tyler claims taxes went as high as 90 cents on every dollar of goods sold; revisionists say it was half or less than half that amount. At any rate, taxes soared to new heights and so did the tempers of many a Southerner.

"They know that it is their import trade that draws the people's pockets $60 million or $70 million per annum, in the shape of duties, to be expanded mainly in the North and in the protection and encouragement of Northern interests," growled one Southern newspaper in 1861.[40]

Then when 64 Congressmen endorsed Hinton Helper's *The Impending Crisis of the South: How to Meet It*, there was no way the Southern states could stay in the union.[41] Revisionists in the last 40 years generally say little about Helper's book other than to focus on two points: Helper's call for an end to slavery and his argument that the price of land would rise enough after abolition to offset the $1.5 billion worth of Southern slaves that owners would lose.

While this angered the small group of large planters, Helper's book had a far more profound impact on the psyche of everyone else in the South. What many revisionists don't discuss is Helper's call for the four million slaves in the South to rise up and "massacre" their masters. "It is for you to decide whether we are to have justice peaceably or by violence, for whatever consequences may follow, we are determined to have it one way or another," he said, addressing slave owners in 1857.[42]

Just a few years earlier slaves had revolted in Haiti, killing their masters, and here was Helper advocating they do the same in the South. Then John Brown, who also called for the slaves to revolt, raided the arsenal at Harper's Ferry, Maryland, on October 16, 1859, with the idea of gathering arms for a campaign of terrorism against the South. The first person he killed in the raid was a free black man trying to stop him. Brown was a bloody murderer whose family had a history of mental illness. Born in Connecticut, he carried the nickname of "Ole Osawatomie," for his part in a massacre where he split open the heads of five slave owners with a broadsword at Osawatomie, Kansas, on May 24, 1856 — a crime for which he was never brought to justice.[43]

Helper's book, along with Brown's diabolical acts convinced Southerners that the radical abolitionsists had pretty much taken over the government. Fear swept through the South. Even though nine out of 10 Southerners did not own slaves, they often knew someone down the road who did. They also knew about the bloody 1832 slave revolt in Haiti where slaves murdered their owners.

The situation in Congress was just as tense. Republicans nominated John Sherman of Ohio, the brother of Union General William T. Sherman, for Speaker of the House. Sherman had been among the 64 Congressmen to endorse Helper's book and had helped get it distributed throughout the North. His nomination triggered heated debate as warfare nearly erupted on the floors of

Congress. Democrats introduced a resolution that anyone endorsing Helper's book wasn't fit to be Speaker. A Republican roared that "slaveholding is worse than robbery, than piracy, than polygamy," that it was the doctrine of Democrats and "the doctrine of devils as well."[44]

When Senator Henry Wilson, a Republican from Massachusetts, read portions of Helper's book in the senate, it caused a similar uproar. Senator Asa Briggs of Helper's home state of North Carolina, charged that Helper was "a thief and had left North Carolina a dishonest... man... catering to a diseased appetite at the North to obtain a miserable living by slander upon the land of his birth."[45]

"So violent is the feeling that the members on both sides are mostly armed with deadly weapons, and it is said that the friends of each are armed in the galleries," one senator wrote. Another said, "I believe every man in both houses is armed with a revolver — some with two — and a Bowie knife."[46] It is no wonder under such circumstances that Southern congressmen started walking out and eventually voted secession.

Some historians have suggested the South's wealthy plantation owners (only about 2,700 — of the South's 5.5 million whites — had more than 100 slaves in 1860) dragged the rest of the region into the war over slavery.[47] That is not true. The Confederate Constitution forbade the importation of slaves and when the states seceded, slave owners' paid a price. Secession meant Southern slave owners forfeited any chance of taking their slaves anywhere other than to sister Confederate states. Far more painful was the plummeting value of slaves in the South following secession. Some estimates put their loss at $430 million.[48]

It cannot be ignored that most of the citizens in the North and South who were not passionate supporters of the abolitionists and wealthy slave owners, far outnumbered those belonging to either extremist group.

The fact of the matter is that when Lincoln ordered the South invaded to enforce the Morrill Tariff and punish it for exercising its Constitutional right to secede, Southerners, in their typical Celtic fashion, refused to submit to such a tyrannical act. When asked by his Union captors why he was fighting, a Confederate soldier in his native Tennessee responded: "Because you're here."

Perhaps this is why the battle flag still comes flying out of Southern homes — often in defiance of government encroachment on their lives. It's a natural reaction for Southerners whenever the federal government raises our taxes or restricts a Constitutional right. The battle flag was made to fly in the face of tyrants.

Then there's another key point that should be made on the slavery issue. If there was animosity between slaves and owners, then why did the soldiers leave their women, children, and crops in the care of their slaves? There were virtually no reports of violence by slaves against white women and children in the South — despite calls for such action by Helper and others.

Though it is rarely taught anymore, Lincoln, like Helper and Brown, hoped the slaves in the South would revolt.

"Lincoln's Emancipation Proclamation was not issued from a humane standpoint," said historian James Ford Rhodes. "Lincoln hoped it would incite the negroes to rise against the women and children."[49]

But of course they didn't. Why? If they wanted to live in the North, they took the Underground Railroad. But many stayed because they were loyal to the South. It was their home, too.

"I am reminded that it was my grandfather and grandmother who kept the home fires burning while the Confederacy waged its war," Douglas said. "Which is why I cannot view loyalty to the South or the desire for independence as being monopolized by either race."[50]

Professor Smith says since there were more than 500,000 free blacks living in the South in 1860, slaves knew freedom was possible. "Slavery was dying on its own," he said. "It would have died had there been no war at all, it just would have taken a little more time. The war simply speeded up the process."[51]

Many white Southerners were trying to figure out a way to end the "peculiar institution" when the intolerant abolitionists went nuts over the issue.

"Had the South been allowed to manage this question unfettered, the slaves would have been, ere this, fully emancipated and that without bloodshed or race problems," said historian Charles Francis Adams Jr.[52]

Despite the voluminous evidence against it, most historians continue to award "the palm of moral superiority to the North," said Ludwell H. Johnson III, a retired history professor from the College of William & Mary in Williamsburg, Virginia. "The simplified 'devil theory' of the era, formerly so dear to the hearts of abolitionists and Radical Republicans, can no longer be sustained in the face of accumulated research."[53]

The fact that blacks fought for the Confederacy is enough to throw the debate over slavery into a vortex of complexities. Add the heated debate over taxes, the ethnic differences between the two regions, varying interpretations of the Constitution, and one can see how entangled the causes surrounding the War for Southern Independence can become. The war's causes, tactics, weapons, politics, and personalities are much too big for anyone to get their arms around. Yet the small anti-flag groups attempt to condense the war into a few inflammatory statements that can be encapsulated on a bumper sticker or in a 15-second sound bite. Such behavior does an injustice to our nation's rich history and the brave men — on both sides — who fought in the war.

Author Bruce Catton cautioned more than three decades ago about simplifying the causes of a war that remains embedded in heart-felt and complex emotions:

> *The deeper meaning of the American Civil War, for the people who lived through it and for us today, goes beyond the historian's grasp. Here was an event so complex, so deeply based in human emotions, so far-reaching in its final effects, that understanding it is likely to be a matter primarily for the emotions rather than for the cold analysis of facts. It was an experience that was probably felt more deeply than anything else that ever happened to us. We cannot hope to understand it unless we share in that feeling, simply because the depth and intensity of the feeling are among the war's principal legacies.[54]*

Princeton's James McPherson put it this way: "Arguments about the causes and consequences of the Civil War, as well as the reasons for northern victory, will continue as long as there are historians to wield the pen — which is, perhaps even for this bloody conflict, mightier than the sword."[55]

That's why so much is still being written about it more than 130 years after Appomattox. On an average, at least one new book has been published on the war every day since 1865. Only Jesus has been the subject of more books than Lincoln.[56] Yet despite the passage of time and the shear volume of new books coming off the presses each year, sales continue to boom, said Kathleen McDermot of the History Book Club, a division of the Book of the Month Club. "There are hundreds of thousands of Confederate history buffs out there," said Lisa Dellwo, marketing director for the University of North Carolina Press.[57]

Occasionally new information is uncovered, but that only triggers intense scrutiny and more debate.

"This interest in the Civil War is just amazing," said James Robertson, history professor at Virginia Tech. Robertson teaches the largest course on the War for Southern Independence in the country. In 1991, university officials asked him to organize a weekend course for alumni. He agreed to do so, but was apprehensive over how many would attend. "I said, 'You're not going to find five idiots willing to come to Blacksburg, Virginia, in the middle of February,'" he said. About 50 showed up the first year. People were turned away from the 1996 class after enrollment hit 330.[58]

Amid this continuing high level of interest in re-examining the war, it is unfortunate that slavery is misused as a political ploy against the Confederate battle flag. I say unfortunate because the battle flag was not — nor will ever be — symbolic of slavery or racism. It was the battle standard of the Confederate Army. Yet many in the media continue to imply otherwise. A reporter in North Carolina wrote a generally balanced story in 1996 about the battle flag debate. In the article the reporter wrote that the Confederacy "involves the always touchy subject of the Civil War."

Since when is history "touchy?"

Later in the story, the following statement is made: "In fact, although most mainstream historians would differ, (Frank) Powell and his SCV brothers maintain that slavery was not the leading cause of what they call the War for Southern Independence." Mainstream? Who is mainstream here? Most historians or the SCV? In a subtle way, it suggests that the SCV's position is not mainstream. And if it's not mainstream, then what is it? Radical? Making such preposterous statements in editorials or opinionated columns is one thing, stating them as fact in news stories or features is another.

Another major newspaper ran the misleading headline, "Some States Reject Racist Songs, Policies, and Confederate Flags."[59] Can you imagine the thousands of people who read that and may keep it in the back of their minds indefinitely? It is an example of the misleading and slanderous things being said about the South even today.

If the news media would really like to help combat bigotry, why don't they look into the subtle racism occurring in the

Northeast where disgraceful zoning ordinances often keep blacks out of white neighborhoods? They reek wih hypocrisy every time they refer to Southern state's resistance to federal desegregation, while never mentioning what was hapening in other regions of the nation at the same time.

The issue of the battle flag has been made a political issue — one most journalists are woefully unprepared to handle. Journalists are trained to go out, get facts, and then come back and write what they heard and saw. Writing about history does not work that way. If they have not studied the war extensively, they become susceptible to special interest groups who will use them to rewrite and distort history to meet the groups' present needs. This is the trap that has ensnared much of the media as it has pandered to the NAACP, who like the revisionists and politically correct patrol, use distortion of facts to advance their arguments.

Their use of distortion is not to be underestimated, especially when it comes to the South's history, because the news media is a powerful force and much of its members are proponents of the politically correct movement, a weird type of morality that has filled the vacuum created by the demise of Marxism. It's goal: to deconstruct the truth.

Ralph Reed, executive director of the Christian Coalition, accurately explains in his book, "Politically Incorrect," how the "PC Patrol" — with the media often leading the way — uses distortion to smear Christians, often portraying them as "poor, uneducated, and easy to command," much the way the "PCers" — and especially Hollywood — characterizes Southerners.[60] Can you imagine the reaction of the "PC" crowd if such a thing was said about another group, such as the NAACP? Why the news media would scream for the 101st Airborne to devour the dastardly perpetrators.

Nashville, Tennessee, columnist Frank Ritter, has observed the politically correct crowd with a keen eye and has exposed the flaws in their attack against the battle flag:

> *The politically correct crowd, which sees only what it wants to see and nothing else, will appropriate any flag — be it the American flag or the Confederate flag — for its own purposes. The PC Police will decide what a flag means despite what honest and well-meaning people say it means, then enforce their rigid orthodoxy with ruthless zeal.*

*The Confederate battle flag should mean what the
honest, well-meaning descendants of Confederate
soldiers say it means: a symbol of freedom from an
oppressive government, a symbol of a distinctive
region of our country which once existed as a
separate nation.*[61]

Georgia historian Mildred Rutherford warned Southerners not
to be apathetic and that such battles to protect the South's true
history would have to be fought. Interestingly she made her
exhortation while engaging in a similar type of struggle more than
70 years ago:

*For over 60 years the civilization of the South
has been almost destroyed by the falsehoods written about it, and now when one has in hand the
authenticated facts to prove these falsehoods to be
false, many of our own Southern people as well as
the press, largely responsible for them, are unfair
and say, 'It will do no good to bring these facts to
light, for you will only stir up strife.' Why not stir up
strife, rather than allow these falsehoods to forever
remain in history? Shall fear of attacks from those
responsible for them silence us? Have we lost our
courage? The truth is all we ask, and when proven
that what we have said is not true, then we will
retract. Prejudice has no part in history.*[62]

Rutherford's persuasive argument was heeded. Other Southerners rallied to the cause; and indeed, history, which had been
one-sided favoring the North, was modified early this century to
tell both sides of the war story. This was not revisionist history
because it was based on provable facts supported by many of the
players who were still alive at the time. It served no political
purpose and, if anything, flew in the face of the Jim Crow laws of
the day. She was among the first Southerners to reiterate the
South's reason for seeking its independence as Jim Crow took
flight in the 20th century South.

One of the key elements in the anti-flaggers distortion strategy
is the Klu Klux Klan. "The Klan and other hate groups fly the
Confederate battle flag," they often yelp. That is true, but it should
be noted the Klan also flies the American flag. Does that make
"Old Glory" a racist symbol? They also fly the Christian flag. Is it
racist, too? If we follow the anti-flaggers logic, then "Old Glory"

will have to come down with the battle flag because it flew over the slave trade for 80 years and American Indians could view it as a symbol of the genocide of their people.

But maybe that's what the anti-flaggers — and especially the politically correct folks — really want. The battle flag is as much a part of America as "Old Glory." Dishonor one and you dishonor both. After all, the Constitution is filled with the signatures of slave owners. So when the anti-flaggers get rid of the Confederate battle flag, will they then bully Americans into changing the name of their nation's capital? That will be followed by a push to rid that city of the Washington and Jefferson Monuments, just before they do away with most of the currency. And while they're at it, they might as well go down the street and knock out the stain class windows at the National Cathedral which feature the Confederate battle flag, Robert E. Lee, and "Stonewall" Jackson. Since Lincoln is believed to have sold some of his family's slaves down the river, that means the Lincoln Monument will go, too, plus the penny and five dollar bill. (But as one Southern wag quipped, "Somehow or another that doesn't bother me as much.") Next will come a facelift for Mount Rushmore, a jackhammer assault on Stone Mountain, Georgia (which features the faces of Davis, Lee, and Jackson), and the burning of all books published prior to 1865 (though "Huckleberry Finn," which was published after the war, is now under attack). Is it hard to imagine these people feeding the Constitution to a shredder? Washington's birthday has already been removed from American calendars, having been replaced with something called "President's Day." All of this looks eerily like what the Communists did to rewrite Russian history after the fall of the Czar.

You should understand that some of those who would destroy the (Confederate) battle flag would burn the American flag. Baton Rouge, Louisiana's Ed Cailleteau had this to say in a Southern newspaper editorial:

> "Both flags are standards under which men answered calls to duty and gave themselves the last measure of devotion. The battle flag is nothing more and nothing less. No individuals wearing bed linens can stain the battle flag in the estimation of the people. If they succeed in doing so, it would speak very little to the educational attainments of a people who would be susceptible to such a corrupting influence.[63]

As I've stated, the Klan and other groups fly the battle flag hoping to gain favor with the Southern people. They know Southerners love the battle flag. They also know down deep that Southerners find Nazism repulsive.

The misuse of the battle flag by hate groups has triggered a growing sense of frustration among the true protectors — and rightful heirs — of the battle flag — the Sons of Confederate Veterans. The SCV has been the most outspoken critic of hate groups misusing the battle flag. It passed a resolution at its national convention in 1992 renouncing "the KKK and all others who promote hate among our people and dishonor our Confederate flag and emblems."

"The Confederate soldier was not a skinhead or a member of a racist or paramilitary group," said Ronald Clemmons, SCV executive director.[64]

"As far as I'm concerned, they're (hate groups) the reason we get stereotyped all the time," said Ronnie Mangrum, an SCV member who is director of a museum in Franklin, Tennessee.

The battle flag is actually caught between two extremes. The Nazi hate groups and the left-wing extremists composed of the "PC Patrol," revisionists, radical blacks, and liberal members of the media. Make no mistake, some members of both extremes would like nothing better than to divide and destroy America. When they say the Confederate battle flag is divisive, consider it hogwash. America has never been stronger. It has survived wars with Spain, Japan, Italy, North Korea, North Vietnam, Iraq and two with Germany. Communism has collapsed and America still stands — all with the Confederate battle flag flying across the South.

Thankfully, some blacks are rallying to the truth. One is Rudolph Young, a Vietnam veteran, and an amateur historian who has been researching blacks in the Confederate Army. Like Winbush, he has become a popular speaker at black churches and SCV meetings.

"This is part of our shared history," Young says. "I am part of that history. I am a Southerner. The Confederate flag per se does not offend me. It stands for what the person holding it wants it to. If I see it at a KKK rally, I know it's a hate flag. If I see it at a Confederate veterans organization, it's a patriotic flag. If it's on the back of a pickup truck, it's being trivialized."[65]

Yet mendacious revisionists, bigots, and the "PC Patrol" are relentless in using distortion to primarily connect slavery and racism to the South's sacred banner. "When you're standing on a hill looking down, you can't tell which guy wearing a gray suit is a racist," said Kelly Alexander, president of the North Carolina chapter of the NAACP, in a 1996 newspaper story about the battle flag. "But we do know that the increased memberships (in the SCV), the increased interest over the last three to five years, has not been driven by a love of history. It's a way to express dissatisfaction and anger, and that's something that we should pay attention to."[66]

People are certainly paying attention to the mean-spirited rhetoric. Among them: Thomas Sowell, a nationally renown columnist who is black. Sowell once wrote:

Demagoguery can be a very lucrative and even glamorous career, as a number of black 'leaders' and 'scholars' demonstrate, But that is not how 33 million black Americans will advance. Despite attempts to picture slavery as something created by white people for black people, the truth is far worse. Slavery was inflicted by every people on every other people they could enslave, all over this planet, and for thousands of years. Only very late in human history, after shipbuilding technology and navigational instruments reached a level that made transoceanic voyages feasible, was such a thing possible as the transplanting of millions of Africans to the Western Hemisphere. But even more millions of Africans were sent in bondage to the Islamic world of North Africa and the Middle East — and other millions were enslaved in Africa by fellow Africans. The notion that white people went ashore in West Africa and started rounding up blacks may fit the emotional needs of today but it does not fit the realities of the time.[67]

The untrue rhetoric linking the flag to slavery by groups like Alexander's is ironic because they're the very people who also badger Southerners about letting go of their past, while at the same time, clinging to it themselves. How many times have they thrown Jim Crow in the faces of today's Southerners, nearly all of whom had nothing to do with it? So what does Jim Crow have to do with the battle flag? The only connection I can see between Jim Crow and the war, much less the flag, is that it may have been the white

Southerners' way of retaliating against some blacks who took advantage of them during the most corrupt and disgraceful period in our nation's history, Reconstruction. Such wrongful retaliation occurs whenever the majority regains control after the minority has abused the majority.

Let me reiterate, slavery was wrong. Reconstruction was wrong. Jim Crow was wrong. For Pete's sake, the war was wrong! All Lincoln had to do was what many Northerners, including abolitionists, wanted him to do and that was simply let the South go in peace. Secession was constitutional. The federal government had been created to serve the states, not to encroach on their sovereign rights as protected by the Constitiution. Fire-breathing abolitionist Wendell Phillips noted secession was well within the Constitutional rights of the South. "Standing with the principles of '76 behind us, who can deny them the right?" he said prior to the war.[68]

Secession is certainly nothing new. Norway had seceded from Sweden, and the United States supported the secession of Panama from Colombia in 1903.[69] The New England states and Massachusetts had argued earlier in the century that they had a right to secede. But when the South tried to do the same she was attacked.

"No people must be forced under sovereignty under which it does not choose to live," President Woodrow Wilson said early in this century.[70]

Yet Lincoln, without the consent of Congress, waged a war on an innocent sovereign nation that cost more than 620,000 lives (360,000 of them Union troops, 260,000 Confederates and an unknown number of Southern civilians since the war was primarily waged in their homeland) and billions of dollars in lost property. And with all that, as Winbush points out, lawmakers still can't settle the states' rights issue as contained in the 10th Amendment of the U.S. Constitution.

Another one of the great distortions the anti-flaggers use in their attempt to link slavery to the battle flag is Lincoln's position on slavery. South-bashing revisionists have long used Lincoln's so-called "compassion" for the slaves to maintain his lofty position in their minds and in the annals of American mythology. For them, Lincoln must be portrayed as having "the moral high ground" so Northern aggression against the South can withstand scrutiny.

The fact that Lincoln was a "flip-flopper" on slavery is well documented. Professor Smith puts it more directly: "Lincoln had a low estimate of black people."[71]

Indeed he did. In an 1858 speech given in Charleston, Illinois, Lincoln sounded more like the "Grand Wizard" of the Klu Klux Klan than the "Great Emanicipator":

> *I am not, nor ever have been in favor of bringing about in any way the social or political equality of the white and black races. I am not now nor ever have been in favor of making voters or jurors of negroes, nor of qualifying them to hold office, nor of intermarriages with white people. There is a physical difference between the white and black races which will forever forbid the two races living together on social or political equality. There must be a position superior and inferior, and I am in favor of assigning the superior position to the white man.*[72]

The Emancipation Proclamation freed no one. It applied only to Southern states, which ignored it until they were subjugated. It did not apply to the one million slaves in Northern states (including those belonging to Union General U.S. Grant), particularly those in Maryland and Delaware. Slavery was not abolished until the states ratified the 13th Amendment to the Constitution.

As for the Emancipation Proclamation, it was simply an after thought. Lincoln decided he could not face the world with the blood of Southerners on his hands because he chose to deny what the Founding Fathers had guaranteed them 85 years earlier. He couldn't say to the world, "I'm going to destroy the South over taxes." So he issued the Emancipation Proclamation to make the war look like some great moral crusade when, in fact, it wasn't that at all.

The Emancipation Proclamation did solidify Lincoln's political standing with the abolition lobby, which was small, but vocal, and two-faced. One of the loudest abolitionists, William Lloyd Garrison of Massachusetts, was considered a gadfly by most Bostonians. They once put a rope around his neck and mockingly paraded him through the streets. After the war, Garrison revealed his true racist colors, ridiculing any guarantees of civil rights for blacks, particularly when it came to voting privileges.[73]

Lincoln expected to lose the 1864 election. He certainly would have been voted out, or thrown out, of office had he not used the army to frighten people from the polls and had there not been military victories by Union Generals William Sherman in Georgia and Philip Sheridan in the Shenadoah Valley.

If Lincoln was so concerned with slavery, why did he wait until the war was nearly two years old before issuing the Emancipation Proclamation? Because the war was about the Constitution and taxes, not slavery.

Lincoln's true colors about the slaves began to resurface as the war ground to a halt. He considered having blacks rounded up and shipped to the malaria-ladened swamps of Panama to begin digging the Panama Canal.[74] But of course, in one of the great ironies of history, John Wilkes Booth, who was not a Confederate, took care of that idea.

Immediately following his death Northern historians rushed to insure Lincoln's lofty place in history — at the expense, of course, of the South's reputation. Today's anti-flag groups simply regurgitate those same old positions, but for a different reason this time around: to smear the South. And at the center of that attempt is the battle flag.

It's interesting to note that Southerners, and particularly the old Confederate veterans, picked up on the attempts to distort history rather quickly in the years immediately following the war. Modern-day Southerners would do well to do the same. *Confederate Veteran* magazine noted in 1894 that there was a proliferation of "unreliable, partisan" history books being produced by "mercenary publishers (who) were diligently placing (them) in Southern schools." "Offensive epithets appear in many works wholly useless in writing history and unquestionably irritating," the magazine noted in 1895. "The secession of the Southern states is stigmatized as a rebellion, and the Southern people are offensively called rebels. "... These epithets, so applied to the course of the Southern states and the conduct of its people, would not be used as reproach by any just jurist, statesman, or historian."

Personally, I still don't like the term "rebel" to describe Confederate soldiers. It was a derrogatory term created, and used frequently, by Lincoln in the same manner England's King George III had used the term to denigrate the Founding Fathers. That's why in most of today's newspapers "rebel" is rarely capitalized. It is used in the lower case form as a derrogatory adjective. The anti-flaggers choose to select only the history that fits their needs. That's why they ignore the fact that secession was not rebellion. The term "rebel" is another example of how distortion can be successfully used to rewrite history. It is astonishing how many Southerners think being called "rebel" is flattering. They should think again, especially after reading historian Lyon Tyler's explanation of the term:

> *This term, as used by the British as well as by Lincoln, meant not merely a political offender but a moral one which ranked the person with thieves and cut-throats, and the use of the word in this sense was kept up by Northern presidents long after the war. Such words (like 'rebel') were greatly objected to by our Revolutionary fathers, and a committee of the Continental Congress imputed to this habit of the British the licentious conduct of the British soldiers. They were taught by these words to look down upon the Americans, to despise them as inferior creatures. And the same influences operated upon the Northern soldiers, who plundered the South. Lincoln taught them.[75]*

This same distorted view of the South is perpetuated everytime Hollywood or Madison Avenue creates a "dumb" character whose key feature is a Southern accent.

Barely 30 years after the war, historians were already distorting the image of Jefferson Davis, labeling him a traitor and asserting that the South's purpose for seceding was to destroy the United States. Of course, Davis was unjustly imprisoned for two years after being charged with treason and as a conspirator in the assassination of Lincoln. He was never brought to trial because U.S. authorities knew the conspiracy charges were untrue and that Davis, as Supreme Court Chief Justice Salmon P. Chase stated, could not be convicted of treason since secession was a violation of neither the law nor the Constitution. Northerners knew that such a trial would vindicate the South and its cause. Davis was finally released, and to a degree, the South's cause was vindicated anyway.

Such distortions of history greatly concerned the Confederate veterans, so much so that they formed a historical committee which produced one of the most outstanding works ever published in behalf of their cause. Entitled *Report of the Historical Committee*, it was issued on April 25, 1906 in New Orleans, Louisiana, and is a 16-page document every history teacher should make mandatory reading for their students. It was prepared for the committee by J.W. Nicholson, professor of history at Louisiana State University.

At about the same time the committee's report was released,

one Confederate veteran after another began to debunk the malicious things being written and said about the South.

"While the North and Northern soldiers are inveighing against all manifestation of sectional feeling, they are erecting monuments to their successful leaders and telling the story very much to their credit and to our detriment," Confederate General Vincent Marmaduke of Missouri, wrote three decades after the war.[76]

A Southerner only has to visit the Shiloh National Battlefield in southern Middle Tennessee to see the evidence of Marmaduke's lament. The park is filled with massive Union monuments, while there are pitifully few honoring the Confederates who fought there. In fact, the dead Union troops are buried individually in a beautiful cemetery overlooking the Tennessee River. The Confederates were pitched into a trench back in the woods. The National Park Service has approved in recent years the flying of the Confederate "Stars and Bars" over the trench as well as sites for new monuments honoring Confederate soldiers from Mississippi and Tennessee. But it will be generations, provided the park service allows it, before the number of Confederate monuments will come close to matching those honoring Union troops. Located in the "Heart of Dixie," Shiloh remains a sacred, but sad place to Southerners.

Fellow Missourian, General J.B. Gantt agreed with Marmaduke's concerns and issued a warning to Southerners that applies still today. "True it is that the South is living in the present and keeping step with the age in which it lives, but the truth remains that it has been enabled to do this through the labors and courage of the fathers of the Old South, and because it still keeps the faith imparted by its fathers. In this talk of a New South there is a veiled insinuation that the Old South was a section of slothful, bigoted people, who did not keep pace with the civilization of their day. This imputation upon the South is iterated and reiterated sometimes brutally, but oftener in cunning insinuations."[77]

This is certainly the picture many people attempt to paint today — particularly those who don't know a thing about the South or its people. In 1995, Nashville Mayor Phil Bredesen, a Democrat who hails from the former slave trade capital of America, New York, caused a firestorm in the "Music City" when he said most people think of haybales, "HeeHaw," and women in gingham dresses when they hear the name "Nashville."

Gantt was prophetic wasn't he?

Even Booker T. Washington would not have stood for such degrading characterizations about his fellow Southerners. When General James H. Wilson toured Tuskegee Institute in 1909, he was surprised to see pictures at the black college of Generals Robert E. Lee and Thomas "Stonewall" Jackson. "Dr. Washington," Wilson asked, "what are you doing with those damn rebels' pictures on the wall?" Washington replied, "Those are pictures of Southern gentlemen, the best friends the negro ever had, and I do not care to hear you speak disrespectfully of them again sir!"[78]

Wilson's cross characterizations of Lee and Jackson shows just how much — by the turn of the century — Northern historians had slandered the reputations of Southern leaders and the cause for which Southerners fought. Such distortions, combined with the devastating effects of the war, set the South back 100 years and had

a profound impact on race relations in our country. Perhaps that is why Reconstruction really didn't end in 1876, but rather in 1964, with the passage of the Civil Rights Act.

Speaking of Reconstruction, it appears that it has gotten a facelift by some modern-day historians. Charles Reagan Wilson of the University of Mississippi claims Reconstruction was "a myth," that it really didn't last as long as historians have written. He says carpetbaggers and scalawags were not as prevalant as history has taught us. Wilson apparently agrees with another author, Carl N. Degler, who wrote that

It's not the battle flag, but federal park officials gave the Sons of Confederate Veterans in Hardin County, Tennessee, permission to raise the Confederacy's first national flag, the so-called "Stars and Bars" over the Confederate graves at Shiloh National Battlefield.

"the tragedy of Reconstruction is that it failed." Degler points out, as Wilson says, "that modern historical scholarship rejects the idea of Reconstruction as a unique period of bad government and oppression, but one should remember that generations of southerners believed the myth."[79]

It appears Wilson was influenced by revisionist historian Kenneth Stampps in the 1950s. "Stampps' 'The Peculiar Institution' (1956) aimed at overturning Ulrich B. Phillips' magisterial 'American Negro Slavery' (1918), which had portrayed slavery as relatively humane and the slaves' yoke as not very burdensome, a view not acceptable to many (with the advent of the Civil Rights Movement) in the late 1950s," said Ludwell Johnson. "A parade of revisionist studies then began and still goes on. Sometimes much to their surprise, revisionist scholars came across evidence that ran counter to the idea of any sharp moral division between North and South. The Civil Rights Movement inspired research into Northern racial attitudes and practices before, during, and after the war, research that showed, as Alexis de Tocqueville had observed long before, that racial prejudice was a nationwide phenomenon. A quantitative study by two Northern scholars tended to confirm Phillips' and undermine Stampps' view of slavery, producing cries of anguish from those to whom the unmitigated cruelty of slavery had become an article of faith."[80]

There is no justification for slavery, but no one has the right to impose late 20th century standards on those who lived in 1860. Nor should they attempt to rewrite history to meet their present needs. It is unfair for anti-flaggers to pronounce judgment on the ancestors of Southerners by labeling them racists or devilish traitors. Such characterizations are offensive to Southerners, the large majority of whom had ancestors fight for Southern independence. It is not known how many Southerners are descendants of Confederate soldiers, but if one's grandparents or great-grandparents were born in the South, the probability is extremely high that some relative fought for Dixie. There are about 27,000 members in the SCV and nearly all of them have parents, brothers and sisters, or other relatives who are descendants of Confederate soldiers as well. The number of people in the South whom the NAACP and other anti-flag groups have offended is staggering. Essentially, they've insulted a nation, one composed largely of people who know their history.

"Chroniclers of Southern history often do not grasp the most elementary concept of sound historiography: the ability to appraise the past by standards other than those of the present," said Southern historian and textbook author Francis Butler Simkins. "They accept a fanatical nationalism which leaves little room for sectional variations, a faith in Darwinian progress which leaves no room for static contentment, and a faith in the American dream of human equality which leaves little room for one person to get ahead of another except in making money."[81]

The anti-flaggers are just the latest in a list of South-bashers who strive to keep blacks and whites at each others' throats. The tactic has long been referred to as "waving the bloody shirt," a term spawned from post-war Republicans who used the term to mock Democrats (most of whom were Southerners) as a way of diverting attention from politically embarrassing issues.

In the process, these small, fanatical groups — some black, some white — have justified their political existence at the expense of racial harmony. Let's face it, there are people in America who do not want the two races to get along, particularly in the South. The South's history makes it an easy target for special interest groups, politicians, and the media, or anyone who thrives on divisiveness in order to advance their agenda or make a buck. For way too long under-educated Southerners have fallen for this ruse. And when it's all said and done, the South is always left in ashes.

Stop and think for a second. If you're a white Southerner, can you name a black person, whom who personally know, that you actually hate? And if you're a black Southerner, can you name a white person, whom you personally know, that you hate?

Probably 99 percent of Southerners would answer no.

Am I suggesting that racism does not exist? Of course not. Unfortunately it is alive and well. And while there are a number of groups, political and ethnic, who contribute to racism today, the anti-flag movement becomes a part of it every time it waves "the bloody shirt."

Organizations like the NAACP do such things in order to draw attention away from the crisis facing its members — namely guns in the hands of their youth, fatherlessness, poverty, and drugs. Today young blacks are more likely to be shot and killed in their own neighborhoods than they would have been walking in the jungles of Vietnam in the late 1960s. It is easier to wave "the bloody shirt" and cry about the battle flag in order to raise funds than it is to deal with real problems.

All of us can sympathize, to an extent, about anything that makes people feel uncomfortable. We're all glad that progress, concerning equal rights, has been made in our country. But there are at least two problems with this particular thought as it is applied by today's anti-flag movement. Many of the people opposing the Confederate battle flag would oppose any flag. Even the American flag would be ridiculed if such behavior fulfilled their purpose. In reality they do oppose the American flag, they just do it in the closet because they know the majority of Americans are not ready for that Orwellian move. You don't see descendants of Confederate soldiers watering down the noun "American" with a hyphen in front of it. The anti-flag movement does not understand the value of sacred symbols like "Old Glory" and the Cross of St. Andrew.

Second, just because a symbol makes a few people uncomfortable is no reason to ban that symbol. What about the First Amendment? America had better wake up because it's pandering too much to people who seem to make a living at getting their feelings hurt. We're becoming a nation of "victims." Everyone's got to complain about something. This often drives wedges between people and could turn America into another version of the Balkan states. In the case of the battle flag, the whining is based on half-truths and lies.

If the truth be known, Southern blacks and whites have more in common than they realize. White Southerners are among the most conservative of all Americans. However, a nation wide poll in 1993 showed that large numbers of blacks are more conservative than many whites believe. The poll showed that 63 percent of blacks declared themselves "born again" Christians, while 80 percent said they prayed daily. Like the majority of white Southerners, the polls showed that blacks are overwhelmingly pro-family, believe in fair treatment for all, and encourage personal responsibility.[82]

No wonder the NAACP (which is largely funded by supporters in Northern cities who don't like to be reminded of the racial sins in their own backyard) has created a needless issue out of the battle flag. Could it be the NAACP is fearful of blacks and whites discovering they have much in common? Such a discovery would render it obsolete. Does it continue to "wave the bloody shirt" because its worried that such discernment could reduce it to insignificance?

"The flag issue keeps racism alive on both sides of the ideological line," notes an Alabamian. "The result has been heightened tensions and hardened feelings, as inflammatory rhetoric streams from the press, the podium, and the pulpit. When Southerners are pitted against each other, no Southerner wins. The winners are those who seek to manipulate and control both blacks and whites."[83]

What Southerners resent is their homeland being villified as if it were the only place where such terrible behavior takes place. Remember the race riots in Los Angeles and Boston? Don't forget, Mark Fuhrman and Louis Farrakkan don't live in Dixie, and white supremists congregate in Montana and Idaho.

As for the politically correctniks, they wave "the bloody shirt" out of fear. They know the Confederate battle flag is the most powerful and enduring symbol standing against their attempts to destroy American history. And the same holds true for what Sowell calls the "counter-culture" news media. By no means are all members of the media part of the counter-culture, but most of them are. If it's perverse, they highlight it. If it's Christian, they secularize it. If it's a majority, they attack it. If it's anti-big government, they smear it. Then there are the revisionists. They are often scholars who fail to discover anything new, so they simply offer "new interpretations" of what is already known. They do this for the "shock" value it produces, which ultimately provides them with the notoriety they seek. However, there is an irony in these "new interpretations" of the war as it pertains to the battle flag. They have produced refreshing debate, and that is good because it forces people back to the original source of the history. And as long as that occurs, the South, its quest for independence, its battle flag, and its ancestors who fought for it, will always be vindicated. And finally, there is "big government." Southerners, by and large, oppose "big government." The South is clearly the most conservative region of the country. It expects the federal government to stick to providing necessities like the currency, national defense, a handful of social programs such as Social Security, Medicare, Veterans Affairs, and a few other basic functions. Otherwise, Southerners believe the federal government should stay out of their lives! When the federal government gets so big that it starts creeping into Southern schools, churches, and homes, then look for the battle flag to "start popping in the wind like an angry cannonball."[84] The thought of this happening terrifies federalists. It always has. The supporters of a big federal government have never known how to deal with the cavalier attitude of Southerners. So they have often reacted with violence, as they did from 1861-1876, or with degrading humor, like they do today. But whatever their reaction, it has always been motivated by fear.

"For some years after the close of that war, whenever the old soldiers of the South assembled for a peaceful celebration of some historic anniversary, there was a great outcry throughout the North that the Confederacy was again mounting, and that some new treason or trouble was to be expected," a Confederate veteran noted in 1906. "But that foolish and unfounded dread was wholly dissipated when the men of the South... eagerly volunteered for the... war with Spain... ."

A Chicago society periodical, sactimoniously entitled "Elite," called for Southerners to stop playing "Dixie" in 1897.[85] The South refused then, but it looks like this time around may be a different story if Southern colleges like the University of Georgia and Virginia Tech are any indication.

Perhaps beyond their wish to see the ridiculing and character assassination against their culture stop, Southerners would most like for America to finally forgive their homeland (though many Southerners would like to know for what)? The Confederacy is still the only nation to be invaded, subjugated, and destroyed by the United States. Yet the United States has forgiven Britain and Germany twice, and Mexico, Spain, Italy, and Japan once.

Even the surrender terms offered to Lee at Appomattox by Grant did not compare with those allowed British General John Burgoyne by U.S. General Horatio Gates at Saratoga on October 17, 1777. The British were allowed to march out of their trenches with all the honors of war, flags flapping, drums beating, and bands playing. No such privileges were granted to Lee and his Confederates. Is it too much to ask that Southerners be allowed to be proud of their heritage and to afford them the right that their brave fathers were denied at Appomattox? Can't America let the battle flag fly? Can't it let "Dixie" be played?

It is only natural that Southerners would hold onto such a hallowed part of its past. While the battle flag was never the national flag of the Confederacy, it was incorporated into the second and third national flags. Many other regions in the world who have been invaded, subjugated, and destroyed fly their banners proudly. The province of Quebec, Canada, still flies the French Fleurs-de-lis and the Canadian government doesn't even burp. No one calls Quebeckers "traitors" and "devils." Scotland still flies its Cross of St. Andrew, and England bears no resentment. Instead they honor it by allowing Scottish troops to wear it on their uniforms. The English, who tried to exterminate the Scots, now go to great lengths to pay tribute to them. It's interesting that the Band of the Royal Air Force frequently plays "Scotland the Brave," yet a high school band in the South is told it had better not play "Dixie."

It should be remembered that the South is the only region in the United States — and one of the few on earth — that must carry out the sad task of observing two Memorial Days — Confederate on April 26 and U.S. on the last Monday of each May.

"I think people need to remember Southerners are the only American citizens who have ever been defeated in war (on their own land)," Virginia Tech's Robertson reminds us. "Winners always forget the war, and losers never do. The South can't get over the Civil War, and they can't let go of that flag."[86]

When anti-flag noisemakers attacked the South's honorable heritage in Nashville, Tennessee in July 1997, businessman Bill Dorris responded appropriately Dorris, a member of the Sons of Confederate Veterans, erected 13 flag poles on his private property next to Interstate 65 between Brentwood and Nashville. Each pole has battle flag and the flags of the 13 states of the Confederacy. Leaders of local politically correct groups went berserk, but Dorris threatened to put up similar displays on his vast real estate holdings around Nashville.

CHAPTER FIVE

THE BRIGADES OF GRAY HAVE THEIR SAY

I can see that banner streaming
In the sunset's glorious gleaming;
You may think that I am dreaming
Of a past that's far away.
Oft the storms of battle tore it
And the breezes bravely bore it,
Men of honor fell before it —
In the old brigades in gray.
                                    – The Old Brigades In Gray
                                       T.C. Harbaugh

"The battlefield was covered with their dead and wounded soldiers," wrote Confederate Private Sam Watkins of the First Tennessee Regiment. "On the final charge that was made, I was shot in the ankle and heel of my foot. I crawled into their abandoned ditch…. The firing raged in front…. While I was sitting there, a cannonball came tearing down the works, cutting a soldier's head off, spattering his brains all over my face and bosom, and mangling and tearing four or five others to shreds."[1]

Such were the horrors experienced by the Confederate soldier. Though Confederate records are incomplete, estimates place battle-caused deaths among Southern troops at 100,000, while 200,000 died from disease. Another 230,000 were wounded. That's 530,000, or 62 percent, of the 850,000 who served.[2] It is likely every Confederate soldier knew someone who had died or was wounded during the war. Most of them, as in Watkins' case, were eyewitnesses to the killing and mutilation. Many of the victims were friends or relatives. The trauma resulting from such ghastly and painful experiences cannot be overemphasized when examining the meaning of the battle flag to the Confederate soldier.

"Southern culture produced the Confederate soldier, the flag, and the emotions that joined the two," said author Richard Rollins. There were many emotions linking the two, the most powerful of which was the Confederate soldier's concern for his compatriots. The Confederate soldier fought for many reasons, Rollins noted, "but most of all he fought for the men around him and the men who had fought before." With each passing battle, the flag became a sacred banner consecrated with the blood of compatriots. Historian Brian Pohanka noted the effects the mounting death toll had on the Confederate soldier's view of his often bullet-riddled standard. "The flag represented the regiment. It represented their cause, but I think above all, those flags represented their comrades, their comrades who had fallen trying to carry that flag into victory, their comrades who had fallen trying to follow those flags."

Yet the anti-flaggers dismiss the sacrifices made by the Confederate soldier as if he were a repulsive beast. They sit on their self-appointed thrones of judgment and hatefully pronounce him a traitor and a supporter of slavery. "I see a symbol of slavery, treason against the United States and opposition to the Constitutional principles of equality," history Professor Bobby Lovett of Tennessee State University said, referring to the battle flag. Of course, none of that is historically true. But isn't it ironic how people claim exclusive interpretation over a symbol they want suppressed, yet know little or nothing about?

It is grossly unfair for anyone to assail the courageous and honorable men of the Confederacy, much less the battle flag they fought and died for. Sneer at them if you must because they dissolved the union. Rant and rave if you differ with them for violently opposing a federal government set on becoming a leviathan. Those things are true and debatable. But that is no reason to smear Confederate soldiers and their battle flag with outlandish untruths and historical distortions. Not even many of the men they fought viewed them in such a disgraceful manner. "The Confederate was a rebel, not a traitor," said Union Captain C.T. Clark. "We are all rebels against laws and institutions we don't like."[3]

Unfortunately, there are people out there who thrive on hate and seek to justify their existence by tinkering with the South's legacy. But there are many sons and daughters of Dixie who know their region's history. They need only to stand up and speak the truth in order to stop this nonsensical character assassination of the Confederate soldier, his flag, and homeland. Southerners also need to start acting like Southerners again and shift their focus from a new Lexus and making "a fast buck" to God, country, family, community, and liberty.

It is interesting that the anti-flaggers, after 135 years, have decided the Confederate soldier and his battle flag deserve to be slandered, yet in 1902 the very men he fought felt otherwise. Union veterans were overwhelmingly in support of returning all captured battle flags to the former Confederate states and understood the affection Southerners had for their sacred banners. "I advocate the return of the flags…," a Union veteran said at the turn of the century. "We cannot see too much of the men whom we ardently admire, even when they were our sworn foes. Respect for bravery cannot be controlled."[4] Another said, "The soldiers cherish no resentment now; and even in the bitterness of strife individuals, when they met, could not forget that they were brothers. I do not see why the flags were not returned long ago."[5]

An assault upon the battle flag is an assault upon the Confederate soldier and the South's heritage; for the battle flag epitomizes everything the Confederate soldier starved, froze, vomited, bled, and died for. Attacks on the battle flag bring into question the South's character and honor — two qualities that are frequently ridiculed in today's society, but still very much alive in the hearts of Southerners. The majority of today's Southerners are descendants — either directly or indirectly — of Confederate soldiers. Desecrating the reputation of the Confederate soldier is offensive to their families — past and present. The time for Southerners to stand up for their ancestors and their heritage is now. A transplanted Northerner warned what a failure to do so might yield. "Today, the Southern accent is blatantly discriminated against in the Atlanta talk media. And every year, more and more people flock from the Northern Rust Belt to the Deep South. Atlanta has even become an international city. If this were any other culture, historians would call this great migration what it very closely resembles: colonization and imperialism. So while I would not necessarily defend the (Georgia) state flag, I have found the blatant attempts to de-Southernize the South to be deeply disturbing. Like French Canadians, Scots, Sicilians and other sub-groups who have been consolidated into larger political units, Southerners feel their traditional culture is threatened, and they're hanging on to whatever they can. It's an entirely human response to wrenching change. I think when it is gone, we will be the poorer for it."[6]

Confederate General John B. Gordon addressed the critics of the South this way: "If those unhappy patriots who find a scarecrow in every faded, riddled Confederate flag would delve deeper into the philosophy of human nature, or rise higher, say to the plane on which McKinley stood, they would be better satisfied with their Southern countrymen, with Southern sentiment, with the breadth and strength of the unobtrusive but sincere Southern patriotism. They would see that man is so constituted, the immutable laws of our being are such, that to stifle the sentiment and extinguish the hallowed memories of a people is to destroy their manhood."[7]

Rather than bad-mouth the Confederate soldier, maybe the anti-flaggers ought to consider what his enemy had to say about

The battle flag is revered throughout the United States — not just in the South. Members of the Ohio Division of the Sons of Confederate veterans adorn all 2,260 Confederate graves at the Camp Chase Prison site in Columbus, Ohio, with Confederate battle flags and American flags during special ceremonies each June. Reenactors proudly display the colors as they prepared to fire a 21-gun salute in honor of the dead. (Photo courtesy of Bob Croye)

him. Union artillery officer William M. Armstrong recalled the following:

> *I have an intense admiration for them (Confederates), and it's odd that this was first awakened during a fierce engagement. Everything was against any who should attempt to come up that line, but a force of Confederates tried it. Their front lines were mowed down by the batteries, but on they came, as though they meant to take everything before them, until one could but wonder what madness possessed them. Again and again they were repulsed by merciless firing, but every time they would reform and come marching back as proudly as if on review, until — would you believe it — they charged us seven times, and every time they came nearer, until in the last desperate assault our defenses were reached, and, clambering upon them, they fought like madmen with the butts of their guns until our batteries swept them down in a heap. I never saw anything that could equal it in my life, and I have seen some thrilling sights. While they were fighting so heroically I felt like cheering them myself. Since then I have always thought that such foes would be worthy having as friends.[8]*

You would think everyone in the South would be proud to have a flag that was carried by such men. Thankfully, most are. Sadly, a few are not; and they are the ones who should heed the advice of a Union colonel after the war, "Thoughtful people do not malign the motives of the Southerners...."[9]

No defense of the battle flag would be complete without examining what the soldiers themselves had to say about their banner. After all, it belonged to them until they entrusted it to their sons, most of whom have passed it on to yet another generation. As a New York member of the Sons of Confederate Veterans said: "For others to tell us what our flag means misses the obvious truth that it is the nature of symbols to mean different things to different people. But those with the last word on the subject should be the people who create and use the symbols to express their identity and their convictions."[10] Yet this irreversible fact continues to be ignored by the NAACP, KKK, ACLU, CBS, ABC, CNN, Illinois Senator Carol Moseley-Braun, Common Cause, the Rainbow

Coalition, Aryan Nation, Hollywood, skinheads, Madison Avenue, the Southern Christian Leadership Conference, the Southern Poverty Law Center, most newspapers, and revisionists.

When it comes to the battle flag, the last word belongs to the Confederate soldiers. Period. Though the last of them died in the 1950s, their words still carry the wallop of 1,000 howitzers.

"I, for one, though I stood alone in the Confederacy, without countenance or aid, would uphold the banner of Southern Independence as long as I had a hand left to grasp the staff, and then die before submitting. Tell my boy when I am gone how I felt and wrote and tell him never to do anything which his father would be ashamed of — never to forget the principles for which his father struggled," wrote Confederate General J.E.B. Stuart to his wife, Flora, in 1862.[11]

Thirty-five years later the Confederate soldier's sentiment toward the flag hadn't changed. "A few of the 'tattered standards of the South,' rent with bullets and shells, and worn with age, were held aloft, and were everywhere, greeted with cheers. All the bands played `Dixie,' nothing but `Dixie,' but none grew tired of it," a grizzled veteran said following a reunion in July 1897.[12]

Captain C.H. Andrews of Company D, Third Georgia, recalled the following, "It was a bright and beautiful morning, May 18, 1862, when this glorious flag was flung to the breeze on the heights of Petersburg. Its colors were then bright, fresh, and pure. Some two years passed, and this flag floated again on these heights; but its folds were torn with shot and rent by shell, and these 'tricolors of liberty' were made dim by the smoke of battles and stained with the blood of the brave. In its worn and tattered condition, it was the more glorious in the love of its defenders for the victories at Richmond, Manassas, and Chancellorsville; and no less sacred for the struggle at Sharpsburg, the slaughter at Gettysburg, and the defense at Cold Harbor."[13]

The battle flag initially served two purposes: it allowed units to communicate with — and identify — each other on the chaotic battlefield, and it served as a source of motivation and inspiration for soldiers who were — on an average — substantially outnumbered in nearly every battle they fought.

To grasp the importance of the battle flag as a means of tactical communication on the battlefield, one must understand the composition of the Confederate Army. Generally it looked this way: Ten companies formed a regiment of about 1,000 men.

Regiments formed brigades, which composed divisions, while divisions made up a corps. Only regiments carried battle flags. Each flag was carried by a color bearer, who was usually a sergeant. He was protected by about a half dozen soldiers, generally corporals. These men formed the color guard of each regiment. A battle between Confederate and Federal armies might best be described as a vortex of indescribable violence. The focal point within this hurricane of metal missiles was the color guards. An experienced soldier explained it this way:

> The post of honor, as well of danger, in a battle is that of the color guard. Attached to the right center company of a regiment, the (color) guard is composed of a sergeant and seven corporals, whose duty it is to carry the colors, and as the colors are most frequently the point of attack it makes them the place of danger, for to lose them is a disgrace, to capture them an honor. In victory they were the salient point of the enemy's attack in their attempts to dislodge the victors, regain their lost ground and capture the colors. In the repulse of a charge they were the rallying point of those who came out with their lives.[14]

A soldier with the Fifth Alabama understood the significance of the job:

> Our commander appeared in our front, with our battle flag in his hand, and said, "Boys, this is our flag; we have no regular color bearer; who will volunteer to carry it? Whoever will let him step out." The 'god of day' was now setting behind the western horizon. All nature seemed to be draped in mourning. It was indeed a solemn time. Every man seemed to realize that it was a dangerous position to occupy. It was only a moment, though, before I stepped out and took it. The officer told me to stand still until he made another call. He then said, "I want five men to volunteer to go with this color bearer as guard." It was not long before the required number volunteered (two were killed the next day at Mechanicsville). I repeat, it was one of the most solemn moments of my life. I knew that to stand under it in time of battle was hazardous, but

I was proud that I had the courage to take the
position, for it was a place of honor.[15]

Defending or capturing a battle flag often meant a promotion, and many times, a medal. It could elevate a soldier to hero status. "This flag whose staff (30th Louisiana) had been shattered by bullets, had changed hands as often as its defenders had fallen, until there was no one left around to protect it, and it remained on the bloody ground (near Ezra Chapel outside Atlanta), close to the enemy's works, surrounded by the bodies of its defenders and thus became a prize in the hands of the 46th Ohio," a Union soldier wrote after the war. Private Henry Davis of the 46th Ohio received the Medal of Honor for capturing the bullet-riddled banner (which his unit, out of respect, returned to Louisiana some 30 years later).[16]

There were two key points that should be made with regard to the Confederate soldier watching the color guard as each battle developed. Both contributed mightily to his feelings toward the battle flag. First, he was able to gauge his position on the battle-field. Amid the noise and smoke, it was often impossible to hear commands or see what units were where. The battle flag fullfilled this purpose, and in some cases probably saved his life. Second, by keeping his eyes on the color guard he became a witness to some of the war's most ferocious fighting — much of it hand-to-hand. To lose a flag was a disgrace, and he certainly hated to see any of the color guard killed or wounded because he likely knew them, plus it placed the flag — and maybe even his unit — in extreme peril.

Hundreds of battle flags were lost by both sides during the war. More than 50 Confederate battle flags were captured by Federal forces during General George Pickett's charge at Gettysburg.[17] Thirteen color bearers of the 26th North Carolina Regiment were killed that day alone. A veteran with the 15th Georgia recalled what he saw within his regiment that same day: "The enemy was in twenty steps of our front line, and the colors had been shot down a half dozen times. Men in Company C, the color company, said that nine were killed with the colors, and they were finally left on the ground, as it was certain death to pick them up."[18]

A color bearer for the Fifth Alabama described what happened to him at the battle of Gaines' Mill:

Just then General Archer waved his sword over
his head and gave the command, "Follow me!" I
moved on — my color guard was near me — until

within about fifteen or twenty paces of their front line, when I looked back to see if the boys were coming; just then I was shot through my right hip. I did not know how badly I was wounded; I only knew that I was shot down. I raised up on my hands, like a lizzard on a fence rail, and took in the situation as best I could. I got up, but I found I could not walk, and if I made the trip (to get away)... I would have to drag my leg. I grasped my wounded leg with my right hand and started. Just then I saw four of the boys lying down, but I could not tell whether they were all dead or not. I made my way back, dragging my leg, under a galling fire, when a minie ball struck my left wrist and tore it up and took off my thumb. I looked back to see if the "Yanks" were coming, and just at that moment (another minie) ball drew a little (blood) under my chin. A few more hops and I tumbled into a gully.[19]

A Confederate officer recalls the following incident involving another brave color bearer at the battle of Cold Harbor:

The day before that great battle, in which 13,500 of the enemy were, in thirty minutes, shot down in front of our fortifications...; (Allen) Woodman, who had been tinkering with his flag for an hour under a tree, brought his colors to me, and said: "Captain, what do you think of that?" The brave fellow had picked up somewhere a stout brass spear, which he had rubbed until it shone like gold, and fastened it securely on the end of his flagstaff. I remarked that it was very pretty. He replied: "It is not only pretty; but if anybody tries to get these colors, I'll run this through him." I ridiculed the idea of one getting that close, but... sure enough, the next morning, the enemy made a rush at daybreak on a weak salient we occupied, and for a brief time overran our position, climbing into our works. Our men would not give one inch, and there was a furious hand-to-hand fight with pistols and clubbed muskets. In the midst of the melee, a Yankee officer, with two men, rushed up to Woodman and said: "Surrender that flag, sir." The

young fellow replied: "This is the way I surren-
der," and charged him with his flagstaff, running
him clear through the body with the spear. The
officer threw up his hands and fell dead. The two
men with him fired into Woodman, and he fell with
two bullets through his body, still holding onto his
staff with a death grip. Then there was a rush for the
flag by the men of both sides, and a fierce scramble
was had over both bodies. But the Confederates
pressed the Union men back; Woodman, opening
his eyes, saw that his precious flag was still safe,
and with one last superhuman effort pulled himself
forward and reaching over, tore the colors from the
staff, threw them behind them, and fell back a
corpse.[20]

The make-up of the regiments can shed further light on the emotional links between the Confederate soldier and his battle flag. Regiments were largely composed of men from the same neighborhoods. This meant units included family members and close friends. In short, the Confederate soldier knew his compatriots intimately. The trials of war brought them even closer together. Of course, their rallying point was always the battle flag.

Regiments often included fathers, sons, brothers, and cousins. This literally made some units feel like family. For example, ten sons and five sons-in-law of the Bledsoe family from Mississippi fought for the Confederacy; Mrs. Enoch Hooper Cook of Alabama saw her husband, ten sons, and two grandsons all wear the gray. Eighteen members of a Bell family served in one company. Eleven died, six in combat and five of disease. All six sons of David Barton of Winchester, Virginia, were soldiers in the Stonewall Brigade. Two were wounded and two were killed, one nearly within sight of his home. Four Timberlake brothers fought with the Bartons. All four were crippled from battle wounds. Four Carpenter brothers from Allegheny County, Virginia, were part of an artillery battery named in honor of the oldest boy. He was killed in 1862 and succeeded in command by the next brother, who lost an arm. The third struggled home with a bullet in his lungs; while the fourth lost a leg near the war's end.[21]

There were cases where fathers saw their sons killed. Initially, the father would stop, often overcome with indescribable sorrow. But his feelings would gradually turn to rage that often resulted in a vengeful blood-thristy charge at the enemy. Such was the case with Captain Michael P. Spessard of the 28th Virginia, who had his son, Hezekiah, with him during Pickett's charge at Gettysburg. The young boy was severely wounded while crossing the field. Another officer noticed Captain Spessard seated on the ground with his son's head in his lap. Spessard looked up in anguish and cried out, "Look at my boy, Colonel." Spessard gently kissed his son, laid his canteen by his side, rose to his feet with sword in hand, and charged the Federal lines. It was noted he fought with ferocity and was among the Confederates who pierced the Union defenses and got inside the stone wall on Seminary Ridge. Hezekiah died about two weeks later. Watching his compatriots — and sometimes family members — die in combat had a profound impact on how the Confederate soldier viewed the battle flag.[22]

We can also see the mortal side of the Confederate soldier through the eyes of Private William Fletcher of Texas, who while at Gettysburg, showed us how he dealt with fear and the concern he felt for fallen compatriots:

> *I tried to force manhood to the front, but fright would drive it back with a shudder. I was in this state of torture for at least fifteen minutes. I was laying behind a rock protection and dropped asleep with fear and disgrace to be my portion. I had slept but a few minutes when our batteries behind opened fire.... When I awoke my fears had gone and when I heard the countermanding order I had a feeling of regret, thinking what a great relief we could be to our wounded by dropping our water canteen by their sides as we went forward and possibly through some unforseen condition we might be able to remove them to the rear.[23]*

While more than half of the soldiers in the Confederate Army were small farmers, the rest came from a variety of backgrounds. Muster rolls indicate they were blacksmiths, retailers, butchers, millers, shoemakers, clerks, doctors, teachers, mechanics, lawyers, cooks, sheriffs, dentists, overseers, and slaves. Many of the companies in each regiment were based on pre-war milita units, some dating back for decades. We still see the remnants of this today. Army National Guard units in the South display streamers on their units' flag, indicating which battles units have participated in — including those fought during the War for Southern Independence. One National Guard unit in Kentucky still uses the battle flag as its regimental colors, while the Louisiana Washington Artillery that received the original battle flag from General Beauregard is still an active unit in the Louisiana National Guard — and its members are not bashful about their unit's rich heritage.

About 75 percent of the men in the Confederate Army did not own any slaves and certainly were not fighting so that others could have them (remember less than 10 percent of all Southerners — black and white — owned slaves). It's not surprising the slavery issue was rarely discussed in the solders' personal writings. The explanation is easy; it was not their reason for fighting. If it were, they would have said so. If anything, slavery had put many of them, especially the small farmers, at a disadvantage because slave labor on the big plantations kept crop prices down. That didn't hurt the big plantations because they prospered thanks to volume sales. In the end, the small farmer had trouble competing.

Some anti-flaggers argue that the planter aristocracy dragged the rest of the South into the war. That's not true. When Grant invaded Tennessee, it left Southerners no choice but to fight. It should also be noted that Jefferson Davis' cabinet contained only one person from the planter aristocracy. The Confederate Congress was controlled by conservatives, who like Davis, "made no effort to appeal to either the fire-eating secessionists or the devoted Unionists," wrote University of Wisconsin historian William B. Hesseltine.[24]

Most Confederate soldiers were young men, many of whom could not read or write. For those men, the Cross of St. Andrew became a powerful sign. They knew the cross on the flag had long been a symbol of good faith, a symbol many of them used as binding signatures. If he didn't know anything else, he could look at the flag and it reminded him of honor and the righteous cause for which he and his compatriots were fighting. In that sense, it helped further instill *esprit de corps* among the gray regiments.

The average age at enlistment was under 24. Records show one recruit was only 13 (one enlisted at age 73). But muster rolls show that more than 80 percent of the soldiers were between the ages of 18 and 35, thus debunking U.S. Grant's slanderous claim that the Confederacy robbed the cradle and the grave to sustain its army.[25]

"In a general way they reflected both the weaknesses and the virtues of the yeoman society from which they sprang," author Bell Wiley noted about the Confederates. "They were naive,... susceptible to prejudice, haphazard in dress, and unpolished in manner; but they were endowed with a good measure of integrity, self-respect, and courage."[26]

Once he got into battle, the Confederate soldier, by and large, fought well. His sense of family, community, and closeness to those around him made him more resolved in his purpose. Often when he looked at the battle flag, it reminded him of home and the loving hands that had made his beloved banner.

Another emotional tie between the Confederate soldier and his flag was his community, which was intensified by his mother and sweetheart back home. Both often made battle flags out of home-spun cloth, or in the case of Beauregard's first battle flag, a dress. The Florida Marion Light Artillery flew a battle flag made from a crimson shawl belonging to Mrs. J.J. Dickison. The rings which held it to the staff were manufactured out of jewelry contributed by the ladies of Orange Lake, Florida; "the ferrule being forged from a superb silver comb contributed by Mrs. Dickison, and worn by the fair donor on her bridal night."[27]

When the South seceded, many Southern ladies and sweet-hearts applied a good deal of pressure on their boyfriends to join the brigades in gray. "I was of the conservatives who had voted steadily against secession and was prepared to maintain my mental equilibrium in almost any kind of political revulsion," said one recruit. "Some of the more enthusiastic women threatened to put petticoats on the young fellows who did not enter the ranks promptly. These same women worked till their fingers were sore in getting the soldiers ready for service. But we are off for Jackson (Tennessee) to be mustered in."[28]

An observer also noticed the irresistible pressure exerted by the women. "They vowed they would themselves march out and meet the Yankee scoundrels. In a land where women are worshipped by the men, such language made them war-mad."[29]

An eyewitness in the town of Tappahannock, Virginia, recalls seeing the 55th Virginia march off for the final time. "There were good-byes and cheery words. Then the drums beat for formation. There was a moment of stir; then silence, then the order 'Forward march!' I can never forget that silence, nor the scrape of feet as the column moved down the silent street. The women on the sidewalks waved and smiled encouragement though there were tears running down their cheeks. Not even a child made a sound. The Regiment was gone! It left a sad little town behind it."[30]

When debate surfaced at the turn of the century over whether the government should return all captured battle flags, Union troops made it clear they understood the emotional ties the Confederate soldier had with his flag. "As to the flags, send them back," said a Union general. "They know as well as we do that their flags represent nothing that exists today, but they are dear to them because of associations connected with painful memories. `All sentiment,' some would say; but it is the kind of sentiment that lurks in many American hearts, and is rather difficult to eradicate."[31] Another expressed similar feelings, "The flags should be given back to those to whom they are dear because of personal associations connected with them."[32]

Historians generally have characterized Confederate soldiers as being honest, straightforward, hard-working rural people who wore their ambitions on their sleeves. They didn't read much, hated politics, but loved music. Their rural background meant they were self-sufficient, excellent horsemen, and good marksmen.

The Confederate soldier was a fierce individualist who could take care of himself. The Confederate Army's motto, "Help yourself and God will help you," was something he put into practice. He traveled lightly and knew how to live off the land. The Confederate soldier's self-sufficent attitude may be the origin of why Southerners still generally view— with contempt — any move by the Federal government to discourage personal responsibility. The Confederate soldier would likely be appalled at the bevy of social programs offered today. If he were to see our nation's current budget and the taxes levied against its citizens, he would be within his rights to shake his head and say, "See, I told you so."

The military prowess of the Confederate calvary is legendary. Men like J.E.B. Stuart, Nathan Bedford Forrest, "Fighting" Joe Wheeler, John Hunt Morgan, and "The Gray Ghost," John Mosby, are considered by military experts to be among the best the world ever witnessed. Forrest, who had more than 20 horses shot out from under him during the war and was called the most "remarkable soldier" the war produced by Union General William Sherman, offered two of the most popular quotes still loved by today's military commanders: "Get there first with the most" and "Get 'em skeered, and then keep the skeer on 'em."

The Confederate calvary's rough appearance, cavalier attitude, and ability to ride is well known. The Confederates were described by a boy in Maryland, who was accustomed to seeing only Union horsemen, as "... the dirtiest men I ever saw, a most ragged, lean and hungry set of wolves. Yet there was a dash about them that the Northern men lacked. They rode like circus riders."[33]

A rural upbringing also meant that the Confederate soldier was proficient with a rifle. This became shockingly apparent to Federal troops fighting at Spotsylvania, Virginia, on May 9, 1864. Union General John Sedgwick began scolding his troops for taking cover as the gray regiments opened fire from a distance. "What — men dodging this way for single bullets!... I am ashamed of you. They couldn't hit an elephant at this distance." A split second later a Confederate bullet struck the burly general under his left eye. The minie ball knocked Sedgwick into his stunned chief of staff, sending both men tumbling to the ground. Blood began pouring out of the hole in Sedgwick's face as medics rushed to his aid. But it was no use. Sedgwick died in a matter of minutes.[34]

Above all else, the Confederate soldier felt it was his duty to protect "his family, home, state, and personal honor and that it was the essence of manhood to do so," Rollins points out. "The invasion of the South was thus a direct attack on their personal honor. Defending it was defending them, and thus identity of self and family became wrapped up in the flag."[35] These feelings were spawned partly from "Southern chivalry," a term we rarely hear anymore. Chivalry meant more than being gracious or defending one's manhood. It was really a code of behavior that was shaped by Southern culture, but is largely ridiculed today. Beyond honor and courage, it came to mean opening a car door for a lady or comforting a freightened child. It meant rising above silly name-calling while always responding with gentility when challenging a rascal to a duel. As Charles Lunsford likes to say, "Be gracious even when you ask him to step outside to whip his a—."

Confederate General George Pickett and his men demonstrated Southern graciousness, even in hostile territory. When a young Maryland lady ran out of her house to taunt the passing Confederates with a United States flag, she yelled, "traitors — traitors, traitors, come and take this flag, the man of you who dares!" Pickett removed his hat, bowed, and then saluted her flag. He then turned and looked at his men "and don't you know," he recalled, "that they were all Virginians and didn't forget it, and that almost every man lifted his cap and cheered the little maiden who, though she kept on waving her flag, ceased calling us traitors, till letting it drop in front of her she cried out: `O, I wish — I wish I had a rebel flag; I'd wave that, too.'"[36]

The Confederate soldier also had a great deal of confidence, maybe too much. Northerners often branded him a cavalier, and he loved playing the part. A member of the Third Virginia commented on the road to Gettysburg, "Our division… has perfect confidence in the leaders and feel themselves to be almost invincible."[37] After what they had accomplished at Manassas, Fredericksburg, and Chancellorsville, such confidence is understandable.

Southerners remain proud of the courage their forefathers exhibited against insurmountable odds. "Can you stand eight to ten feet behind an artillery piece, hear it fire, feel the ground shake beneath you while its retort echoes in your very bones, and not marvel at the conviction it would take to stand in front of one? What determination, resolution, and conviction does that take?" Sandy Hazelwood asked in a letter to the editor of a Memphis newspaper.[38]

Not only were they outnumbered on the battlefield, but the manufacturing output in the North was 10 times greater than in the South. Raw materials like copper, coal, and iron ore were plentiful in the North to manufacture quality tools and arms.[39] The same materials were scarce in the South as a Confederate private, who was wounded in the hip at Second Manassas, painfully discovered. "I was satisfied I had located the bullet; and I asked one of the boys to hunt a doctor, as I was suffering greatly. Without further question they commenced to cut and from the way the knife pulled the muscle, I took it to be very dull, and was expressing my views in very forcible terms."[40]

The North had two and half times the railroad mileage of the South and an established Navy. The North also had a functioning government to mobilize its resources, while the South had to build its government from scratch. Most banks were located in the North and that meant financial woes for the South.[41] No wonder Abraham Lincoln thought he could defeat the South in 90 days. He was wrong — and much of the reason can be found wrapped within the Confederate battle flag. The only edge the South had was its experienced officer corps (many officers like Robert E. Lee and George Pickett had served in the Mexican War) and the resolute Confederate soldier. Together they baffled a much larger, well-equipped army for four years. They won their share of battles, and aside from the fiasco at Fort Donelson, denied the Union Army a clear-cut victory in any battle. But in the end, they could not withstand the weight of the men and materiel thrown against them year after year.

But there was more. The Confederate soldier saw the battle flag as a symbol of Southern Independence, particularly in the context of the American Revolution. As author Bruce Catton said, the Confederate "put a special meaning on such a word as `patriotism;'" it was not something you talked about very much, just a living force that you instinctively responded to."[42]

The Confederate soldier was not a traitor, but viewed himself as a defender of the Constitution as it had been written by the Founding Fathers. The South had played an integral part in the forming of America. The contributions Southerners made to the Revolution were taught in Southern schools. George Washington, Francis Marion, Patrick Henry, Thomas Jefferson, James Madison, and many others were portrayed heroically. Southerners had frozen at Valley Forge and were proud that the British Army's surrender came on Southern soil at Yorktown, Virginia. Perhaps no Confederate soldier had a stronger link to the Founding Fathers than Robert E. Lee. Two of his ancestors had signed the Declara-

At left, Philip Kaufman, commander of SCV Camp 1535 near Columbus, Ohio, joings SCV Ohio Division Commander Bob Croye in placing battle flags on the graves of Confederate dead at Camp Chase.

tion of Independence, his father had served on Washington's staff, and he married Washington's great-granddaughter, Mary Custis.

Breaking from the Union was a deeply emotional act for the South. Southerners had paid for the old Union with their blood in two wars with Britain. Southerners like Andrew Jackson and James K. Polk had been instrumental in the development of their new nation. Yet they were once again seeking freedom and the right to self-government.

Much of the language used by Southerners during their struggle for independence was strikingly similar to that used by the colonies during the Revolutionary War. A good deal of it compared the North to Great Britian and referred to the conflict as the North's "war of subjugation against the South." To Southerners, Abraham Lincoln played the part of King George III. To this day, many Southerners still view Lincoln as a despot who mocked the Constitution and destroyed the Republic as it was designed by the Founding Fathers.

A Virginia officer spoke confidently about the Confederacy's ability to win this "second War for American Independence" because "Tyranny cannot prosper in the nineteenth century" against "people fighting for their liberties."[43] An Alabamian summed up his feelings on July 4, 1862, "This is the anniversary of the independence of the U.S. Although not a citizen of the U.S. now, yet I feel that we of the South are more entitled to celebrate and hold sacred the day than the people of the North. The declaration was the product of the Southern mind, and it was for the principles contained in that instrument that induced me to take arms."[44]

When explaining why he felt the Confederate soldier fought, Sam Watkins put it this way:

> The half has not been told, but it will give you
> a faint idea of the hard battles and privations and
> hardships of the soldiers in that stormy epoch —
> who died, grandly, gloriously;… while doing what?
> Only trying to protect their homes and families,
> their property, their constitution and their laws,
> that had been guaranteed to them as a heritage
> forever by their forefathers. They died for the faith
> that each state was a separate sovereign govern-
> ment, as laid down by the Declaration of Indepen-
> dence and the Constitution of our fathers.[45]

Thus the battle flag also became a symbol of Southern

independence and defiance against federal tyranny. *Sic Semper Tyrannis* became a popular motto among Virginians in 1861. Those same words were eventually placed on the Virginia state flag. The battle flag became a second "Stars and Stripes," just like the first one in 1776.

When the Confederate soldier looked at his battle flag, he saw the Cross of St. Andrew. And as the war wore on, it came to reflect many things, including his religion. The cross is symbolic of Andrew, the disciple of Jesus. This solidified the Confederate soldier's religious beliefs which helped sustain him and intensify his "will to fight" — even to the point of death. A Northern minister who attended to Confederate prisoners after Gettysburg commented on the powerful impact religion had on the captives:

> *Every (Confederate) soldier is taught to feel that the cause in which he contends is one that God approves; that if he is faithful to God, His almighty arm will protect and his infinite strength insure success. Thus believing that God's arm of protection is thrown around him, that God's banner of love is over him, that God's eye of approval is on him, the southern soldier enters the field of battle nerved with a power of endurance and a fearlessness of death which nothing else can give... ."*[46]

Much of the language used by the veterans after the war to express their affection for the battle flag included allusions to religion:

> *These flags, with tongues of flame, voice the story of (the South's) achievement. They are sacred to her, for now they are holy, "holy because they were planted amid the whirlwind of shot and shell upon many a victorious battlement by the Southern troops...; holy because the men who fought with Lee and Jackson, with Johnston and Beauregard, with Johnston and Hood, with Forrest and Stuart wreathed them around with glory," — holy because they were once the banners of soldiers who rode into the presence of their Maker with not one blot upon their knightly shields; holy because they moved steady upon the crested front of the billows of death at the command of their great leaders.*[47]

Prayers were not uncommon before and after battles. A

Confederate artillery sergeant called for prayer for the dead following Shiloh and remembered the reaction by his compatriots. "If daylight had suddenly broken upon us, it would have discovered tears stealing down the cheeks of nearly all present."[48] Another Confederate from Virginia explained his inner feelings about religion and combat prior to the battle of Gettysburg, "My mood was so calm that my calculations were perfectly rational. I felt that the Lord's hand was with me, that his shield was over me and that whatever befell me would be by his agency or permission, and therefore it would all be well with me."[49] Private John Moseley of the Third Alabama was mortally wounded and captured at Gettysburg. As he lay dying behind enemy lines, he penned a farewell letter to his mother. In it he shares his deepest thoughts and all that he felt the Confederate battle flag stood for:

> I am here a prisoner of war & mortally wounded. I can live but a few hours more at farthest — I was shot fifty yards (from) the enemy's lines. They have been exceedingly kind to me.
>
> I have no doubts as to the final results of this battle and I hope I may live long enough to hear the shouts of victory yet, before I die.
>
> I am very weak. Do not mourn my loss. I had hoped to have been spared, but a righteous God has ordered it otherwise and I feel prepared to trust my case in his hands.
>
> Farewell to you all. Pray that God may receive my soul.
>
> Your unfortunate son John.[50]

"The Southern cultural matrix became bound up in, and a part of, the Confederate battle flag," Rollins said. "When he saw the flag, it symbolized his emotional ties to his family and community; he comprehended it within the framework of the heritage of the Revolution, the doctrine of states' rights and individualism as he understood them. He felt he had to display the central tenets of the code of behavior he had been brought up with: honor and courage. His belief in evangelical Protestantism helped him face death and fight with little fear and a good deal of elan."[51]

Confederate Private Carleton McCarthy noted the complexities surrounding the Confederate soldier's reasons for fighting: "The heart is greater than the mind. No man can exactly define the cause for which the Confederate soldier fought. He was above human reason and above human law, secure in his own rectitude of purpose; accountable to God only, having assumed for himself a 'nationality,' which he was minded to defend with his life and his property, and thereto pledged his sacred honor."[52]

Perhaps no single incident demonstrated better the deep affection the Confederate soldier had for his battle flag than when the Army of Northern Virginia surrendered at Appomattox. The Confederate soldier showed no emotion when he was forced to stack his rifle, but he cut loose with tears, curses, and cries when he was forced to lay his flag down. Some distraught compatriots tore their flags from their staffs and hid them in their shirts until Union officers stepped in and put a stop to the practice. Still others cut their battle flags to pieces so they could become framed heirlooms in Southern homes.[53]

Union General Joshua Chamberlain described the historic scene, "... lastly, reluctantly, with agony of expression, they fold their flags, battle-worn, bloodstained, heart-holding colors, and lay them down, clinging to them, pressing them to their lips.... How could we help falling on our knees, all of us together, and praying God to pity and forgive us all."[54]

One Confederate remembered it this way, "Many grizzled veterans wept like women, and my own eyes were as blind as my voice was dumb."[55]

How can the South turn its back on such men? And how can it turn its back on the flag they loved so much?

CHAPTER SIX

'OH MY GOD, THEY SHOT ME'

Young as the youngest who donned the gray,
True as the truest who wore it,
Brave as the bravest he marched away,
(Hot tears on the cheeks of his mother lay,)
Triumphant waved our flag one day,
He fell in the front before it.
                              – The Southern Soldier Boy
                              Unknown

"I'd like to buy one, but... I'm afraid to fly it outside." Those are the words flag retailer Tom Tucker says customers sometimes use when they stop by his Columbia, Tennessee, store and see the Confederate battle flags on display. "They'll look at them, talk about them, but then they end up not buying. I guess some people really are afraid."

Their fear of flying a Confederate battle flag can be traced to the January 14, 1995, shooting death of Michael Westerman of Todd County, Kentucky. The 19-year-old father of infant twins was shot in the heart after he and his wife, Hannah, both white, were targeted during a high-speed chase on a rural Tennessee highway by two car loads of blacks, mostly teenagers. One of them, 17-year-old Freddie Morrow, a native of Chicago who had moved to Todd County, possessed a cheap .32-caliber pistol.[1] And when Morrow fired the bullet that clipped Michael's heart, it sent shock waves through the South and brought normally tranquil Todd County unwelcomed national scrutiny. But even more than that, it brought immeasurable sorrow to the Westerman family.

Why did Morrow pull the trigger? Because Michael was flying a Confederate battle flag in the back of his pickup truck. "It's a flag for people that liked slaves," said one of the seven blacks involved in the incident. "I've talked to all of them and the only thing that might have motivated them was the fact that the truck had a Rebel flag on it," said Detective David Benton a few days after the shooting.[2]

Todd County is composed of about a dozen rural communities. It is located in southwest Kentucky next to the Tennessee state line about 50 miles north of Nashville. Railroad ties, clothing, and cardboard are manufactured there, but it's farming that remains a way of life for many Todd countians. The Black Patch War over low tobacco prices raged around Todd County in the early part of this century. For a few years, the Planters' Protection Association met in the town of Guthrie. The final meeting drew 25,000 farmers.[3] The "Trail of Tears" passes through Todd County (Wonder how many Todd residents know that some of the American Indians, forced to move by the United States government, brought their black slaves with them?).

Some would say the communities in Todd County have been bypassed by progress. There are a handful of factories, like Guthrie Garment, where Michael's mother, JoAnn, runs a sewing machine. But Todd countians still love their community, despite the lack of high-paying factory jobs. Michael McKnight, a local insurance salesman who is black, says the people of Todd County are "good folks." "I eat in their houses. My company had doubts about how I was gonna be accepted here. After a week I told them you can't find any better people anywhere." McKnight said he understands and respects the Confederate battle flag's history, noting that about five out of every 10 houses in the area fly the battle flag.[4]

The town of Guthrie sits on the county's southern edge next to the state line. On the outskirts of town is a sign: "Welcome to Guthrie, Birthplace of Robert Penn Warren, First Poet Laureate of the United States." The home where Warren was born in 1905 is still there and open to the public. Warren was a three-time Pulitzer Prizer-winning poet and a member of the famous Agrarians, a group of Southern literary scholars who earlier this century opposed the industrialization of the South. Their views remain

Michael Westerman (left) and Hannah Westerman (right), Michael's widow, holds the couple's twins during a Christmas gathering nearly a year after Michael's death. Hannah has since remarried.

popular with some Southerners who feel the so-called "New South" has sold its soul for 30 pieces of silver.

On the far western edge of Todd County is the community of Fairview, birthplace of Confederate President Jefferson Davis. Davis lived in a log home at the site until the age of two. A 351-foot obelisk marks the spot. The huge concrete monument serves as a backdrop each June for the crowning of a local teenager as Miss Confederacy.

Back to the east and in the center of the county is Elkton, the county seat and home of Todd County Central High School. Michael and Hannah attended Todd County High. Hannah played on the girls' basketball team, while Michael was selected Future Homemakers of America Sweetheart his senior year. Since 1963 the nickname of the schools' athletic teams has been the "Rebels." The school mascot is two pudgy Confederate soldiers and the battle flag. The mascots are painted on walls in the school and even on the band director's podium. If there was ever a place where the battle flag could be classified ubiquitous, it's Todd County.

About 10 miles directly north of Elkton is Clifty, where Michael and Hannah settled down. The two had met during a 1992 school trip to Fort Donelson, Tennessee, the site of a disasterous Confederate defeat in February 1862. It was during the bus ride that Michael and Hannah realized they were more than friends. "We were sitting there just talking," she recalled. "And then he started kissing on me for nothing. And he just kept on." They graduated in 1993, married six months later, and went to work at her father's sawmill. "Our lives were filled with good times," Hannah said.[5] Her father, Billy Laster, said "Michael was a hard worker and took great interest in every job that he did. He had already worked up to a level that most 25-year-old men haven't made."[6]

Michael was a good-looking young man nearly six-feet two-inches tall, weighing a muscular 226 pounds. He was the middle of David and JoAnn Westerman's three children, Cynthia being the oldest, and April the youngest. Often referred to as "Smiley," Michael had dark hair and was known for his playful nature. "Michael picked and plucked at people and laughed at everything," said Hannah's mother, Nancy Laster.[7] He loved comedian Jeff Foxworthy and driving his four-wheeler, though he had less time for it after the twins, Michael Austin and Michaela Adrianna, were born prematurely in December 1994. He frequently wore a black cowboy hat and black Levis and cowboy boots. Michael was so attached to the hat and Levis that he wore both with a bow tie and tuxedo jacket when he took Hannah to their senior prom. He sported a small tattoo on his arm of the cartoon character Tasmanian Devil clutching the Confederate battle flag.

Michael Westerman's pickup truck just a few days after he was shot and killed by two men for flying the Confederate battle flag.

Three small battle flags decorated Michael's grave after the shooting.

Michael was a fourth generation Westerman to work on A.J. and Andrew Gray's sprawling farm in Todd County. Michael's father, David, still works there just as he has since 1976. JoAnn recalled how her late son reacted when he got his first pay check from the farm. "Michael was 12 years old when he started working in tobacco on the Grays' farm," she said. "He took me to Ponderosa (Steak House) with his first check. I'll never forget how big he acted. 'Now I'm buying, so you pick out anything you want,' he said to me as he took my hand and led me around. That showed me he was responsible and wanted to share. He acted so grown-up."[8]

Michael was best known for his big red 1986 four-wheel-drive Chevrolet pickup which had a Confederate battle flag flying from its bed. There have been different explanations offered as to what the battle flag meant to Michael, but those who knew him say it had nothing to do with racism. "He'd do anything to make his truck look sharp," Hannah said. "The truck's red. The flag's red. They match."[9] She also said it showed school pride.[10] David agreed, saying Michael flew it as a sign of loyalty to his alma mater.[11] Still his aunt and the family's historian, Brenda Arms, said Michael was interested in his Southern heritage and that he had always had a battle flag. She recalled Michael putting the battle flag on his first car. "He treasured that flag," she said. "Michael's display of the flag at the time of the shooting was a sign of his Southerness and the fact that he graduated from Todd County High School."[12] JoAnn said Michael always had a battle flag on his bedroom wall. "He used to ride around with a small Confederate flag on his three-wheeler even before he and Hannah met. He'd ride these fields with that flag on the back of it."[13]

The Confederate battle flag had never been an issue with Todd countians — until 1993. That's when a black woman who graduated in 1982 returned to the area and was quoted in a local newspaper, calling it offensive.[14] Almost simultaneously, the Kentucky Conference of the NAACP "piggy-backed" the national organization's 1991 resolution and called for schools to stop using Confederate mascots. That year the school removed the two "Rebel" mascots painted on the basketball court. Art Douglas, who was principal at the time, said the complaints from the NAACP was not the reason for the mascots being removed.[15]

But something changed black attitudes about the battle flag. "It never dawned on me what the flag represented," said Kim Gardner, a black 1980 graduate.[16] Marcus Flippin, a black coach who began teaching at Todd Central in 1992, complained that opponents were whipping their players into a tizzy because of Todd County's mascot and the school's nickname of "Rebels." Flippin said they would say, "You know that that flag represents slavery and the Klan. We have to go over and show those racists."[17] With its preemptive attack well underway throughout the South, the NAACP enjoyed some initial successes, many of which were hailed in newspapers far and wide. Such stories must have caught the eyes of a few young blacks in Todd County. Flippin said black students at Todd Central started asking questions. "They'd ask, `How can they get away with it here in Todd?'"[18] When Flippin told school officials what was happening, they agreed to paint over the "Rebel" mascots on the gym floor, replacing it with an outline of Todd County. Clearly, the NAACP's hate proganda was reaching a zenith in Todd County. It took a lot of unsuspecting people off guard.

Garland Lester, a young white man who graduated from Todd Central in 1994, volunteered to do the repainting. "There are several people who walk around with an edge on their shoulder all the time," he said after Michael was shot. "It's the kids that don't have much education, the younger people."[19] No one apparently raised any objection when the gym floor was painted over. Why? Probably because none of the school's other mascots were painted over and no attempt was made to change the school's nickname. Such strategy has been used by anti-flaggers throughout the South ever since the battle flag debate surfaced. In short, their strategy is this: Go in and agitate; get rid of what you can and then pull back; wait for things to calm down, then return to wipe out the rest. It's doubtful that many Todd countians knew about the NAACP resolution and the attacks on Southern heritage sweeping their region. Like throughout the South, flag supporters were caught off guard and were woefully rusty on the true history of the battle flag and other Confederate symbols. But flag supporter Frances Chapman of Guthrie sensed what was going on when the Todd mascot controversy flared in 1995. "If they (intimidated school officials) had left it alone two years ago and refused (to remove the symbols) then, we wouldn't be going through this now," she said. "Sometimes you have to nip this in the bud and say 'No, we're not going to take away the flag.'"[20]

Insinuations continued to surface that the battle flag and mascot were adopted in 1963 in defiance of the civil rights movement. Nothing could have been further from the truth. "Our reasons for the decision were that the rebel soldier represented the spirit of a true fighter and the prominence of the Jefferson Davis monument in Todd County's history," said Dr. A.G. Campbell, a Todd County physician who chaired the mascot committee in 1963. "At that time the civil rights movement was at its height; however, we did not feel the "Rebel" and the colors "red and gray" would be considered racist or offensive," Campbell said. "For more than 30 years, no issue was made of that decision until the last two years. At that time a few individuals decided to make it an issue. I submit that those individuals like all liberals pick issues so they can project their power. There is nothing liberals like better than power — power to intimidate...."[21] They like to deconstruct the truth.

For schools to select a nickname like "Rebels" in 1963 was indicative of what was happening throughout the nation. Starting around 1955 and continuing through 1964, our nation observed the 100th anniversary of the War for Southern Independence. Many activities were taking place commemorating the war. New monuments were erected, reenactments exploded on the scene, books were produced by the thousands, Georgia changed its state flag, and new markers were placed along highways to refresh our memories of the war — particularly in the South where most battles took place. Even President John F. Kennedy got caught up in the excitement. History now teaches us that he really wanted to go to Gettysburg in mid-November 1963 for festivities marking the centennial anniversary of that great battle. But he was unable to attend because of preparations being completed for his fateful visit to Dallas, Texas, a few days later.[22]

The needless agitation surrounding Todd Central's mascot and the battle flag caught the attention of Morrow and Damien Darden, another 17-year-old who drove the car from which Morrow fired the shot that killed Michael.

Though neither one belonged to an anti-flag group, testimony at their trial and subsequent interviews with the news media indicated both men were familiar with the debate over the battle flag. "They was telling me about how they had a war for it back in the days and all this," Morrow said. "It means white pride and continued slavery."[23] Wonder who Morrow was making reference to when he said "They?"

Though he was not writing about the Westerman case, insightful black columnist Thomas Sowell offered some words of advice to young black Americans three months after the shooting and, unfortunately, too late for Morrow and Darden:

> Black identity-mongers... are creating a pho-
> ney history and phoney traditions as escapes from
> very real problems of drugs, violence and social
> degeneration in the ghettos of the 1990s. Worse,
> they are turning young blacks' attention backward
> toward slavery instead of forward toward the op-
> portunities and demands of the high-tech world of
> the twenty-first century. If you want to spend your
> time navel-gazing about `roots,' while other are
> learning square roots, and contemplating chains
> while others are mastering computers, do not be
> surprised if the whole parade into the future leaves
> you behind, mired in squalor, imprisoned by igno-
> rance and misled by demagogues. Demagoguery
> can be a very lucrative and even glamorous career,
> as a number of black 'leaders' and 'scholars'
> demonstrate. But that is not how 33 million black
> Americans will advance.[24]

The shooting took place on a rainy Saturday around 5 p.m., after Michael and Hannah decided to go out for a night of dining and shopping. It was their first night out since the birth of their five-week-old twins. They left them with Michael's parents and headed to nearby Clarksville, Tennessee, for some fast food before traveling to Springfield, Tennessee, and Nashville. The most convenient route from Clarksville to Nashville is Interstate 24, but the Westermans decided to take winding U.S. 79 to Guthrie, before picking up U.S. 41 into Springfield. "There's nothing to look at on the interstate," Hannah said. "And we were in no hurry."[25]

When they reached Guthrie, Michael pulled up to the gasoline pumps at Janie's Market, a convenience store on the state line where Tennesseans join Kentuckians in buying lottery tickets. Michael went inside and paid for the gas and a pack of gum as Hannah sat in the truck. When he returned, they opened the gum and talked for a minute. Nothing seemed out of the ordinary.

Earlier in the day, Tony Andrews, a 17-year-old junior fullback on the Todd Central football team, got his hair cut. He hopped in the car with Damien Darden before they picked up Freddie Morrow and a 15-year-old friend. They rode around Guthrie and talked about going to see "Higher Learning," a movie about racial problems on a college campus in which whites gather around the battle flag and shoot a black student.[26] At their trial, the teens claimed they had seen a truck like Westerman's riding through the black community in Guthrie, though no one else corroborated their story. And even if someone had, the teens made it clear they felt the flag justified some type of violent reaction. When Darden stopped for a moment along a main street in Guthrie, Michael and Hannah just happened to drive by before pulling into Janie's Market. "Let's go whip that dude," Darden said, according to Andrews.[27] Darden, who had borrowed his mother's 1989 Geo Prizm, sped off to find more friends to help in the up-coming fight. The quartet was joined by another car carrying three former or current black residents of Guthrie, Robert "Bobo" Bell, 26, and driver of the vehicle, Michael Mimms, and Ricky Lynn Williams, both 19.

Just as the Westermans started to pull off from Janie's, Hannah noticed a black person hanging out the back window of a small car, laughing and pointing at them. Then Darden pulled up near the truck, which had dark-tinted glass so he nor any of the others could see who was inside. "The suspects thought there were several males in the truck," Benton said after he questioned the teens shortly following their arrests. "They didn't know until later that they had known Michael."[28] Andrews, a childhood neighbor of the

Westermans who played with Michael, was in the front seat with Darden. The back seat carried the 15-year-old on the passenger side, with Morrow behind Darden. Darden later said that he was "a fighter, but not a killer and I just wanted to fight that dude that had the flag on his truck."[29] Morrow said a hand reached through the truck's sliding rear window and shook the flag. Then, he said, someone shouted "Niggers!"[30] But Hannah said she nor Michael said or did anything. The 15-year-old, who was sitting beside Morrow, later testified that he did not see the flag being shaken and did not hear anyone say anything in the truck.[31] Even if they had, it seemed that Morrow was implying that such speech justified pointing a loaded gun at the offender and pulling the trigger. But as prosecutor Dent Morriss said, "There is no right to chase someone down... because of an offensive symbol and kill them," adding that race was an issue, but only where Morrow was concerned.[32]

Hannah noticed Darden following them as they pulled out and drove south on U.S. 41 into Tennessee. She noticed the second car, which had been parked across the street from Janie's, pull out to follow as well. Even though the Westermans had a head start, Hannah noticed both cars gaining on them — fast. "Kick it!" she said as Michael pressed the accelerator to the floor.[33] The needle on his speedometer reached its peak of 85 mph, but both cars — with Bell's initially in the lead — continued to close in.

Morrow mentioned to the others that he had a gun. "No you don't!" they taunted.[34] Morrow reached under his shirt and produced a Czech semiautomatic he purchased for $50. Morrow had purchased the gun after an argument with a former friend who had called him "weak" and "a nobody." "I am not weak; I am somebody," Morrow said at the trial.[35] "It just felt like all my worries were through (when he bought the gun)," he recalled later while in jail.[36] Morrow fired two shots wildly into the air as Darden passed Bell. The gun jammed just as Darden pulled up beside the Westermans, while the other car remained behind the truck. Michael pushed Hannah down into the floorboard as he and Darden sped down the highway side-by-side in the rain. Morrow pointed the gun out the passenger-side window as the 15-year-old ducked. Morrow fired at the truck. Hannah did not hear the shot that struck Michael, but she got up when she heard her husband moan. He reached around to his back and felt blood. "Oh God, I've been shot," he told her.[37] Hannah crawled behind the wheel as Michael lay bleeding. He began to pray. She noticed that Darden had stopped ahead and that Morrow was hanging out the left rear car window. He was pointing the gun at the truck. Andrews testified that Morrow then said, "Now I've got him," as a fourth shot was fired.[38] Hannah veered off the road, bounced into a ditch nearly flipping the truck over, then made a U-turn and bumped back onto the highway behind the other chasing cars and headed in the opposite direction. Hannah said she made the U-turn because the second car had stopped in a nearby parking lot and its three occupants were walking toward her and Michael. "I was trying to get away from them," she said.[39] The two cars did not give chase as Hannah headed for Clarksville Memorial Hospital 20 minutes away.

By the time they arrived at the hospital Michael was in shock. The bullet had pierced his heart. Surgeons closed the wound and transferred him by ambulance to Vanderbilt University Medical Center in Nashville. Michael never regained consciousness. He died the next day. While searching the truck, police found a single bullet hole in the driver-side door, a loaded, but unfired, .380 automatic pistol belonging to the Westermans, and Michael's black cowboy hat with a piece of gum still stuck to the brim.[40]

Morrow, Darden, and the others never made it to their movie. All of them returned to Guthrie and went their separate ways. Morrow said he went home and placed the gun under the mattress in his bedroom before going to his girlfriend's house to "lay low." Morrow said he started getting "a bad feeling in his stomach" and went back to get his gun. He then hid it under a trailer in the community.[41] The next day Morrow, Darden, Andrews and the 15-year-old turned themselves in to police. Morrow told police the gun was his and that he had fired it. A ballistics expert later confirmed that Morrow's gun had been fired and that a .32-caliber bullet had been removed from Michael's right lung. All four teens cooperated with police, contending they never intended to hurt anyone. Three weeks later a Robertson County grand jury indicted all of them, including the three men in the second car, on charges of felony murder, civil rights intimidation, and attempted aggravated kidnapping. Morrow and Darden were also charged with first-degree murder. Morrow, Darden, Andrews, and the other teen were immediately jailed. Morrow remained incarcerated until the trial, while Darden, Andrews, and the other teen were released on $100,000 bond on Feb 17, 1995.[42] Bell was arrested 23 days after the shooting at his place of employment. Mimms was taken into custody at Todd Central High the same day as was Williams, who was served with his arrest warrant at the Todd County jail, where he was being held on unrelated charges.[43] Bell and Mimms were eventually released after the $250,000 bonds were reduced. Prosecutors said they believed a third car followed the Westermans, carrying two more people, but no charges were filed against them. The murder charges stemmed from the shooting death of Michael, the civil rights intimidation charges stemmed from the Westermans' being denied their First Amendment right to fly the flag, and the kidnapping charges stemmed from the defendants' trying to imprison Hannah in the truck. The trial would take place in circuit court in Robertson County, Tennessee, where the shooting occurred.

There were many grieving and anxious moments for the Westerman family during the 11 months between the shooting and the trial. "I'd just like to have Michael back for an hour," David said as he mourned the loss of his only son.[44] Three weeks after the shooting, David's mother passed away. "Their (David's and JoAnn's) lives have been completely wrecked," said David's brother, Freddy, who had to be treated by doctors for severe depression.[45] "They don't eat or sleep like they should and they are moody and depressed a lot," he said, referring to David and JoAnn. "I miss seeing my parents laugh, joke, and cut-up," said Cynthia, Michael's older sister.[46]

Friends rallied around Hannah as she struggled to survive with two infants on $99 a month. "I have a lot of nightmares about it every night I go to bed," Hannah said about two months after the shooting. "It's hard to forget. I don't want to be alone."[47] She began receiving anonymous phone calls from men asking for "Michael." Hannah rarely ventured out. "Hannah lives an imprisoned life," said Tanya Henson, a family friend. "She is constantly looking over her shoulder and jumping when a car starts to pass her on the road. I can understand why after all that has happened." Henson told Circuit Court Judge Robert Wedemeyer, who presided over the murder trial, that some of those involved in the shooting who were out on bond, followed her and some friends, including Hannah and the twins, around a shopping mall in Clarksville. "They followed us through the mall, to the car, and chased us to our next destination. We all feared for our safety and the safety of our children."[48] Joyce Laster, Hannah's sister, described the same incident.[49] Another of Hannah's sisters, Sarah Belanger, also told Wedemeyer about their encounter at the mall, identifying the two as Mimms and the 15-year-old. She said they followed them back to Elkton "going 80 mph with their lights off."[50] The stress took its toll on Hannah. "I don't ever recall seeing her (Hannah) weak," said long-time friend Shelly Haley. "It wasn't part of her disposition. All of that had changed in such a short time though."[51] Family and friends took turns staying with her and the twins as the months leading to the trial passed by.

Prosecutors sought to have Morrow, Darden, and the other two teens tried as adults, a request that was approved by a juvenile court judge two weeks after the shooting. Then in April 1995, lead detective David Benton suddenly died of a heart attack. Authorities also mourned the loss of Benton's distraught son, who went to his father's grave on Father's Day and killed himself.

Meanwhile, Andrews struck a deal with prosecutors, agreeing to testify against the others in exchange for two years probation. The trials for Morrow, Darden, and the 15-year-old were scheduled to begin in July before Wedemeyer, but they were pushed back when Morrow's mother could no longer pay the private lawyer she had hired. A public defender took over the case as a result. "The longer it goes the more it hurts," JoAnn said in June 1995.[52]

Another delay came in September 1995 when Darden and the 15-year-old, who had been released on bond, were arrested and charged in Elkton with felony weapons possessions, trafficking drugs on school property, and trafficking in cocaine. Both were among five people in a Cadillac stopped by police outside a Todd Central football game after a teacher alerted police that she had smelled marijuana. A search of the car uncovered four loaded guns and about 60 rocks of crack cocaine.[53] "You can pretty well see the type of people we're dealing with," roared Montgomery County Distict Attorney General John Carney. "They were involved with the violent death of Michael Westerman... (and) released back into society on bond. And now they are apparently showing their lack of respect for our society."[54]

Darden and the teen were not the only ones involved in the Westerman shooting who had additional run-ins with the law. Williams was indicted by a Christian County, Kentucky, grand jury August 30, 1995, on charges stemming from the theft of a Springfield vehicle. He was charged with receiving stolen property over $300, theft of a motor vehicle license plate, and one count each of first- and third-degree criminal mischief.[55]

Motions were also filed for a change in venue as defense attorneys argued about the excessive media coverage and the inability to find enough qualified black jurors. But Wedemeyer denied the motions. He also ruled that Morrow, Darden, and the 15-year-old would be tried together. A trial date was set for early January 1996.

In the meantime, Todd County became the site of a media circus, and amid all their sorrow, the Westermans found themselves smack in the middle of it.

It's unclear why, but generally, the larger news organizations showed little interest during the first few days following the Westerman shooting. A columnist noted that the smaller newspapers around Todd County reported it in a timely manner, but some of the larger regional publications seemed to hesitate: "Sometime during the day of the (Michael's) funeral a small cross was burned by the road in front of the gunman's home. Suddenly the event was newsworthy. The cross burning, that is, not the shooting."[56]

Sure enough, reporters from New York to Atlanta seemed to crawl out from under every rock, pointing out every little sin in Todd County. In reality, Todd County has fewer blemishes than most counties its size. Out-of-town reporters eventually discovered this, forcing them to desperately search for some racist and anti-flag angle to hang their stories. That is the only way they could draw attention from the real issues surrounding Michael's death and the battle flag. So in order to whet their appetites, the intrepid journalists high-tailed-it to nearby Montgomery County, Tennessee. Redbone's Saloon, a rough and ready biker's bar that seemingly loved to incite visiting news media with its "unique decor" and "lively" clientele, was a popular spot for "inquiring minds" from Nashville to New York. Redbone's, in its unabashed way, routinely posted flyers on the wall inviting people to events like a "Thank God for James Earl Ray Party." One sniffing reporter from New York claims he nearly had an arm jerked off as he scampered out the bar's front door after asking one too many questions to a burly customer who must have been having a bad day.[57] Of course, Redbone's had nothing to do with Michael's death and it is certainly not indicative of the citizenry of Todd County, but what the heck, it made good copy. What was so funny about the reporters who bugged the folks at Redbone's is that they didn't have to go all the way to Montgomery County, Tennessee, to find such a colorful establishment. They have 100 times the number in their own sanctimonious backyards. At least everyone at Redbone's kept their clothes on, unlike the plethora of disgusting "watering holes" that litter the polluted metropolises the visiting reporters called home. (One can point a finger, but there will always be three pointing back.)

Some news hounds began characterizing Todd County as a nest of racial strife, focusing particularly on the local high school where "ugly" symbols of the "Old South" are still mascots. The media may have gotten what it needed, but it began to annoy Todd countians. These feelings were exacerbated when the F.B.I. arrived to investigate the so-called cross burnings. "The F.B.I. is sending agents to Todd County to check on (cross burning) violations, while a young white male, with wife and kids, was buried on Wednesday," wrote Ed Radford of Hopkinsville. "He was shot by... black kids who did not like what he was... carrying in the back of his truck. Maybe I am wrong (as I usually am), but something has got to be done to wake up the USA to the crime going on and penalize the criminals and not someone burning kindling."[58] The crosses were made of tiny pieces of wood. Authorities dismissed them, saying they had been made by amateurs. "If there are any racial problems, they are coming from outside (Todd County)," said Guthrie Police Chief Robert Whittlesey.[59]

Joe Johnson, a black resident of Todd County, expressed dismay with the press. "If the media quits blowing it up out of proportion, calling it racial tension, everything will be all right," he said.[60]

Pauline McCormick, who is white, added this, "We don't have any trouble with black people. We treat them nice, and they treat us nice."[61]

Greg Glass, a black teacher at the school said the racial climate has always been amiable. "We've always gotten along, with the exception of a few incidents, like in any community. Most of the hoopla, it didn't come from people in Todd County."[62]

It was amid this circus atmosphere that the Westermans found themselves as they suffered in what seemed like a bottomless pit of grief and despair.

The Westermans were disturbed by some reports characterizing Michael as being "rowdy" and a "hellraiser," yet the only run-in Michael ever had with police resulted in one speeding ticket. The Westermans point to a white female student at Todd County High who was reported to have described Michael as "a loudmouth" to a newspaper reporter, as an example of how their son was sometimes mischaracterized. When quizzed by the Westermans about her comment, the girl denied making the statement, denounced the publication which printed the remark, and then admitted she didn't even know Michael.[63] "How many other people who didn't even know Michael have been quoted in newspapers?" David angrily asked.[64]

Many Southerners felt insinuations were made that Michael "had it coming," providing an unnecessary stench to the tragedy. "Michael Westerman was a working man, a model citizen, and a family man with an unblemished record, but to some people there is a perception that he was a racist who got what was coming to him," a disgusted SCV member told *The Washington Times*.[65] There was a growing sense that Michael was the one being put on trial.

As if that weren't enough, the Westermans were then subjected to vicious stories concerning Hannah and Michael's relationship. One of the more sickening stories floated around town was that Hannah and Michael had fought the day of the shooting because she had been with one of the blacks involved in the incident.[66] Of course, the story was untrue, but the Westermans expressed concern that the story might trigger retalitory violence from people supporting Hannah and the family. "You don't know how much trouble I went through trying to keep the peace in Guthrie ," David said about the city, which has a population that is 60 percent white and 40 percent black. "You don't know how many telephone calls came in where I said, 'Naw, let's let justice take its course.' They were ready to come in and clean house."[67] A local newspaper lauded the Westermans for their calls for peace, stating, "If anyone has a right to feel any bitterness, racial or otherwise, it would be (Michael) Westerman's wife and the couple's parents and relatives. From the beginning, however, it is they who have led the appeal for racial harmony. In their remarkably restrained response to the tragedy, they have set a standard for all to follow."[68]

Then came the shocking comments from a Kentucky human rights official two days before Morrow and Darden were to go on trial. In a response to a letter from the Sons of Confederate Veterans, the state's highest ranking human rights official had the unmitigated gall to blame Michael's death on the citizens of Todd County. "The Confederate flag as a symbol is directly linked to the murder of one Kentuckian (Michael) in 1995," wrote Beverly L. Watts, executive director, Kentucky Commission on Human Rights. "Had the victim's community been more attuned to the flag's present symbolism than to its alleged glorious history, that tragedy might have been averted."[69] What ought to frighten the citizens of Kentucky is Watts' failure to defend Michael's First Amendment and civil rights, much less her ignorance with regard to American history.

The shooting plunged Todd countians into another unwanted debate, this one over Todd County Central High School's long-time mascot. The flap created a firestorm of protest and weeks of debate following Michael's death.

"I feel like, why not change the flag," said Gayle Petrie, one of about a half dozen blacks who attended an emotionally charged school board meeting to discuss the issue about a month after Michael's death.[70] Among the 400 whites packed into the meeting was Frances Chapman, a retired nurse from Guthrie who garnered 3,800 signatures on a petition in support of keeping the "Rebel" mascot. "It's something special in the South that other parts of the country don't have." Chapman urged people to "learn that this flag does not have a connotation to slavery or hatred."[71]

In the end, a community committee decided to keep the "Rebel" mascot at the beleaguered school. But the controversy was enough to encourage out-of-town civil rights activist Louis Coleman to file a complaint with the U.S. Department of Education's civil rights office in Missouri, which oversees Kentucky.[72] Coleman wanted all Confederate symbols removed at 18 different high schools throughout Kentucky, including the "Rebel" mascot at Todd County. It also diverted attention from the atrocity committed against Michael.

The Westermans' misery mounted with the arrival to Todd County of the Klu Klux Klan. Just like when the NAACP arrives, the Kluxers have a knack for throwing gasoline on a fire. They tried to recruit new members and distributed literature featuring Michael's photograph. "I want that to stop — now," David said. "They have been nice to us, but I don't want my son on their literature." The Klan complied.

Then some guy started selling unauthorized T-shirts with Michael's name for $65 a pop and "not a penny was going to the twins," David said. "Our lawyers put a stop to that." The only group authorized to sell anything associated with Michael was an

SCV camp which sold similar T-shirts for $12. All of the proceeds went to the trust fund set up for the Westerman twins.[73]

Not even the Westermans' home failed to miss scrutiny by the press. One reporter, in a story carried by a national magazine, referred to the Westermans' cozy den as being "cluttered." "That hurt our feelings," said David. Their den walls are covered with Confederate items, but to describe them as being "cluttered," seemed rude if not inaccurate.[74]

For months reporters called or showed up at the Westermans' farm home. Some wanting interviews to write books, others wanting them to appear — with Morrow's and Darden's families — on television shows like Montel Williams and Jerry Springer. Wisdom prevailed, and all offers were declined.

The trial finally began January 9, 1996. When no black jurors could be found, defense attorneys waived their defendants' rights to a jury trial just three days before the proceedings were to begin, leaving the verdict in the hands of Wedemeyer. Bill Goodman, a public defender from Springfield assigned to defend the 15-year-old, said neither expediency nor pre-trial publicity were factors in the decision to waive a jury trial. "The decision, we feel, would be the best way to proceed," he said, adding that Wedemeyer was more than capable to render verdicts.[75]

In opening arguments, defense attorneys agreed the shooting was a tragedy, but that it was not planned. Goodman said his client had just started hanging out "with the big boys" and was in the wrong place at the wrong time.[76] "You've got a bunch of stupid kids caught up in the heat of the moment acting out of control," said Jerry Converse, a Springfield attorney representing Darden.[77] Springfield attorney Collier Goodlett and Carlton Lewis, a black attorney from Nashville who teamed-up to represent Morrow, called the incident a case of "horrible luck."[78] But whatever arguments were chosen, they seemed moot based on the incriminating statements the defendants gave police the day after the shooting. Plus two potent witnesses, Hannah and Andrews, added powerful testimony to the prosecution's case. Andrews identified Darden as the instigator and Morrow as the willing gunman. Converse called Andrews "the state's whore," who was trying to "save his own butt" by making a deal for two years probation in exchange for his testimony against the others.[79]

But prosecutors remained confident about their case. The shooting would not have happened "if Mr. Morrow hadn't been in the Guthrie community, a little street punk from Chicago with a prior history," prosecutor Morriss argued.[80] "Mr. Morrow has an attitude, your honor ..," he added later. "He has a gang tattoo on his arm, a 'gangster disciple' tattoo. He certainly has lived up to his aspirations in life."[81] Morriss' prosecuting colleague, Art Beiber said Darden initiated the chase by driving to two locations to solicit help in "jumping the dude in the truck." "He's the one telling people about some redneck waving a Rebel flag and shouting racial epithets," Beiber said. "He was too chicken to jump the dude until there were nine-plus-a-gun on one."[82]

The judge deliberated about 90 minutes. When he returned, more than a dozen uniformed and civilian-dressed law enforcement officers lined the packed courtroom. His verdict for Morrow: Guilty of civil rights intimidation, attempted aggravated kidnapping, and felony murder. He was acquitted of premeditated murder. "By law the court imposes sentence of imprisonment for life," Wedemeyer said. He found Darden guilty of the same three offenses and sentenced him to life in prison as well. Both will not be eligible for parole for at least 25 years. The 15-year-old was found innocent.

The Westermans burst into tears before exiting the courtroom to a horde of reporters. "I feel everyone should have got what the two got," Hannah said. "They got what they deserved — well, they deserved to die."[83] It's about time someone who's white got to stand up and say, 'Our civil rights were violated.'"[84]

Bell and Mimms were given two years probation in February 1996 and told never to make contact, including chance encounters, with the Westermans again. "If you run into each other at the mall, turn around and go the other way," Bell was warned by his attorney, Edward DeWerff.[85] The incident will be removed from their records in two years, but if they violate their probation at any time they can be brought back for trial on the civil rights intimidation charge. Williams continued to serve time in the Christian County, Kentucky, jail on unrelated charges.

But the convictions of Morrow and Darden for murder were not enough for David who wasted no time in pressing the federal government to file civil rights charges against all seven. But his efforts — supported by many in the South — were met with a seemingly lackadaisical attitude by the U.S. Justice Department. Nearly two years after the shooting David was still trying to get the agency to act. He even raised the issue with a visiting producer from ABC News in July 1996 in hopes the network might do something.[86]

In a May 1996 letter to Michael's widow, Hannah, Deval L. Patrick, assistant attorney general for civil rights, said, "One aspect of that decision (to prosecute) will be determining whether federal jurisdiction exists, since federal criminal civil rights charges can be brought in a crime of violence such as the death of your husband only where there is both a racial motive and interference with a federally protected right. In other words, it is not enough for the purposes of federal criminal civil rights law simply that a victim was selected because of his or her race; in order for federal jurisdiction to be present, the accused must have interferred with a federal protected right as well." In response to why it has taken so long for his office to reach a prosecutive decision, Patrick replied, "When a parallel state prosecution is pending, the federal government defers a prosecutive decision until the conclusion of the state proceeding, since it is our preference, barring exceptional circumstances, that local authorities have the first opportunity to bring the accused swiftly and vigorously to justice."[87]

But *The Washington Times*, after looking into the Westerman case, discovered that Patrick wasted no time in filing federal murder charges, under the hate-crime statute, against two Hispanic and one white for killing a black man in Lubbock, Texas, just two months after Michael was killed. The charges were filed even though Texas had already filed charges against the three men. "This indictment shows that racially motivated killings are not a thing of the past," Patrick said, referring to the Texas case. A Justice Department spokesman told *The Times* that at no time during the first three and one-half years of the (Bill) Clinton administration has a black been prosecuted for a hate crime involving a white.[88] By May 1996, an official with the department's Civil Rights Division told David that the department was reviewing the transcripts from the trial, a process that would take some time. "But please be assured that the task remains a priority matter," the official said.[89]

David did not understand the delay. From his point of view and most Southerners as well, Michael was shot because he flew a Confederate battle flag, which identified his Southern ethnicity. His federally protected right of free speech, as guaranteed in the First Amendment, was clearly violated. Interestingly, the NAACP agreed. For someone "to kill a man because he flew a Confederate flag is clearly a violation of his First Amendment rights," said Neal Darby, executive secretary of the Nashville chapter of the NAACP. "That man (Michael) had a right to fly any type of flag that he chose, even if we don't like that flag."[90] Darby's comments were a surprise given the inflammatory and hateful language the NAACP had been using against the flag.

David has called Patrick's office many times in an effort to get them to do something. Many friends have written letters asking for the same. Even though a federal official attended the trial, for two years all they ever said was that they were "monitoring" or "studying" the case. Their perceived stonewalling hasn't caused David to give up. "I promised my son before we unplugged the life support that I would make sure the people responsible for doing this to him would be brought to justice," he said with tears in his eyes. "The U.S. Justice Department hopes I will go away. But they might as well realize right now that I'm not going away. I promised my boy, and I'm going to keep that promise."[91]

If he is anything, David Westerman is a fighter. He has experienced enough tragedy in his life to have crushed most men. "We have come a long way," he told his Compassionate Friends group at the First Baptist Church of Hopkinsville. Compassionate Friends is a support group the Westermans have joined. It includes parents who have had children die. "When we got married (in 1973) I was making $7 a day," David said. "We had three children; we lost two houses to fires... and we lost my mother (to a heart attack) one month after Michael was murdered. It was more than she could handle. But through all of this, Michael's loss has taken away a part of me."[92]

The death of his 65-year-old mother, Ivy Pearl Westerman, just three weeks after Michael was killed was especially bitter. "It (the shooting) had a greater effect on Michael's grandmother," wrote her sister, Margaret Evans, in a letter to Judge Wedemeyer, asking that he impose life sentences on Morrow and Darden. "She was very close to Michael. She worried and grieved over it until she had a fatal heart attack. We not only lost Michael, but lost his grandmother due to this nonsense."[93]

Two weeks before she died, the twins' grandmother left the two infants a letter for them to read when they get older. "I just want to tell you what your Daddy meant to me," she wrote. "He was a joy from the time he came into this world. He could make you laugh if you didn't want to laugh. As you grow up you will learn more about Daddy, (about) how much he loved you and Mommie. Sorry he had to be taken so soon. Austin, he had so many plans for you and himself. Andrianna, he was so proud of you, he loved you so much. Always keep his memory written in your hearts. Love, Grandma Westerman."[94]

Two years after the shooting, the pain is still felt by the Westermans. "Our friends tell us the grieving process may take six to eight years," says JoAnn. "I really can't imagine it ever ending. Some nights I go to bed and go to sleep. Other nights I just lay there and cry."[95]

David and JoAnn both resented part of a published article they felt implied that their marriage of 23-plus years was in trouble. "As soon as you wake up in the morning you know if it's going to be a good day or a bad day," David said. "If one of us is having a bad day, we've learned to give the other some space." David said they were instructed at a 1996 Compassionate Friends meeting to write notes to their deceased children, put them inside helium balloons, and release them to the sky. David took his yellow balloon and tied it to JoAnn's red one. "I told her I was going to pull her through this mess just like my yellow balloon was going to pull her red one to the clouds."[96]

Friends have noticed how much the ordeal has taken its toll on the Westermans. "I feel closer to the Westerman family than most employers would as they have worked for us for almost 50 years," said A.J. Gray. "Feeling as close to the Westermans as I do, the loss of Michael was painful for our whole family."[97] Andrew Gray described David as a valued and trusted employee. "During this long ordeal David's dedication to us and his job has not lacked, but… nights of poor rest have taken its toll with a look of fatigue and days of just being there. To David's credit, when needed he has always been there to get the job done and we know that has not always been easy as we could see the pain he was in."[98]

JoAnn has often gone to Compassionate Friends twice a month, driving to Fort Campbell, Kentucky, for additional support. She spends some days still going through Michael's childhood things. She has kept an essay he wrote in school and frequently curls up in her favorite den chair and reads it over and over. Though she is often moved to tears, JoAnn, when pushed to the limit, has a fighter's streak as well. "I'm so sick of the Civil War and slavery being an excuse," she said. "My step-father was killed in the Vietnam War. Does that mean I should hate all Vietnamese?"[99]

The mothers of both convicted men apparently asked for assistance in trying to overturn their sons' convictions from the NAACP, American Civil Liberties Union, Jesse Jackson's Operation PUSH, the Black Entertainment Network, and the Congress of Racial Equality. Their requests were reportedly rejected. "But what they don't understand is they killed a redneck in redneck country," Darden's mother, Louise Terry, said in an astonishingly callous manner, adding that she didn't regret teaching Darden to fight. "I'd rather him come out on top," she said. "I'd rather be Ms. Terry right now than Mrs. Westerman. It's survival."[100]

Much like John Brown's murderous raid on Harper's Ferry and call for blacks to kill white Southerners in 1859, the Westerman murder seemed to serve as a close-striking lightning bolt to Southerners. Most Southerners had been too pre-occupied with other matters to get involved in the battle flag debate. Others, in their quintessentially Southern ways, graciously listened to the hate rhetoric spewed by the NAACP and other anti-flag groups. For a large number of Southerners, the flag has been a secondary issue to what they feel are more pressing problems like rising taxes, dwindling paychecks, education, and breakdown of the family. Consequently the debate has been left to groups like the NAACP and the SCV. But with Michael's death, other Southerners began joining in. As one Southerner put it, "They thought we were done, but when they stuck their fork in us, we woke up."

Read Majors of Lebanon, Tennessee, expressed the sentiments of a growing number of Southerners in a letter to a newspaper. "If we are to throw out every offensive thing in this country, who will be the judge? Who will decide what goes and what stays — the government, the churches, the various advocacy groups? Is anybody out there willing to put this endangered freedom in somebody else's hands? You may despise me and my symbols, but when mine go, yours are next."[101]

Carlie Butler of Hopkinsville, Kentucky, put it this way:

Now, the issue is not whether the Confederate symbol is offensive to some; the issue is whether public officials can be blackmailed into action by criminal behavior. The Confederate flag, in truth, is not about racism, it's about states' rights. We are in danger today of a different type of enslavement, which threatens to destroy our nation. This is the enslavement of ideas, the theory of politically cor-

*rectness. We cannot allow other people to tell us
what we must think.*[102]

Support even came from Northern states, like the letter written
to a Southern publication by Father Peter M. Donish, a Catholic
priest from Beaver Meadows, Pennsylvania:

> *I'm a staunch supporter of the Confederate
> battle flag. Critics say it is a symbol of racism, etc.
> I say that it is a symbol of all that was good and is
> good of the South: bravery, dedication, loyalty,
> Christian moral values....*[103]

The brouhaha over the flag — and Michael's death — has
given rise to new organizations across the South. The Southern
League, which is composed largely of professors and scholars
from Southern universities, started having their views published in
newspapers like the *Washington Post.* Lobbying efforts for the
preservation of Southern heritage took flight due to new groups
like The Confederate Society of America, the Heritage Preservation Association in Georgia, the Confederate Heritage Fund in
Alabama, and Preserving Our Heritage, Inc., in Florida. A network
of Southern attorneys — spanning six Southern states plus New
Jersey — formed the Southern Attorney's Council to provide
badly needed legal expertise. Southerners showed renewed interest in heritage organizations like the SCV, the United Daughters of
the Confederacy, Order of Confederate Rose (wives of SCV
members), and the Children of the Confederacy.

Whether the number of changed attitudes in the South is
sufficient in quantity and quality to save the battle flag and Dixie's
heritage remains to be seen. But this much is known, for the first
time, the Westerman shooting made it appear that some anti-flag
people are willing to use violence to impose and enforce their
views on the matter. Their crocodile tears linking the flag to slavery
will not stand up to historic truth. When Morrow shot Michael, he
might as well have shot the South. Ultimately, the battle flag and
the South are inseparable. "It's an especially critical time for us to
clear the air because of the Westerman trial," said Mark Choate of
Brentwood, Tennessee. "A lot of people are watching it and
believe wrong things about the symbol. If I choose to fly a flag in
my yard or have a decal on my vehicle, which I do, what is to stop
them from taking a gun and going after me and others when we
have no desire or wish to upset anyone of either race."[104]

Then, on August 17, 1995, it happened again. A car load of

black men pulled into a youth recreation center in Evansville, Indiana, stopping at least three times to ask what two Confederate flags in the back of a nearby pick-up truck meant. "I think they were just looking for trouble," said the center's manager, Carson Harl. "That's what they came here for, to find out what the flags stood for, why the kids had them." When they stopped the final time, they reportedly asked if anyone wanted to fight. Jeremy Mabis, a 19-year-old white man stepped forward with some others and asked them to leave. Two blacks, one with a gun, jumped out of the car. One reportedly pinned Mabis against a car while the other fired one shot with a Ruger 9mm semi-automatic handgun, grazing Mabis's neck and striking a finger. Both of Mabis's attackers were charged with attempted murder.[105] "We explained it to them (teens at the rec center), that it's (the flag) offensive to some people," Harl said. "I think they understand because what happened was so serious."[106] Several of the youth at the center said they did not fly the flag as a racial statement, but that some flew it to proclaim their Southern heritage, while others displayed it as a symbol of freedom or just for the fun of it. "The bottom line is that there could be a dozen different reasons," said Evansville Police Detective David Wires. "There were kids out there with a gun, and they shot this kid. That's the bottom line."[107]

Much more than any previous acts of violence, the two shootings were a severe blow to the anti-flag movement. Michael's death, in particular, cost the anti-flaggers the moral high ground. How could the anti-flaggers continue to condemn the battle flag without looking like anti-First Amendment lunatics who condone murder? Yet a black college student, who was an acquaintance of the one of the men arrested in the Indiana shooting, had this chilling comment about the flag and the First Amendment: "I think the Confederate flag should be illegal, just like it's illegal to yell fire in a crowded building. They wave their flag, call people niggers and then when something happens, they turn it around and call themselves victims and say they're just exercising their freedom of speech."[108]

The NAACP seemed to be its usual contradictory self following the two shootings. Since Michael was killed, it had no choice but to acknowledge his right to fly the flag. But after the Indiana incident, Nelson B. Rivers, southeast director of the NAACP, resorted to his organization's typical demagoguery. "Anyone who suggests that it is not a symbol of racism and segregation does not understand history or is just lying," he said. "Children need to understand that the flag represents people who committed treason against the United States. That's the flag that was flown above the army that attacked the United States government. The Confederate flag was the celebration of the enslavement of African-Americans in this country. It was the symbol of the force that was delivered to maintain that system. People who argue that the Civil War was not about slavery are just lying."[109]

The anti-flaggers' only salvation to date has been a largely sympathetic news media, who continues to express views much like those of Rivers. One talk show host in Nashville frequently likens the battle flag to a Nazi swastika, while a public television station talk show host in the same city grudgedly concedes the First Amendment issue on the battle flag, but then says the "Confederate flag means nigger." Isn't it interesting how it's the anti-flaggers who use the "N" word, not the Southern preservationists who denounce its usage? Since Michael's death, the South's large metropolitan newspapers have excoriated the flag in unprecedented numbers, adding fuel to an already acrimonious debate.

Renewed interest by Southerners in saving their heritage seems to have unnerved liberal members of the press. An over-wrought reporter with a New York publication wrote that there is a struggle underway in the South "fueled by a burgeoning and sophisticated cadre of Southern 'nationalists' who feed on modern fears of dwindling status and on nostalgic images of a South that is cohesive, distinct, and independent from the rest of America."[110] An ultra-liberal "alternative" tabloid in Nashville hysterically proclaimed "a streak of Confederate Nationalism that reinforces the feeling that the conflict between North and South was never resolved."[111]

The SCV seemed to be a primary target of the media. An *Atlanta Journal Constitution* article claimed the SCV was promoting sedition. A Nasvhille television reporter ended a report on the Westerman murder by saying "this trial proves the Confederate flag is still a problem." That remark, possibly innocent, sparked phone calls of protest to the station. David Westerman called the reporter, saying he interpreted the report to mean that "Michael was at fault for exercising his Constitutional right to fly the battle flag." The shaken reporter stood by the story and acknowledged that was not what was meant. "The problem is they murdered my son," David said. "They are the ones with the problem." The reporter apologized.[112] Then another reporter with *New Yorker* magazine accused "'Southern-heritage' groups (among them the Sons of Confederate Veterans)... (of) exploiting Westerman's murder." David, a member of the SCV, said that was untrue. The SCV established a trust fund for the Westermans' surviving twins. By mid-1996 the fund had received more than $43,000 in donations and funds were still being accepted. Exploitive? "They (SCV members) are the only people who check on us anymore," David said. "I don't know what we would have done without them. We tried to send thank you cards to all the camps, but we may have missed some. I want them to know that we appreciate everything they've done."[113] Hannah agreed. "The Sons of Confederate Veterans were real respectful," she said when the organization sponsored a large memorial service about two months after the shooting. "They didn't want to do anything that would embarrass us."[114]

A few months after the trial, *The Tennessean,* a politically liberal newspaper in generally conservative Middle Tennessee, printed a story examining how the families involved in the Westerman tragedy were coping. Late in the story, the writer seemed to take aim at the SCV: "Getting the most mileage out of Michael's death are the Sons of Confederate Veterans, who attract white supremacists and separatists."[115] Members of the heritage organization went ballistic. Many SCV members throughout Tennessee called the newspaper, while others wrote angry letters to the editor. Norman Dasinger, then SCV commander-in-chief, bypassed the editor and responded directly to the newspaper's publisher. "This statement by your newspaper about the SCV is false and defamatory. It is extremely unfortunate that (the reporters) did not, to my best knowledge and belief, make any attempt to talk to any spokesman of the SCV before slandering my charitable organization. The SCV demands and anticipates receiving from *The Tennessean* a full and complete public apology and retraction of its libelous statements made against the SCV."[116] Dasinger's letter was accompanied by a more legal explanation from an attorney representing the SCV.

A few days later a positive article about the SCV appeared, making it clear the organization is not like the Klu Klux Klan and does not seek to attract racists. Meanwhile, local media critic Richard Pride picked up on the controversy for the rival and more politically moderate *Nashville Banner.* Editors at *The Tennessean* confessed to Pride that the SCV had been "miscast" and responded with the story differentiating the SCV from the Klan. Pride lauded

The Tennessean for its action, but added, "It would have been better still if *The Tennessean* had told readers, straight out, what it was doing and why. Paradoxically, only by admitting errors and making corrections openly will newspapers be fully trusted."[117]

About three weeks after the two stories were published, a lawyer for *The Tennessean,* in a letter to the SCV, offered the organization an opportunity to write a second piece describing its nature and purpose, presumably if it would drop the matter.[118] The SCV accepted the offer, but the guest column by SCV member Wes Shofner, a Nashville attorney and Harvard graduate, ended up being a searing attack on the politically correct movement. "Under the dual banners of 'sensitivity' and 'tolerance,' the politically correct attack those with whom they disagree. But such attacks are rarely armed with either logic or history. Instead, the politically correct employ the invective. As one of millions of Americans who venerate their Confederate ancestors, I, along with my fellow Southerners, have suffered needlessly from the ceaseless harangues of the politically correct. Recent local examples of such attacks are the following: the 'sensitive' pronouncement by Professor Bobby Lovett of Tennessee State University that the 'Confederacy was evil then and is evil now;' the 'tolerant' proclamation by John Seigenthaler, the grand pooh-bah of free speech, that the 'Confederate flag means nigger;' the vile murder of Michael Westerman for displaying his Confederate flag; and the statement by *The Tennessean* that the SCV 'attracts white supremacists and separatists.' If this, the bloodiest of all centuries, has taught us anything, I hope and pray that it has taught us that by projecting evil onto one people, we are unleashing the evil in ourselves. Struggling against the evil in oneself is struggle enough. It is time for all of us to cease being politically correct and start being truly tolerant."[119]

Things settled down between Nashville's morning newspaper and the SCV, but the heated exchange between the two was a classic example of how one pro-flag group and the largely anti-flag news media clashed. It was another example of the profound impact Michael's death had on the South.

There were, however, a handful of Southern newspapers which defended the battle flag after the shooting. *The Augusta (Georgia) Chronicle* called on other newspapers "to use photos and images of the battle flag accurately and judiciously when reporting on issues with racial overtones. Always associating the historical battle flag with hate groups is misleading, inaccurate and often inflammatory."[120] *The Sun News* of Myrtle Beach, South Carolina, chastised hate groups for misusing the battle flag, stating it "should be separated from the Klan, which had no business using it."[121] The *Kentucky New Era* of Hopkinsville encouraged Todd countians to "quit focusing on the Confederate flag as the source of racial conflict" and to refrain from making a hasty decision on banishing a long-time Confederate mascot from Todd County High School.[122] "Any immediate capitulation on the Rebel flag and soldier sends the wrong message that violence is a viable option in formenting change," the newspaper stated.[123]

Much has happened since the Westerman trial. Morrow had nine years added onto his life sentence because of the kidnapping and civil rights intimidation charges. Darden had four years added to his time for the same offenses. "It must be made clear that this type of senseless violence cannot be tolerated and must be dealt with severely," Judge Wedemeyer said in adding the sentences.[124] Appeals for a new trial were filed in behalf of Morrow and Darden in August 1996. Both were denied. Meanwhile, Hannah filed a $12 million wrongful death lawsuit against Morrow, Darden, Andrews, and the 15-year-old. "Some people in prison write stories, sell books, and sometimes make movies. If they do that, and we have a judgment against them, Hannah and the children will collect it," said Nashville attorney, Lucien Dale, who represented Hannah in the suit. "In this case, that likelihood certainly exists. Of course two of them aren't in prison and they'll be out working, I hope. A portion of their wages will be garnished for a very long time, if the judgment against them is declared."[125]

Rueters news service reported in December 1996 that a Hollywood director was interested in making yet another film about racism in the South. Norman Jewison, who was nominated for an Oscar for best director for "In the Heat of the Night" in 1967, wants to focus the film on the Westerman shooting.

Many Southerners are already bracing themselves, fearful Jewison will make Westerman look like the bad guy. They have good reason given all the South-bashing Hollywood has slopped on the silver screen in recent years. News of the impending film made one SCV computer hacker to lament on the Internet, "The Westerman project will portray Southerners as we are now, when we do mean things like vote Republican, wave our forefathers' flag, and believe in Jesus."

Jewison need not expect a parade when he arrives in Todd County (except from maybe the KKK or the NAACP). Todd countians would just as soon Jewison choke on his idea. But that seemed unlikely as the curtain fell on 1996. Said Jewison colleague Gayle Fraser-Baigelman: "It's an attempt to re-examine something he's looked at in the past with an idea toward the future."

Some southerners held a glimmer of hope that Jewison's film might tell the truth. He reportedly hired Robby Henson, a documentaty filmmaker as his script writer. Henson wrote and directed a feature film called "In Pharoah's Army," a movie generally viewed as pro-Southern. Still, given Hollywood's obsession with revisionist history and anti-Southern films, most people in Dixie remained apprehensive about the Jewison project.

Hannah has also remarried. She married Joe Pewitt of Lyles, Tennessee, June 1, 1996. They met when Pewitt sold some insurance to Hannah's father for his saw mill. Both David and JoAnn Westerman attended the wedding. "We're happy for Hannah," said David. "She still has a whole life ahead of her."[126]

While the debate over the battle flag continues to rage around them, the Westermans remain an integral part of that discourse. But to them, it's something far more profound than just a debate over the battle flag; for in the midst of the often heated discussion, their only son was killed.

David keeps a notebook filled with articles about Michael's death. "I've kept these clippings because I want the twins to know what happened to their daddy," he says, wiping the tears from his face. Then with a grin he recalls the first deer Michael killed — just a few weeks before his death. "It was a 10-point buck, but he never got to see it mounted. But it's mounted now."[127]

It is one of many fitting tributes to Michael that have been saved for the Westerman twins, a sure-to-be cherished heirloom from their father whom they will never know.

ENDNOTES

CHAPTER ONE

1. Davis, Jefferson. *Rise and Fall of the Confederate Government.*

2. McPherson, James M. *Battle Cry of Freedom.* New York, Oxford: Oxford University Press, 1988. 287-288.

3. Rutherford, Mildred Lewis. *The South Must Have Her Rightful Place In History.* Athens, Georgia, 1923. 5.

4. McPherson. *Battle Cry.* 560, quote from Wood Gray, *The Hidden Civil War: The Story of the Copperheads* (New York, 1942), 112.

5. McPherson. *Battle Cry.* 561.

6. McPherson. *Battle Cry.* 609-610.

7. McPherson. *Battle Cry.* 287-289.

8. Safire, William. Freedom. Garden City, New York: Doubleday & Company, Inc. 1987) taken from *John Hay's real diary for September 25, 1864,* also in Donn Piatt's *Memories of the Men Who Saved the Union.* 291-295.

9. April 1995 Associated Press article concerning study conducted by Dr. John Shelton Reed of the University of North Carolina-Chapel Hill.

10. Thomas, Jo. "New history standards reflect critics' attacks." *New York Times* April 1996.

11. Chambers, Herbert O. III. Letter to the editor, *Southern Partisan.* 4th quarter 1994. 3.

12. Simmons, Henry E. *The Concise Encyclopedia of the Civil War.* New York: The Fairfax Press, 1986. 103-105.

13. Goolsby, Charles. "To Live and Die For Dixie." *Southern Partisan.* 4th quarter 1994. 16, 20-21.

14. Smith, Whitney. *Flags Through the Ages and Across the World.* New York, 1975. 124.

15. Blackaby, Henry T. and King, Claude V. *The Experiencing God Study Bible*, Nashville: Broadman & Holman Publishers, 1994), 1467.

16. Foxe, John. *Foxe's Book of Martyrs.* Philadelphia. 30.

17. Smith, *Flags Through the Ages.* 175.

18. Mackie, J.D. *A History of Scotland.* London: Penguin Books, 1991. 18.

19. Carr, H. Gresham. *Flags of the World.* London, 1953. 34-35.

20. DuRocher, Steve. Article, *Southern Partisan.* 2nd quarter, 1995. 45.

21. Carr. *Flags.* 32-33.

22. Smith. *Flags Through the Ages.*

23. Carr. *Flags.* 32-33.

24. Davis, Jefferson. Speech as presented by the Memphis Commerical Appeal, delivered in Memphis on St. Andrew's Day 1875.

25. Carr. *Flags.* 32-33

26. Mackie. *A History of Scotland.* 16.

27. Carr. *Flags.* 32-33.

28. Kennedy, Billy. *The Scots-Irish in the Hills of Tennessee.* Londonderry: Causeway Press, 1995.

29. Herm, Gerhard. *The Celts: The People Who Came Out of the Darkness.* New York: St. Martin's Press, 1975).

30. McWhiney, Grady. *Cracker Culture: Celtic Ways in the Old South.* Tuscaloosa and London: The University of Alabama Press, 1988. xiii.

31. Grenier, Richard. "Braveheart: Legacy of a People," *Reader's Digest* March 1996, 69.

32. Grenier. "Braveheart." *Reader's Digest* March 1996, 69.

33. Kennedy. *The Scots-Irish.* 17.

34. McWhiney. *Cracker Culture.* xiii.

35. McWhiney. *Cracker Culture.* xiv.

36. Chaplin, Joyce E. *"Climate and Southern Pessimism."* The South as an American Problem. Ed. Larry J. Griffin and Don H. Doyle. Athens and London: University of Georgia Press, 1995. 69.

37. Watkins, Samuel R. Co. Aytch: *A Side Show of the Big Show.* Wilmington: Broadfoot Publishing Co. 1987. 49.

38. *Confederate Veteran.* "Historical Committee Report." 25 April 1906.

39. Grenier. "Braveheart." *Reader's Digest.* March 1996, 69.

40. Kennedy. *The Scots-Irish.* 30.

41. Grenier, "Braveheart." *Reader's Digest.* March 1996. 69.

42. Herm. *The Celts.* 3.

43. Herm. *The Celts.* 4.

44. McPherson. *Battle Cry.* 344.

45. *Confederate Veteran.* "Flag History." April 1896. 116.

46. Barrett, Samuel. *Letter from the William Porcher Miles Papers, Southern Historical Collection,* the library of the University of North Carolina at Chapel Hill.

47. Kennedy. *The Scots-Irish.* 18.

48. Romero, Sidney J. *Religion in the Rebel Ranks.* Lanham, Maryland, 1983. 3-4.

49. Romero. *Religion.* 5-6.

50. *Confederate Veteran.* "Religion in the Southern Army." January 1893. 15.

51. Norton, Herman. *Rebel Religion: The Story of Confederate Chaplains.* The Bethany Press, 1961. 64-65.

52. Norton, *Rebel Religion.* 65.

53. "Sermon Before The Reunion" by Rev. J.B. Hawthorne of First Baptist Church of Atlanta. *Confederate Veteran.* August 1897. 411-412.

54. Hawthorne sermon. *Confederate Veteran.* 411.

55. Hawthorne sermon. *Confederate Veteran.* 411.

56. "Cutting the Flag in Two — A Clever Suggestion." *Confederate Veteran.* April 1896. 116-117.

57. Journal of the Provisional Congress. 4 March 1861. 101-102.

58. Cannon, Devereaux D. Jr. *The Flags of the Confederacy.* (Gretna, Louisiana: Pelican Publishing Co. 1994. 7.

59. Cannon. *The Flags.* 7-8.

60. *Southern Historical Society Papers.* Vol. 38, "The Flag of the Confederate States of America." 251-252.

61. *Southern Historical Society Papers.* Vol. 38, "The Flag of the Confederate States of America. 252.

62. *Southern Historical Society Papers.* Vol. 38, "The Flag of the Confederate States of America." 253.

63. *Southern Historical Society Papers.* Vol. 38, "The Flag of the Confederate States of America. 252.

64. *Journal of the Provisional Congress.* 4 March 1861. 101.

65. *Southern Historical Society Papers.* Vol. 38, "The Flag of the Confederate States of America. 4 March 1861. 255.

66. Cannon. *The Flags of the Confederacy.* 8.

67. Cannon. *The Flags of the Confederacy.* 7.

68. Eggenberger, David. *Flags of the U.S.A.* Thomas Y. Crowell Co. 1959. 138.

69. *Southern Historical Society Papers.* Vol. 8, "Origin of the Confederate Battle Flag." 497-499.

70. *Southern Historical Society Papers.* Vol. 38, "Flags of the Confederate States of America." 259.

71. *Southern Historical Society Papers.* Vol. 38, "Flags of the Confederate States of America." 259.

72. *Southern Historical Society Papers.* Vol. 38, "Flags of the Confederate States of America." 259.

73. *Southern Historical Society Papers.* Vol. 38, "Flags of the Confederate States of America." 259.

74. *Southern Historical Society Papers.* Vol. 12, "Flag Presentation to the Washington Artillery." 29-30.

75. *Southern Historical Society Papers.* Vol. 38, "Flags of the Confederate States of America." 259-260.

76. *Southern Historical Society Papers.* Vol. 12, "Flag Presentation to the Washington Artillery." 29.

77. *Southern Historical Society Papers.* Vol. 38, "Flags of the Confederate States of America." 260.

78. *Journal of the Provisional Congress* 4 March 1861. 102.

79. *Southern Historical Society Papers.* Vol. 8, "Origin of the Confederate Battle Flag. 499.

80. *Southern Historical Society Papers.* Vol. 12, "Flag Presentation to the Washington Artillery." 31.

81. *Southern Historical Society Papers.* Vol. 12, "Flag Presentation to the Washington Artillery." 31-32.

82. *Southern Historical Society Papers.* Vol. 12, "Flag Presentation to the Washington Artillery." 32.

CHAPTER TWO

1. Jennings, Bill. Telephone interview with author, March 28, 1996.

2. Jennings, Bill. Telephone interview with author, March 28, 1996.

3. Zeirke, James W. Letter to the editor. *Southern Partisan.* 3rd Quarter, 1995.

4. Buchanan, Patrick J. "Battle over a flag." *New York Post,* July 27, 1994.

5. Sandel, Matthew. "In Defense of Dixie and Our Flag" cassette tape, All-Media, 1992.

6. Rutherford, Mildred Lewis. *The South Must Have Her Rightful Place in History.* March 1923, 1.

7. "Confederate Flag Not Infamous." *Confederate Veteran.* April 1897, 161.

8. "Confederate Flag Not Infamous." *Confederate Veteran.* April 1897, 161.

9. "Confederate Flag Not Infamous." *Confederate Veteran.* April 1897, 161.

10. "Confederate Flag Not Infamous." *Confederate Veteran.* April 1897, 161.

11. "Confederate Flag Not Infamous." *Confederate Veteran.* April 1897, 161.

12. Rollins, Richard. *The Flags of the Confederate Armies.* Redondo Beach, California: Rank and File Publications, 1995.

13. "Banners of Glory." Arts and Entertainment Network special, spring 1996.

14. Rollins, Richard. *The Flags of the Confederate Armies.* Redondo Beach, California: Rank and File Publications, 1995.

15. Tanner, James. *Washington Post,* Letter to the Editor reprinted in *Confederate Veteran.* July 1898, 338.

16. Carroon, Robert Girard. Letter to William Crowley, museum administrator, State Historical Museum, 28 December 1992.

17. Survey, *U.S. News & World Report,* August 15, 1994.

18. McPherson, James M. *Battle Cry of Freedom.* New York and Oxford: Oxford University Press, 1988, 854, 856.

19. Lewellen, Faye. "Limbs Made and Unmade by War." *America's Civil War,* September 1995. 38-39.

20. Lewellen, Faye. "Aid For Disabled Veterans." *America's Civil War,* September 1995. 40.

21. Hesseltine, William B. *The South in American History.* New York: Prentice-Hall Inc. 1943.

22. Hanley, Ray. *Civil War Times Illustrated* January-February 1992. 45.

23. Andrews, Gene. Telephone interview. 29 March 1996.

24. Beauregard, G.T. Letter contained in *Southern Historical Society Papers,* Vol. 38, 259-260.

25. Coski, John M. "The Confederate Battle Flag in American History and Culture." *Southern Cultures,* Vol. 2, No. 2, 1996.

26. Horwitz, Tony. "A Death For Dixie." *The New Yorker,* 18 March 1996. 72.

27. Dasinger, Norman. Telephone interview. 3 April 1996.

28. Coski, John M. "The Confederate Battle Flag in American History and Culture." *Southern Cultures,* Vol. 2, No. 2, 1996.

29. *The Huntsville Times,* April 21, 1996 (some information taken from the *Montgomery Advertiser,* April 1963).

30. Roberts, Timothy. "Lest We Forget." *Nashville Scene* 25 February 1993.

31. Coski, John M. "The Confederate Battle Flag in American History and Culture." *Southern Cultures,* Vol. 2, No. 2, 1996.

32. Hesseltine, William B. *The South in American History*: New York Prentice-Hall Inc. 1943, 267-268.

33. Winbush, Nelson. Personal interview with author, 21 May 1996.

34. Coski, John M. "The Confederate Battle Flag in American History and Culture." *Southern Cultures,* Vol. 2, No. 2, 1996.

35. Coski, John M. "The Confederate Battle Flag in American History and Culture." *Southern Cultures,* Vol. 2, No. 2, 1996. (Originally appeared in Woodward's "The Burden of Southern

36. Roberts, Timothy. "Lest We Forget." *Nashville Scene* 25 February 1993.

37. Coski, John M. "The Confederate Battle Flag in American History and Culture." *Southern Cultures,* Vol. 2, No. 2, 1996.

38. Coski, John M. "The Confederate Battle Flag in American History and Culture." *Southern Cultures,* Vol. 2, No. 2, 1996.

39. Coski, John M. "The Confederate Battle Flag in American History and Culture." *Southern Cultures,* Vol. 2, No. 2, 1996.

40. Stuart, J.E.B. IV. Telephone interview 4 April 1996.

41. Clemmons, Ronald T. Telephone interview 3 April 1996.

42. Reed, John Shelton. Telephone interview 11 April 1996.

43. Dasinger, Norman. Telephone interview 3 April 1996.

44. Douglas, W. Earl. "Don't Furl the Flag!" *Southern Partisan.* (Richard Quinn column) reprint of Douglas' April 27, 1979 column in *The Charleston (S.C.) News and Courier,* 2nd Quarter 1991, 5.

45. Coski, John M. "The Confederate Battle Flag in American History and Culture." *Southern Cultures,* Vol. 2, No. 2, 1996.

46. Sheehan, Ruth. "Roots or Racism?" *San Francisco Examiner* 5 May 1996.

47. Massey, Jeff. Telephone interview 4 April 1996.

48. Dasinger, Norman. Telephone interview 3 April 1996.

49. Dasinger, Norman. Telephone interview 3 April 1996.

50. Thomas, Wendi C. "A Murder's Legacy." *The Tennessean* 21 April 1996, 12A.

51. Buchanan, Patrick J. "Battle Over A Flag." *New York Post* 27 July 1994.

52. Buchanan, Patrick J. "Battle Over A Flag." *New York Post* 27 July 1994.

53. Eads, Brian. "Slavery's Shameful Return to Africa." *Reader's Digest* March 1996, 77-81.

54. Coski, John M. "The Confederate Battle Flag in American History and Culture." *Southern Cultures,* Vol. 2, No. 2, 1996.

CHAPTER 3

1. Lincoln's violations of the Constitution are contained in Mildred Rutherford's *The South Must Have Her Rightful Place in History.* March 1923, 5. The casualty figure comes from James McPherson's *Battle Cry of Freedom.* New York and Oxford: Oxford University Press, 1988, 854. Lincoln's alleged lack of Christian beliefs comes from Rutherford's book and William Safire's *Freedom.* Garden City, New York: Doubleday & Company, Inc. 1987.

2. Reagan, John H. "Reconstruction." *Confederate Veteran.* July 1897, 346.

3. Roberts, Timothy. "Lest We Forget." *Nashville Scene* 25 February 1993, 10.

4. Smith, Ed. Video lecture produced by Preserving Our Heritage Inc. spring 1996.

5. Rice, Marc. "Will the Georgia flag fly? Flag's foes threatening to protest Super Bowl." The Associated Press 27 January 1994.

6. Rice, Marc. "Will the Georgia flag fly?" The Associated Press 27 January 1994.

7. "Confederate son fights for battle flag." The Associated Press 31 January 1994.

8. "Confederate son fights for battle flag." The Associated Press 31 January 1994.

9. Jackson quote in *Los Angeles Times* 19 July 1995.

10. Coski, John M. "The Confederate Battle Flag in American History and Culture." *Southern Cultures,* Vol. 2, No. 2, 1996.

11. Bragg, Rick. "Frankly, my dear, Scarlett's not part of Atlanta Olympic plans." *The Tennessean* from the *New York Times* News Service 19 May 1996, 2D.

12. Bragg, Rick. "Frankly, my dear, Scarlett's not part of Atlanta Olympic plans." *The Tennessean* from the *New York Times* News Service 19 May 1996.

13. Rice, Marc. "Will the Georgia flag fly?" The Associated Press 27 January 1994.

14. Rice, Marc. "Will the Georgia flag fly?" The Associated Press 27 January 1994.

15. Reynolds, Jim. Telephone interview 16 July 1996.

16. February 1996 SCV newsletter taken from *Philadelphia Inquirer* story published 19 January 1996.

17. Reynolds, Jim. Telephone interview 16 July 1996.

18. "Suit Against Flag Dismissed." The Associated Press 4 January 1996.

19. Buchanan, Patrick J. "Battle Over A Flag." *New York Post* 27 July 1994.

20. SCV newsletter which contains quote from conversation between Mr. Smith and SCV member John Courtney.

21. Sullivan, Chris. "Hootie and the Blowfish Update." *The Carolina Confederate* November/December 1995. Rucker's "asinine" quote taken from *Rolling Stone* magazine.

22. Robertson, John. Letter to the editor. *Southern Partisan.* 3rd Quarter 1994.

23. Sullivan, Bill. "A Disaster in Alabama." *Grey Matter* newsletter January 1995.

24. Kesten, Fred. Letter to the editor. *Southern Partisan.* 2nd Quarter 1995.

25. Personal letter from Nathan Bedford Forrest Camp No. 125 of SCV to James Anderson, 3 January 1996.

26. Thomas, William. "Quote skirmish pits student, yearbook." *Memphis Commercial Appeal* 25 January 1994.

27. "National Heritage Violations Listing." *Dixie Messenger* 9 January 1996.

28. "National Heritage Violations Listing." *Dixie Messenger* 9 January 1996. Also Associated Press reports.

29. "Boy Suspended for wearing flag jacket to troubled school." The Associated Press 16 January 1996.

30. Berryhill, Bill. "Confederate Flag Lapel Pin Causes Harnett High School Student Removal." *The Carolina Confederate* March/April 1996.

31. Reynolds, Jim. Telephone interview 17 July 1996.

32. "Todd flag draws complaint." *Kentucky New Era* 23 June 1995.

33. "Blackville Flag Lawsuit Settled." *The Carolina Confederate* March/April 1996.

34. Lambert, Marion. Telephone interview 11 June 1996.

35. Lambert, Marion. Telephone interview 11 June 1996.

36. Corley, Mike. Telephone interview 9 April 1996.

37. Hurst, Jack. *Nathan Bedford Forrest: A Biography.* New York: Alfred A. Knopf. 1993. 97-103.

38. "Confederate flag gone." The Associated Press 29 October 1993.

39. Higgins Randall. "Still Drawing Fire: Defiant Confederate descendants fly banner." *The Chattanooga Times* 29 July 1995. A1, A3.

40. Higgins, Randall. "Still Drawing Fire." *The Chattanooga Times* 29 July 1995. A1.

41. Higgins, Randall. "Still Drawing Fire." *The Chattanooga Times* 29 July 1995. A3.

42. Turnbull, Amy E. "Flag Flying: Confederates Say Visit Positive." *Chattanooga Free Press* 30 July 1995. A1.

43. Turnbull, Amy E. "Flag Flying: Confederates Say Visit Positive." *Chattanooga Free Press* 30 July 1995. 1A.

44. SCV paid advertisement. *Chattanooga Free Press* 30 July 1995.

45. "Smile, You're On Candid Camera." *SCV Gray Line* September 1995 taken from Chattanooga Free Press 7 September 1995.

46. Roberts, Gene. Letter to Lawrence Fafarman 22 September 1995.

47. Fafarman, Lawrence. Letter to Mayor Gene Roberts.

48. Moore, Kimberly C. "Rebel flag talk sways senators." *Nashville Banner* 26 July 1993.

49. Moore, Kimberly C. "Rebel flag talk sways senators." *Nashville Banner* 26 July 1993.

50. "Consistency Not The Trademark of Senator Moseley-Braun." *The Gray Line* newsletter August 1995.

51. "Who really has Grace Under Fire?" *Southern Partisan.* 3rd Quarter 1995. 11.

52. "Heritage Chairman Debates South Carolina Activist." *Confederate Veteran.* Vol. 2, 1996.

53. Tucker Tom. Telephone interview 11 April 1996.

54. Lambert, Marion. Telephone interview 11 June 1996.

55. "Confederate flag waves at Danville." *Southern Partisan.* 1st Quarter 1995.

56. Mitchell, R.M. Jr. Letter to H. Wayne Bibee 2 January 1996.

57. Stocker, Carol. "Young rebel's flag meets with protest at Harvard." *The Charlotte (N.C.) Observer* 15 April 1991.

58. Jones, Michael Dan. "The Battle of Lake Charles: A Case Study For Saving A Confederate Monument." *Confederate Veteran.* Vol. 1 1996. 21-24.

59. Ferris, William D. Jr. Letter to ABC Television 29 March 1996.

60. Francis, Samuel. "North carries banner for cultural warriors." Tribune Media Services Inc. 1 October 1994.

61. Smith, Eugene. "Kirkpatrick: Remove the Confederate Flag." *Crestview News Leader* 14 February 1996.

62. Coleman, Anthony. "New nickname a part of Belmont's move up." *The Tennessean* 23 September 1995.

63. Lambert, Marion. Telephone interview 6 June 1996,

64. "U.S. Army Orders Confederate Flag Removed." *The Carolina Confederate* March/April 1996.
65. Mortham, Sandra B. "Confederate Flag A Historical Record." *St. Petersburg Times* Op/Ed page 27 April 1996.
66. "Group wants to fly `Stars and Bars.' The Associated Press 25 March 1996.
67. "Judge at South Carolina Hearing Defends the Confederacy." *The Carolina Confederate* March/April 1996.
68. "Ed Hooper Receives Two Awards." *The Knoxville Guard* May 1996 newsletter taken from the Metro Pulse.
69. "Wise Council." *Southern Partisan.* 3rd Quarter 1994.
70. Robinson, Bob. Letter to the editor. *Southern Partisan.* 1st Quarter 1995. 3-4.
71. Powell, Frank. Letter to Governor James B. Hunt 8 April 1996.
72. Meetze, Ralph. Telephone interview 3 April 1996.
73. Vanauken, Sheldon. "Warning Symbol." *Southern Partisan.* 3rd Quarter 1994.
74. *Philadelphia Inquirer* article 22 August 1994.
75. "Victory Parade!" *Aide-De-Camp* newsletter July 1996.

CHAPTER 4

1. Nelson Winbush speech given to SCV Sam Watkins Camp No. 29 in Columbia, Tennessee 20 May 1996.
2. Winbush speech.
3. Winbush speech.
4. Schmich, Mary. "Patriot flies flag in face of threat." *Chicago Tribune* 16 February 1994.
5. Schmich, Mary. "Patriot flies flag in face of threat." *Chicago Tribune* 16 February 1994.
6. Schmich, Mary. "Patriot flies flag in face of threat." *Chicago Tribune* 16 February 1994.
7. "Flag Flies Again in Danville." *The Captain's Call* SCV newsletter April 1995.
8. Interview with Patrick M. McSweeney. *Southern Partisan.* 2nd Quarter 1995. 35.
9. Smith, Ed. Video tape lecture produced in Florida by Preserving Our Heritage Inc. spring 1996.
10. Smith video, spring 1996.
11. Douglas, W. Earl. "Don't Furl the Flag." *The Charleston (S.C.) News and Courier* 27 April 1979. This was taken from a reprinted version contained in a Richard Quinn column in *Southern Partisan.* 2nd Quarter 1991. 5.
12. "Flag Flies Again in Danville." *The Captain's Call* SCV newsletter April 1995.
13. Smith video, spring 1996.
14. Jordan, Ervin L. *Black Confederates and Afro-Yankees in Civil War Virginia:* University of Virginia Press, 1995. Also taken from interview with *Atlanta Journal-Constitution* reporter Bill Hendrick in 1995.
15. McPherson, James M. Battle Cry of Freedom. New York and Oxford: Oxford University Press, 1988. 859.
16. Smith video, spring 1996.
17. Jordan, Ervin L. *Black Confederates and Afro-Yankees in Civil War Virginia:* University of Virginia Press, 1995.
18. Smith video, spring 1996.
19. Jordan, Ervin L. *Black Confederates and Afro-Yankees in Civil War Virginia:* University of Virginia Press. 1995.
20. Interview with Patrick M. McSweeney in *Southern Partisan.* 2nd Quarter 1995. 35.
21. Catton, Bruce. *Bruce Catton's Civil War,* 3 vols. *A Stillness at Appomattox.* New York: The Fairfax Press, 1953. 468-471. Also page 692 in Catton's footnotes.
22. Funkhouser, Karl M. Letter to the editor. *The Washington Times* 4 April 1992. Funkhouser obtained his numbers from H.R. Blackerby's Blacks in Blue and Gray.
23. Smith video, spring 1996.
24. Hesseltine, William B. *The South in American History.* New York: Prentice-Hall Inc. 1943.
25. Hesseltine, William B. *The South in American History.* New York: Prentice-Hall Inc. 1943.
26. Adams, James T. *The March of Democracy,* 3 vols. New York: Charles Scribner's Sons, 1965. 9.
27. Winbush speech, 20 May 1996.
28. Kappa, Omikron. "Something of slavery as it existed." *Confederate Veteran.* June 1893.
29. Sowell, Thomas. "In the Sweep of History, Slavery Isn't Race Issue." *Richmond (Va.) Times-Dispatch* 30 October 1995.

30. Trindal, Elizabeth. "Emancipating the Truth About History." *Southern Partisan.* 1st Quarter 1995. 42. The information on Picaud was taken from the *Christian Examiner,* a New York newspaper published in March 1859.

31. Hesseltine, William B. *The South In American History.* New York: Prentice-Hall, 1943. 271.

32.Sowell, Thomas. "In the Sweep of History, Slavery Isn't Race Issue." *Richmond (Va,) Times-Dispatch* 30 October 1995.

33. Kennedy, Ron. "Yankee Hypocrisy." *The Southern Heritage* August 1993.

34. Tyler, Lyon G. *A Confederate Catechism: The War for Southern Self Government. Holdcroft,* Virginia, 6th ed. February 1931. 20.

35. Ashe, Samuel A. *A Southern View of the Invasion of the Southern States and War of 1861-65* 4th ed. Captain J.J. Dickison Camp 1387 SCV, Melbourne, Florida, 1994. 12.

36. Morris, Richard B. ed. *Encylopedia of American History.* New York: Harper & Row, 6th ed, 1982.

37. Buchanan, Patrick J. "Sham by Great Emancipator." *The Tennessean,* 1995.

38. Buchanan, Patrick J. "Sham by Great Emancipator." *The Tennessean,* 1995. Quotes taken from Charles Adams' book *Good and Evil, The Impact of Taxes on the Course of Civilization,* Madison Books, 1995.

39. Tyler, Lyon G. *A Confederate Catechism: The War for Southern Self Government.* Holdcroft, Virginia: 6th ed. 28 February 1931.

40. Adams, James T. *The March of Democracy,* vol. 3, New York: Charles Scribner's Sons, 1965. Reprint of an article from *New Orleans Daily Crescent* 21 January 1861.

41. Ashe, Samuel A. *A Southern View of the Invasion of the Southern States and War of 1861-65,* 1994. 15.

42. Ashe, Samuel A. *A Southern View of the Invasion of the Southern States and War of 1861-65,* 1994. 14.

43. Simmons, Henry E. *A Concise Encyclopedia of the Civil War.* New York: The Fairfax Press, 1986. 41-43, 103-105.

44. Ashe, Samuel A. *A Southern View of the Invasion of the Southern States and War of 1861-65,* 1994, 14-15.

45. Craven, Avery O. ed. *A History of the South,* vol. 6, Baton Rouge: Lousiana State University Press, 1953. 251.

46. Ashe, Samuel A. *A Southern View of the Invasion of the Southern States and War of 1861-65,* 1994. 14-15.

47. Hesseltine, William B. *The South in American History.* New York: Prentice-Hall, Inc. 1943. 267.

48. Adams, James T. *The March of Democracy,* vol. 3, New York: Charles Scribner's Sons, 1965.

49. Rutherford, Mildred Lewis. *The South Must Have Her Rightful Place in History.* Athens, Georgia, March 1923. 19. She quotes Rhodes from his History of the United States, vol. 4, 344.

50. Douglas, W. Earl. *Don't Furl the Flag!* Reprint of a Douglas column which orginally ran in the *Charleston News and Courier* 27 April 1979. It was contained in a Richard Quinn column in *Southern Partisan.* 2ns Quarter 1991. 5.

51. Smith video, spring 1996.

52. Rutherford, Mildred Lewis. *The South Must Have Her Rightful Place in History.* Athens, Georgia, March 1923. 19.

53. Johnson, Ludwell H. III. "Is the Confederacy Obsolete?" *Southern Partisan.* 3rd Quarter 1994. 22. The article was based on an address given by Johnson in November 1993 at the Museum of the Confederacy in Richmond.

54. Rollins, Richard. "The Damned Red Flags of the Rebellion: The Capture of Confederate Battle Flags at Gettysburg." Unpublished manuscript, Redondo Beach, California, 1994. Quoted from Bruce Catton's Prefaces to History.

55. McPherson, James M. *Battle Cry of Freedom.* New York and Oxford: Oxford University Press, 1988. 859.

56. Smith video, spring 1996.

57. Sheehan, Ruth. "Roots or Racism?" *San Francisco Examiner* 5 May 1996. A10.

58. Sheehan, Ruth. "Roots or Racism?" *San Francisco Examiner* 5 May 1996.

59. Headline in *Christian Science Monitor,* 23 June 1995.

60. Reed, Ralph. *Politically Incorrect: The Emerging Faith Factor in American Politics.* Dallas, London, Melbourne, Vancouver: Word Publishing, 1994. 9.

61. Ritter, Frank. "Power of a flag: Abdul-Rauf's blatant disrespect for anthem shjows how symbols can be manipulated." *The Tennessean* 20 March 1996 Op/Ed page.

62. Rutherford, Mildred Lewis. *The South Must Have Her Rightful Place in History.* Athens, Georgia, March 1923.

63. Cailleteau, Ed. "Revisionist view of Civil War must be refuted." *Memphis Commercial Appeal* 2 September 1990. Op/Ed page.

64. Floyd, Tony. "Separating fact from fiction." *The Douglas Dispatch* SCV newsletter April 1996.

65. Johnson, Ludwell H. III. "Is the Confederacy Obsolete?" *Southern Partisan.* 3rd Quarter 1994. 25.

66. Sheehan, Ruth. "Roots or Racism?" *San Francisco Examiner* 5 May 1996.

67. Sowell, Thomas. "Whatever anyone may think, the past is gone." *The Washington Times* 5 April 1995 Op/Ed page.

68. Griffin, Larry J. and Doyle, Don H. eds. *The South as an American Problem.* "Slavery, Secession and Reconstruction as American Problems" by Doyle. Athens and London: The University of Georgia Press, 1995. 108-109.

69. Tyler, Lyon G. A Confederate Catechism: *The War for Southern Self Government.* Holdcroft, Virginia, 6th ed. 28 February 1931. 5.

70. Tyler, Lyon G. *A Confederate Catechism: The War for Southern Self Government,* Holdcroft, Virginia, 6th ed. 28 February 1931. 5.

71. Smith video, spring 1996.

72. Rutherford, Mildred Lewis. *The South Must Have Her Rightful Place in History.* Athens, Georgia, March 1923. 21.

73. Griffin, Larry J. and Doyle, Don H. eds. *The South as an American Problem.* Athens and London: The University of Georgia Press, 1995. Essay "Slavery, Secession, and Reconstruction as American Problems." 112-113,

74. Rutherford, Mildred Lewis. *The South Must Have Her Rightful Place in History.* Athens, Georgia, March 1923. 21.

75. Tyler, Lyon G. *A Confederate Catechism: The War for Southern Self Government.* 6th Ed. Holdcroft, Virginia, February 28, 1931. 52.

76. Marmaduke, Vincent. Letter to *Confederate Veteran.* April 1898. 29.

77. Gantt, J.B. *Confederate Veteran.* May 1906 published from a speech given 25 April 1906. 49.

78. *The Knoxville Guard* SCV newletter, December 1995. Taken from Swank, Walbrook D. Confederate War Stories. 71.

79. Wilson, Charles Reagan and Ferris, William. Eds. *Encyclopedia of Southern Culture: History and Manners.* Chapel Hill and London: University of North Carolina Press, 1989. 658-659.

80. Johnson, Ludwell H. III. "Is the Confederacy Obsolete?" *Southern Partisan.* 3rd Quarter 1994. 22.

81. McWhiney, Grady. Article on Francis Butler Simkins, *Southern Partisan.* 2nd Quarter 1995. 23.

82. Reed, Ralph. *Politically Incorrect: The Emerging Faith Factor in American Politics.* Dallas, London, Vancouver, Melbourne: Word Publishing, 1994. 12.

83. Mills, Gary B. "Dispelling Southern Myths." *The Southern Patriot* newsletter, Vol. 1 No. 1, 1995.

84. Taken from Shennedoah's song "Sunday in the South."

85. *Confederate Veteran.* "Time to Call Off `Dixie.'" March 1897. 113.

86. Sheehan, Ruth. "Roots or Racism." *San Francisco Examiner* 5 May 1996.

CHAPTER 5

1. Watkins, Samuel R. Co. Aytch: *A Side Show of the Big Show.* Nashville: Cumberland Presbyterian Publishing House, 1882. 179.

2. Johnson, Ludwell H. III."North Against South 1861-1865." *Southern Partisan.* 1st Quarter 1995. 21.

3. "Much About Returning Confederate Flags." *Confederate Veteran.* June 1898. 254.

4. "Much About Returning Confederate Flags." *Confederate Veteran.* June 1898. 254.

5. "Much About Returning Confederate Flags." *Confederate Veteran.* June 1898. 254.

6. "Preserving the South." David Walter Leinweber's letter to the editor, *The Atlanta Constitution* 4 March 1996.

7. Gordon, John B. "Confederate Symbols and Patriotism." *Rebel Yell* SCV newsletter taken from *Civil War* magazine which quoted it from Gordon's orginal work published around 1900.

8. "Much About Returning Confederate Flags." *Confederate Veteran.* June 1898. 253.

9. "Much About Returning Confederate Flags." *Confederate Veteran.* June 1898. 254.

10. Kogan, Michael S. *The New York Compatriot* SCV newsletter, fall 1995.

11. Stuart, J.E.B. Personal letter to wife, Flora, March 1862.

12. Hoss, E.E. "Comment On Nashville Reunion." *Confederate Veteran.* September 1897. 463.

13. Andrews, C.H. "Flag of the Third Georgia Regiment." *Confederate Veteran.* July 1894. 201.

14. Smart, C.H. "Fate of Two Flags." *Confederate Veteran.* September 1893.

15. Ledbetter, M.T. "Mechanicsville and Gaines' Mill." *Confederate Veteran.* August 1893. 244.

16. Taken from a flag display at Memorial Hall Museum in New Orleans, Louisiana 25 May 1996.

17. Rollins, Richard. "The Damned Red Flags of the Rebellion: The Capture of Confederate Battle Flags at Gettysburg." Unpublished manuscript, Redondo Beach, California, 1994.

18. Flanagan, W.A. "Account of How Some Flags Were Captured." *Confederate Veteran.* June 1905. 250.

19. Ledbetter, M.T. "Mechanicsville and Gaines' Mill." *Confederate Veteran.* August 1893. 244.

20. Morton, T.C. "Gave His Life For His Flag." *Confederate Veteran.* February 1904. 70-71.

21. Robertson, James I. *The Stonewall Brigade.* Baton Rouge, Louisiana, 1963. Also Eaton, Clement. *A History of the Southern Confederacy.* New York, 1954. Also Wiley, Bell Irvin. *Confederate Women.* Westport, Connecticutt, 1975.

22. Hunton, Eppa. *Autobiogaphy of Eppa Hunton.* Richmond: William Byrd Press, 1933. Also Georg, Kathleen R. and Busey, John W. *Nothing But Glory: Pickett's Division at Gettysburg.* Highstown, New Jersey, 1987.

23. Fletcher, William A. *Rebel Private: Front and Rear.* Penguin Books USA Inc. 1995. 82-83.

24. Hesseltine, William B. *The South in American History.* New York: Prentice-Hall Inc. 1943. 397.

25. Wiley, Bell Irvin. *The Life of Johnny Reb: The Common Soldier of the Confederacy.* Baton Rouge: Louisiana State University Press, 1943. 3.

26. Wiley, Bell Irvin. *The Life of Johnny Reb: The Common Soldier of the Confederacy.* Baton Rouge: Louisiana State University Press, 1943. 4.

27. "The Flag of the Florida Battery." *Confederate Veteran.* March 1895, 73.

28. Hubbard, John Milton. *Notes of a Private.* Memphis: University of Memphis, 1973. 10.

29. Stanley, Henry. *The Autobiography of Sir Henry M. Stanley.* Stanley, Dorothy ed. Boston: Little, Brown, 1909. 165.

30. Ward, Evelyn D. *The Children of Bladensfield.* New York: The Viking Press, 1978. 48-49.

31. "Much About Returning Confederate Flags." *Confederate Veteran.* June 1898. 252.

32. "Much About Returning Confederate Flags." *Confederate Veteran.* June 1898. 253.

33. Flood, Charles Bracelen. *Lee: The Last Years.* Boston: Houghton Mifflin Co. 1981. 15.

34. Hemingway, Al. "General John Sedgwick built a luxurious retirement home in Cornwall Hollow, but he did not live to use it." *America's Civil War* March 1995. 75-76.

35. Rollins, Richard. "The Damned Red Flags of the Rebellion: The Capture of Confederate Battle Flags at Gettysburg." Unpublished manuscript, Redondo Beach, California, 1994.

36. Pickett, George. *The Heart of a Soldier.* New York: Seth Moyle, 1913. 82-83.

37. Wallace, Lee A. *Third Virginia.* Lynchburg, Virginia: H.E. Howard, 1986. 36.

38. Hazelwood, Sandy. Letter to the editor, *Memphis (Tenn.) Commercial Appeal* May 1996.

39. Johnson, Ludwell H. III. "North Against South: 1861-1865." *Southern Partisan.* 1st Quarter 1995. 21.

40. Fletcher, William A. *Rebel Private: Front and Rear.* Penguin Books USA Inc. 1995. 56.

41. Johnson, Ludwell H. III. "North Against South: 1861-1865." *Southern Partisan.* 1st Quarter 1995. 21.

42. Rollins, Richard. "The Damned Red Flags of the Rebellion: The Capture of Confederate Battle Flags at Gettysburg." Unpublished manuscript, Redondo Beach, California, 1994.

43. McPherson, James M. *What They Fought For.* Baton Rouge: Louisiana State University Press, 1994. 9.

44. Barton, Michael. "Did the Confederacy Change Southern Soldiers?" in Owens, Harry P.

and Cook, James J. eds. *The Old South In The Crucible of War.* Jackson: University of Mississippi Press, 1983.

45. Watkins, Samuel R. Co. Aytch: *A Side Show of the Big Show.* Nashville: Cumberland Presbyterian Publishing House, 1882.

46. Bennett, William W. *A Narrative of the Great Revival Which Prevailed in the Southern Armies ... .* Philadelphia: Claxton, Remsen and Haffelfinger, 1877. 367.

47. Hood, John J. "Return of Confederate Battle Flags." *Confederate Veteran.* December 1905. 551.

48. Daniel, Larry J. *Soldiering in the Army of Tennessee.* Chapel Hill: University of North Carolina Press, 1991. 150.

49. Bennett, William W. *A Narrative of the Great Revival Which Prevailed in the Southern Armies ... .* Philadelphia: Claxton, Remsen and Haffelfinger, 1877. 175.

50. Moseley, John. Letter to his mother, 4 July 1863, Virginia State Library.

51. Rollins, Richard. "The Damned Red Flags of the Rebellion: The Capture of Confederate Battle Flags at Gettysburg." Unpublished manuscript, Redondo Beach, California, 1994.

52. McCarthy, Carlton. *Detailed Minutiae of Soldier Life In The Army of Northern Virginia, 1861-1865.* Lincoln: The University of Nebraska press, 1993. Original privately printed, 1882.

53. Flood, Charles Bracelen. *Lee: The Last Years.* Boston: Houghton Mifflin Co. 1981. 27.

54. Johnson, Ludwell H. III. "Is the Confederacy Obsolete?" *Southern Partisan.* 3rd Quarter 1994. 26.

55. Flood, Charles Bracelen. *Lee: The Last Years.* Boston: Houghton Mifflin Co. 1981. 27.

CHAPTER 6

1. Malone, James. "2 of 3 guilty of killing man flying flag." *The Courier-Journal,* Louisville, Kentucky, 13 January 1996, P.1

2. Associated Press story. "Police link flag to death of teen." High Point Enterprise, 21 January 1995. P.5A.

3. Mead, Andy. "Rural killing heightens racial tensions: School's Rebel flag under review." *New Orleans Times Picayune,* 12 February 1995.

4. Parsons, Clark. "A community comes to temrs with a killing." *The Tennessean*, Nashville, 8 October 1995, P.1,8A.

5. Goodwin, M. David. "Woman haunted by husband's slaying." *Louisville Courier-Journal,* 12 March 1995, P.1, 17.

6. Laster, Billy. Letter to Judge Robert Wedemeyer. 1 February 1996.

7. Horwitz, Tony. "A death for Dixie." *The New Yorker,* 18 March 1996, 67.

8. Westerman, JoAnn. Personel interview with author. 25 June 1996.

9. Horwitz, Tony. "A death for Dixie." *The New Yorker,* 18 March 1996, 68.

10. David Russell Ross. "Widow says slaying not provoked." *The Leaf-Chronicle*, Clarksville, Tennessee, 10 January 1996, A1.

11. Westerman, David. Personal interview with author. 25 June 1996.

12. Arms, Brenda. Telephone interview with author, 18 June 1996.

13. Westerman, JoAnn. Personal interview with author. 25 June 1996.

14. Goodwin, M. David, and Malone, James. "Todd County flag flap exposes fissure." *Louisville Courier-Journal*, 29 January 1995.

15. Goodwin, M. David, and Malone, James. "Todd County flag flap exposes fissure." *Louisville Courier-Journal.*

16. Horwitz, Tony. "A death for Dixie." *The New Yorker,* 18 March 1996, 66.

17. Horwitz, Tony. "A death for Dixie." *The New Yorker,* 18 March 1996, 66.

18. Horwitz, Tony. "A death for Dixie." *The New Yorker,* 18 March 1996, 66.

19. Parson, Clark. "A community comes to terms with a killing." *The Tennessean*, Nashville, 8 October 1995.

20. Elvin, Kris. "Flag issue delayed until Feb. 9." *The Leaf-Chonicle,* Clarksville, Tennessee, 31 January 1995, A1-A2.

21. Campbell, A.G. Letter to the editor, *Todd County Standard*, 1995, 2A.

22. Smith, Ed. Video taped lecture in Hollywood, Florida, by Preserving Our Heritage Inc. 1996.

23. Horwitz, Tony. "A death for Dixie." *The New Yorker,* 18 March 1996, 68.

24. Sowell, Thomas. "Whatever anyone may think, the past is gone." *The Washington Times* Op/Ed page, 5 April 1995.

197

25. Hedges, Michael. "Death ends first date after births." *The Washington Times*, 29 March 1995, A18.

26. Horwitz, Tony. "A death for Dixie." *The New Yorker*, 18 March 1996, 65.

27. Blackburn, David, "Defendent testifies in flag trial." *Kentucky New Era*, Hopkinsville, Kentucky, 11 January 1996, 1A. Horwitz, Tony. "A death for Dixie." *The New Yorker*, 18 March 1996, 64.

28. Davis, Donna. "Rebel flag is fatal attack's 'only' motive, black suspects knew victim with school emblem on truck." Associated Press report in *The Commercial Appeal*, Memphis, Tennessee, 21 January 1995, 1B.

29. Boone, Evelyn. "Two are given life sentences in Westerman murder; youngest defendant is acquitted." *Todd County Standard*, 17 January 1996, 1.

30. Blackburn, David. "Flag trial prosecutors continue." *Kentucky New Era*, Hopkinsville, Kentucky, 10 January 1995, 1A,3A.

31. Blackburn, David. "Flag trial prosecutors continue." *Kentucky New Era*, Hopkinsville, Kentucky, 10 January 1995, 3A.

32. Davis, Donna. "Rebel flag is fatal attack's 'only' motive, black suspects knew victim with school emblem on truck." Associated Press story in *The Commercial Appeal*, Memphis, Tennessee, 21 January 1995, 1B. Blackburn, David. "Guilty Verdict." *Kentucky New Era*, Hopkinsville, Kentucky, 13 January 1996, 2A.

33. Dew, Toni. "Flag was to 'look sharp,' not taunt, widow testifies in teens' murder trial." *The Nashville Banner*, 10 January 1996, A1, A5.

34. Horwitz, Tony. "A death for Dixie." *The New Yorker*, 18 March 1996, 64.

35. Boone, Evelyn. "Two are given life sentences in Westerman murder; youngest defendant is acquitted." *Todd County Standard*, 17 January 1996, A8.

36. Horwitz, Tony. "A death for Dixie." *The New Yorker*, 18 March 1996, 68.

37. Hedges, Michael. "Death ends first date after births." *The Washington Times*, 29 March 1995, A18.

38. Ross, David Russell. "Trial heated outside courtroom." *The Leaf Chronicle*, Clarksville, Tennessee, 12 January 1996, A11.

39. Ross, David Russell. "Widow says slaying not provoked." *The Leaf Chronicle*, Clarksville, Tennessee, 10 January 1996, A1, A3.

40. Horwitz, Tony. "A death for Dixie." *The New Yorker*, 18 March 1996, 64.

41. Boone, Evelyn. "Two are given life sentences in Westerman murder; youngest defendant is acquitted." *Todd County Standard*, 17 January 1996, A1.

42. Warren, Beth. "Three charged in flag shooting released from jail on bond." *The Tennessean*, Nashville, Tennessee, 18 February 1995, 2B.

43. Warren, Beth. "Civil rights charges filed in flag case." *The Tennessean*, Nashville, Tennessee, 13 March 1995, 2A.

44. Westerman, David. Personal interview with author, 25 June 1996.

45. Westerman, Freddy. Letter to Judge Robert Wedemeyer, February 1996.

46. Westerman, Cynthia. Personal letter to Judge Robert Wedemeyer, February 1996.

47. Goodwin, M. David. "Woman haunted by husband's slaying." *The Courier-Journal*, Louisville, Kentucky, 12 March 1995, 1.

48. Henson, Tanya. Personal letter to Judge Robert Wedemeyer, February 1996.

49. Laster, Joyce. Personal letter to Judge Robert Wedemeyer, February 1996.

50. Belanger, Sarah. Personal letter to Judge Robert Wedemeyer, February 1996.

51. Haley, Shelly. Personal letter to Judge Robert Wedemeyer, February 1996.

52. Thomas, Wendi C. "Westerman trials won't be moved." *The Tennessean*, Nashville, Tennessee, 7 June 1995, 2A.

53. Loggins, Kirk and Thomas, Wendi C. "Teens' arrest leads to flag trial delay." *The Tennessean*, Nashville, Tennessee, 23 September 1995, 1B.

54. Thompson, Richelle. *The Leaf-Chronicle*, Clarksville, Tennessee, 19 September 1995, A10.

55. Blackburn, David. "New charges face flag death suspects." *Kentucky New Era*, Hopkinsville, Kentucky, 20 September 1995.

56. Cannon, Devereaux. "To live and die for Dixie." *Southern Partisan*. 4th Quarter 1994, 17-19.

57. Horwitz, Tony. "A death for Dixie." *The New Yorker*, 18 March 1996, 66.

58. Radford, Ed. Letter to the editor. *Kentucky New Era*, January 1995.

59. Goodwin, M. David. "Funeral, fiery crosses raise tension in Guthrie." *The Courier-Journal*, Louisville, Kentucky, 19 January 1995, 1,3.

198   ENDNOTES

60. Darnell, Catherine. "Pining for sleepy days." *The Tennessean,* Nashville, Tennessee, January 1995.
61. Darnell, Catherine. "Pining for sleepy days." *The Tennessean,* Nashville, Tennessee, January 1995.
62. Parsons, Clark. "A community comes to terms with a killing." *The Tennessean,* 8 October 1995, 8A.
63. Parsons, Clark. "A community comes to terms with a killing." *The Tennessean,* 8 October 1995, 8A. Also, taped telephone conversation between Hannah Westerman and the female student.
64. Westerman, David. Personal interview with author, 22 July 1996.
65. Hedges, Michael. "Killing blamed on Rebel flag unfurls racial tension in Kentucky." *The Washington Times,* 29 March 1995, A18.
66. Westerman, JoAnn. Personal interview with author, 22 July 1996.
67. Thomas, Wendi C. "A murder's legacy." *The Tennessean,* Nashville, Tennessee, 21 April 1996, 12A.
68. "Heed family's plea for calm." *Kentucky New Era,* Hopkinsville, Kentucky, January 1995. Op/Ed page.
69. Watts, Beverly L. Personal letter to Jeffery W. Massey, 12 January 1996.
70. Goodwin, M. David. "400 pack Todd County gym, speak up for Rebel mascot." *The Courier Journal,* 10 February 1995, B1.
71. Elvin, Kris. "Flag issue delayed until Feb. 9." *The Leaf-Chronicle,* Clarksville, Tennessee, 31 January 1995, A2.
72. "Todd flag draws complaint." *Kentucky New Era,* Hopkinsville, Kentucky, 23 June 1995.
73. Westerman, David. Personal interview with author, 25 June 1996.
74. Westerman, David. Personal interview with author, 22 July 1996.
75. Blackburn, David. "Judge — not jury — to decide Rebel flag case." *Kentucky New Era,* Hopkinsville, Kentucky, 6 January 1996, 3A.
76. Blackburn, David. "Flag trial prosecutors continue." *Kentucky New Era,* Hopkinsville, Kentucky, 10 January 1995, 1A.
77. Blackburn, David. "Flag trial prosecutors continue." *Kentucky New Era,* Hopkinsville, Kentucky, 10 January 1995, 1A.
78. Blackburn, David. "Flag trial prosecutors continue." *Kentucky New Era,* Hopkinsville, Kentucky, 10 January 1995, 1A, 3A.
79. Blackburn, David. "Guilty verdict." *Kentucky New Era,* Hopkinsville, Kentucky, 13 January 1996, 2A.
80. Blackburn, David. "Guilty verdict." *Kentucky New Era,* Hopkinsville, Kentucky, 13 January 1996, 2A.
81. Warren, Beth. "Teens' terms exceed life." *The Tennessean,* Nashville, Tennessee, 27 April 1996, 1B.
82. Ross, David Russell. "Teens get life sentences." *The Leaf-Chronicle,* Clarksville, Tennessee, 27 April 1996, A11.
83. Blackburn, David. "Guilty verdict." *Kentucky New Era,* Hopkinsville, Kentucky, 13 January 1996, 1A.
84. Sack, Kevin. "Symbol of the Old South divides the New South." *New York Times,* 21 January 1996.
85. Hooks, Marc I. and Ross, David Russell. "Two get probation in rebel flag death." *The Leaf-Chronicle,* Clarksville, Tennessee, February 1996.
86. Westerman, David. Personal interview with author, 22 July 1996.
87. Patrick, Deval L. Personal letter to Hannah Westerman, 21 May 1996.
88. Hedges, Michael. "Killing blamed on Rebel flag unfurls racial tension in Kentucky." *The Washington Times,* 29 March 1995, A18.
89. Thayer, Nelson S.T. Personal cover letter to Patrick's letter to David Westerman, 21 May 1996.
90. Warren, Beth. "Civil rights charges filed in flag case." *The Tennessean,* 7 February 1995, 1A.
91. Westerman, David. Personal interview with author, 25 June 1996.
92. Westerman, David. Personal letter to Compassionate Friends support group, June 1996.
93. Evans, Margaret. Personal letter to Judge Robert Wedemeyer, 3 February 1996.
94. Westerman, Ivy Pearl. Personal letter to Westerman twins, February 1995.
95. Westerman, JoAnn. Personal interview with author, 25 June 1996.
96. Westerman, David. Personal interview with author, 25 June 1996.

97. Gray, A.J. Personal letter to Judge Robert Wedemeyer, 29 January 1996.

98. Gray, Andrew J. Personal letter to Judge Robert Wedemeyer, 29 January 1996.

99. Hedges, Michael. "Killing blamed on Rebel flag unfurls racial tension in Kentucky." *The Washington Times,* 29 March 1995, A18.

100. Thomas, Wendi C. "A murder's legacy." *The Tennessean,* 21 April 1996, 12A.

101. Majors, Read. Letter to the editor, *The Nashville Banner.*

102. Butler, Carlie. Letter to the editor, *Kentucky New Era,* Hopkinsville, Kentucky.

103. Donish, Father Peter M. Letter to the editor, *Southern Partisan.* 2nd Quarter 1995, 6.

104. de la Cruz, Bonna M. "The same banner, different beliefs." *The Tennessean,* 23 April 1996, 2A.

105. Merrill, Kathleen. "Shooting at teen hangout may lower flag on East Side rec center." *The Evansville Press,* Evansville, Indiana, 19 August 1995, 1.

106. "Confederate flags not to be displayed." *The Evansville Press,* Evansville, Indiana, 23 August 1995.

107. Beck, Jim. "Symbol or slur: 130 years after Civil War, rebel flag is still dividing people." *The Evansville Courier,* 24 September 1995, A8.

108. Beck, Jim. "Symbol or slur: 130 years after Civil War, rebel flag is still dividing people." *The Evansville Courier,* 24 September 1995, A8.

109. Beck, Jim. "Symbol or slur: 130 years after Civil War, rebel flag is still dividing people." *The Evansville Courier,* 24 September 1995, A8.

110. Horwitz, Tony. "A death for Dixie." *The New Yorker,* 18 March 1996, 65.

111. Roberts, Timothy. "Lest we forget: The battle over the Civil War and its symbols rages on." *Nashville Scene,* 25 February 1993, 9.

112. Westerman, David. Personal interview with author and information from taped telephone interview he had with reporter, 22 July 1996.

113. Westerman, David. Personal interview with author, 25 June 1996.

114. Sherrill, Tracy. "Rally touching for the family of slaying victim." *Kentucky New Era,* 6 March 1995, 1A.

115. Thomas, Wendi C. "A murder's legacy." *The Tennessean,* 21 April 1996, 12A.

116. Dasinger, Norman. Personal letter to Craig Moon, publisher of *The Tennessean,* 25 April 1996.

117. Pride, Richard. "After the news: A news `peg' on which to hang a correction." *The Nashville Banner,* 30 April 1996, Op/Ed page.

118. Knight, Alfred H. Personal letter to William E. Shofner, 21 May 1996.

119. Shofner, William E. "Nashville Eye" column submitted for Op/Ed page.

120. "Historic symbols deserve respect." *The Augusta Chronicle,* Augusta, Georgia.

121. "Laurens proving racism unwanted." *The Sun News,* Myrtle Beach, South Carolina.

122. "Flag debate hides true key to racial strife." *Kentucky New Era,* Hopkinsville, Kentucky.

123. "Todd school's logo proposal poorly timed." *Kentucky New Era,* Hopkinsville, Kentucky.

124. Warren, Beth. "Teens' terms exceed life." *The Tennessean,* 27 April 1996, 1B.

125. Ross, David Russell. "Westerman widow files suit." *The Leaf-Chronicle,* 16 January 1996, A1.

126. Westerman, David. Personal interview with author, 22 July 1996.

127. Westerman, David. Personal interview with author, 25 June 1996.

TURNER PUBLISHING COMPANY has published comemorative history books for more than 400 military veterans associations spanning WW I to the Persian Gulf. We have also published a number of county history titles as well as several special interest titles. Call today to order your catalog featuring our military and special interest titles.

also available from Turner Publishing Company

SONS OF CONFEDERATE VETERANS: THE FIRST 100 YEARS - CENTENNIAL EDITION

SONS OF UNION VETERANS OF THE CIVIL WAR

SONS OF THE AMERICAN REVOLUTION: 1889-1989

DAUGHTERS OF THE REPUBLIC OF TEXAS

TODD COUNTY, KENTUCKY HISTORY

TODD COUNTY, KENTUCKY PICTORIAL

THE SILENT BRIGADE: HOW ONE WOMAN OUTWITTED THE NIGHT RIDERS

LET US TELL IT... HOW IT WAS, HOW IT IS, AND HOW IT WILL BE IN THE FUTURE

TENKO! RANGOON JAIL: SGT JOHN BOYD'S SURVIVAL IN A JAPANESE PRISON CAMP

INSIDE THE BEVERLY HILLS SUPPER CLUB FIRE

———————— *to order your books or a catalog write or call* ————————

TURNER PUBLISHING COMPANY
412 BROADWAY • P.O. BOX 3101
PADUCAH, KENTUCKY 42002-3131

ORDER TOLL FREE 8:00-4:30 CT M-F
FOR ORDERS CHARGED TO YOUR VISA/MASTERCARD
1-800-788-3350 (orders only)
FAX ORDERS (502) 443-0335
CUSTOMER SERVICE (502) 443-0121